Contemporary Views on the Holocaust

Holocaust Studies Series

Randolph L. Braham,
Series Editor

The Graduate School and University Center,
The City University of New York

Previously published:
Perspectives on the Holocaust, 1983

The Holocaust Studies Series is published in cooperation with the Jack P. Eisner Institute for Holocaust Studies. These books are outgrowths of lectures, conferences, and research projects sponsored by the Institute. It is the purpose of the series to subject the events and circumstances of the Holocaust to scrutiny by a variety of academics who bring different scholarly disciplines to the study.

Contemporary Views on the Holocaust

Randolph L. Braham, Editor

Kluwer·Nijhoff Publishing
a member of the Kluwer Academic Publishers Group
Boston The Hague Dordrecht Lancaster

Distributors for North America:
Kluwer Boston, Inc.
190 Old Derby Street
Hingham, MA 02043, U.S.A.

Distributors outside North America:
Kluwer Academic Publishers Group
Distribution Centre
P.O. Box 322
3300AH Dordrecht, The Netherlands

Library of Congress Cataloging in Publication Data
Main entry under title:

Contemporary views on the Holocaust.

  (Holocaust studies series)
  1. Holocaust, Jewish (1939–1945) — Addresses, essays,
lectures.   2. Holocaust, Jewish (1939–1945)
— Historiography — Addresses, essays, lectures.   I. Braham,
Randolph L.   II. Series.
D810.J4C67   1983   940.53′15′03924   83-177
ISBN 0-89838-141-X

Printed in the United States of America

Contents

Preface

This book is the second in a series of studies published under the auspices of the Institute for Holocaust Studies of the Graduate School and University Center of The City University of New York. Like the first book, it is an outgrowth of the lectures and special studies sponsored by the institute during the 1981–82 and 1982–83 academic years.

This volume is divided into five parts. Part I, *Ethics and the Holocaust*, contains a pioneering investigation of one of the most neglected areas in Holocaust studies. Francine Klagsbrun, a well-known writer and popular lecturer, provides an erudite overview of the value of life in Jewish thought and tradition. With full understanding of the talmudic scholars' position on Jewish ethics and using concrete examples of the life-and-death dilemmas that confronted many Jews in their concentration camp experiences, Klagsbrun provides dramatic evidence of the triumph of moral and ethical principles over the forces of evil during the Holocaust, this darkest period in Jewish history.

The next two chapters, grouped under the heading *The Allies and the Holocaust*, deal with the failure of the Western Allies to respond to the desperate needs of the persecuted Jews of Europe during the Second World War. The first is by Professor Bela Vago, an authority on the Holocaust and East Central European history at the University of Haifa. It is a thoroughly documented account, demonstrating the reluctance of the Allies, and especially the British, to engage in rescue activities on behalf of the beleaguered Jews in Nazi-dominated Europe. In Vago's chapter, the offer made by Admiral Miklós Horthy, the Regent of Hungary, during the summer of 1944 to allow the emigration of thousands of Jews is used as a case study to prove that the Allies were not really ready to provide any meaningful assistance to the Jews. Professor Monty Penkower of Touro College in New York goes even further, showing that the Allies, and above all once again the British, were opposed even to the establishment of a Jewish fighting force envisioned to participate in the common war effort against the Axis. As Penkower skillfully demonstrates, the British, guided by narrowly interpreted considerations of national interests, were fearful of the potential danger that the nucleus of a Palestinian Jewish army might represent to their long range interests in the Middle East.

Part III, *The Holocaust: Selected Areas*, includes two contrasting studies. The chapter by Professor David Kranzler of Queensborough Community College is a scholarly account of how the Japanese, their peculiar brand of wartime anti-Semitism notwithstanding, saved some 18,000 Jews during the Holocaust. It is a study full of fascinating insights into the mentality and peculiarities of the Japanese "experts" dealing with the Jewish question during the war. The chapter by Professor Samuel Abrahamsen of Brooklyn College, on the other hand, is devoted to a very tragic chapter of the Holocaust — the destruction of the Jews of Norway. Abrahamsen demonstrates in a fully documented fashion that no other Scandinavian Jewish community suffered such staggering losses as the Jews of Norway.

Part IV, *Reactions to the Holocaust*, details the postwar attitudes toward the Holocaust in the Soviet Union and the Federal Republic of Germany. Dr. William Korey, an expert on the Soviet bloc, analyzes the treatment of the Holocaust in Soviet historiography, demonstrating how Soviet officials and historians distorted the historical record to suit the changing political interests of the regime. Korey's paper makes clear that the official Soviet attempt to denigrate, if not totally erase, the Jewish component of the Holocaust is a culmination of the drive launched in the late 1940s against cosmopolitanism and Zionism. Professor Walter Renn of Wheeling College reviews the treatment of the Holocaust in selected textbooks used in various educational institutions in the Federal Republic of Germany. While he finds that most of the textbooks analyzed continue to basically repress the Nazi past, he concludes with an expression of hope that the current generation of textbook authors will make headway toward coming to grips with both the Holocaust and the National Socialist legacy.

The last part of this book, *Crime and Punishment*, contains two overviews relating to war criminals and retribution. Peter R. Black provides a portrait of Ernst Kaltenbrunner, the former head of the Reich Security Main Office and one of the leading architects of the Final Solution program. Black identifies not only the factors that shaped the man, but also the role he played in the destruction of European Jewry. Allan A. Ryan, Jr., the head of the Office of Special Investigations, U.S. Department of Justice, offers an authoritative review of the American position on the prosecution of war criminals who entered the United States, presumably illegally, after the war. His study focuses on the activities and accomplishments of the Office of Special Investigations since its establishment by the Attorney General in 1979. It is complemented by a valuable appendix that contains a digest of the cases in litigation as of December 1, 1982.

Acknowledgments

Thanks are due to the many people without whose support and cooperation this book could not have been published. First and foremost, I want to express my appreciation to the contributors who agreed to revise and update the lectures they gave under the auspices of the Institute for Holocaust Studies. Further, this is an appropriate occasion to acknowledge with gratitude the consistent and unqualified support for the Institute provided by the administration of the Graduate School and University Center, and above all President Harold M. Proshansky, Provost Stanley Waren, and Dean Solomon Goldstein. I also want to express my thanks to the Holocaust Survivors Memorial Foundation for its consistent financial support. Finally, I want to acknowledge the valuable advice and wholehearted cooperation I received from Philip D. Jones and Bernadine Richey of Kluwer-Nijhoff Publishing.

I ETHICS AND THE HOLOCAUST

1 THE VALUE OF LIFE: Jewish Ethics and the Holocaust

Francine Klagsbrun

In Auschwitz, on the eve of the Jewish New Year in 1944, about fourteen hundred teenage boys were rounded up and locked into a cell. Plans were made to destroy them in the crematorium the next evening. All during the day, parents and friends of the boys sealed in the cell bargained for their release with the *kapos,* those prisoners who had been placed in charge of the other inmates. People who had managed to smuggle diamonds or money into the camp bribed the *kapos* to set their boys free. Because the *kapos* were held responsible for the number of boys locked up, every time they released one child they immediately seized another in his place. The inmates in the camp knew that each time they saved a youngster, they condemned another to death. Rabbi Zevi Hirsch Meisels, a highly respected Hungarian rabbi interned in the camp at the time, later wrote the following account of an incident that occurred in the midst of the frantic bargaining for lives:

> A simple Jew from Oberland approached me and said: "Rabbi, my only son, who is dearer to me than the pupil of my eye, is among the boys destined to be burned. I have the wherewithal to redeem him, but I know, without a doubt, that the *kapos* would take another in his place. I ask you, Rabbi, to give me a

ruling, according to the Torah. Am I permitted to redeem my son? Whatever you tell me I will do.''

When I heard the question I began to tremble and I answered him: "My dear man, how can I give you a clear ruling on such a question? Even in the days when the Temple was standing, questions such as this one that deals with life and death would be brought before the Sanhedrin. And here I am in Auschwitz, without a single book on Jewish law, with no other rabbis, and without peace of mind because of the terrible troubles and tragedies here."

If the system of the *kapos* had been first to free one boy and then substitute another for him I might have had room to maneuver a bit. I might have been able to reason that it was not certain that each boy released was replaced by another. The *kapos* were, after all, Jewish, and Jewish law so strongly forbids taking one life in order to save another. Perhaps, I might have argued, at the last moment, their Jewish consciousness might be awakened, and they would not violate this important law. . . .

Unfortunately, I knew with certainty that the method of the *kapos* was always to seize a replacement first, and then to release a redeemed child. In that way, they protected themselves and kept the number constant. So I had no way to get around the situation.

The man who approached me kept after me, "Rabbi, you must make a decision for me," he insisted. And again I pleaded with him: "My dear man, leave me with this question because I cannot give you an answer. . . ."

Finally, the man said to me with great emotion: "Rabbi, I have done what the Torah commanded me. I have asked my rabbi for a decision, and there is no other rabbi I can consult. If you cannot give me an answer about whether I may redeem my son, that's a sign to me that according to the law you were not able to permit it, for if it were permitted, you would certainly have told me so. I take it for granted, then, that according to Jewish law I must not do it. That's enough for me. My only child will be burned in fulfillment of the laws of the Torah. I accept this decision with love and with joy. . . .''[1]

I begin with this incident to set the stage for the subject: the value of life in Jewish law and ethics and the application of related moral and ethical principles during the Holocaust. On one level, this story points up that even in the midst of the inhumanity and degradation that engulfed Holocaust victims, there were individuals — and not just a few — who still turned to the law and to tradition to help guide them. More important, for our purposes, the incident highlights the fact that there is a system of values in Judaism, a consistent approach to the meaning and worth of human life, that envelops even the most nightmarish questions of life and death. The system does not always solve specific problems in a specific time and place, but it does provide a framework, a conglomerate of principles, within which to form attitudes and draw conclusions. Rabbi Meisels could not bring himself to tell the man directly that he was forbidden to substitute another child's life for the life of his son, but from the rabbi's behavior, the man could surmise what the law was. With almost superhuman dedication, he abided by it.

What are the attitudes of Judaism toward human life? What is the significance of life in Jewish thought? At its most fundamental level, Judaism regards life as a precious gift from God; precious not only because it is a gift from God but because, for humans, there is a uniqueness attached to that gift. Of all the creatures on earth, Judaism teaches, only humans are created in the image of God. Our lives are sacred and precious because we carry within us the Divine Image, and with it, unlimited potential.[2] One of the most profound sayings of the Mishnah has been so often repeated that we tend to take it for granted, yet it is a stunning summary of Jewish thought: "Man was created as a single individual to teach us that anyone who destroys a single life is as though he destroyed an entire world; and anyone who preserves a single life is as though he preserved an entire world."[3] Every life is a potential world, Jewish tradition holds, and every life is unique unto itself. "A man stamps many coins from a single die," the rabbis said, "and they are all alike, but God has stamped every man with the die of Adam, yet not one of them is like his fellow. Therefore every person is obliged to say, 'For my sake was the world created.'"[4] The heart of the Jewish view of human life, then, is that the world was created for the sake of each one of us, and each of us is a world unto ourselves.

The sources for this enormous emphasis on the value of human life can be traced back to the Bible itself. Biblical law is uncompromising in its strictures against homicide. "A person who murders another shall surely be put to death," the book of Leviticus commands.[5] There are no compromises and few mitigating circumstances. Only if a person murders another accidentally may a fine by substituted for the payment of life. Even if an ox gores a human being, the ox must be stoned and killed. These biblical laws of homicide have been criticized for their harshness — even their barbarism — because they are so unrelenting. Yet, the research of biblical scholars, and most especially the work of Moshe Greenberg,[6] have shown that the biblical rulings grow from very basic principles about the value of each individual, the importance of each life. Other ancient legal codes have similar laws, but with crucial differences. In those codes, a murderer who could afford it could strike a bargain with the family of the slain person. He might pay a fine or substitute others to be slain in his place — a wife, a slave, a brother or sister. In biblical law, such substitutions may never be made. In biblical law, the destruction of a human life is considered an absolute wrong, a sin against God — because humans are created in the image of God — and that life may not be measured either in monetary terms or in the equivalencies of other persons. In biblical law, human life is invaluable, and the death penalty comes not as compensation for it, but as punishment for destroying it. Then too, in other Near Eastern codes, crimes against property may be punished by death. In biblical law, offenses against property never entail the death penalty. In biblical law, the taking of life cannot be recompensed by any amount of property, nor can property, under any circumstances, be considered equal to the value of a life.

Paradoxically, the rabbis of post–biblical times, having absorbed the biblical emphasis on the invaluableness of human life, carried that lesson to the next level, and tried to circumvent the death penalty as much as possible. They set up so many restrictions and limitations that it became almost impossible in Jewish law to convict someone of murder. Courts, for example, would examine witnesses so thoroughly that rarely could a witness in a capital case give incriminating testimony against a defendant. In defining circumstantial evidence, for instance, a judge might say to a witness: "Perhaps you saw a man pursuing his fellow into a ruin. You followed him and found him sword in hand with blood dripping from it, while the murdered man lay writhing in pain. If this is what you saw, you saw nothing."[7]

And many of the rabbis of the Talmud so disapproved of capital punishment that they said, "A court that orders an execution once in seven years is branded a murderous court. Rabbi Eleazar ben Azariah said, "or even once in seventy years." Rabbi Tarfon and Rabbi Akiva said, "Had we been members of the Sanhedrin, no person would ever have been put to death."[8]

Life is precious, life is vital, and in order to preserve life almost every law may be broken, including all the laws of the Sabbath, because, the rabbis said, these laws were given to us that we may live by them and not die because of them.[9] In fact, so much more significant is life than law that the more eagerly one goes about breaking the Sabbath in order to save a life, the more worthy is that person of praise.[10]

So far so good. The emphasis placed on the value of human life is clearcut. The rulings discussed above are logical and not terribly controversial. Issues become muddied and decisions harder to make, however, in situations that have to do not only with preserving life but with judging between lives, with weighing one life against another. What do you do if two people need kidney transplants, but there is a kidney available for only one? Or how far do you go in risking your own life in order to save someone else's life? Or what decision do you make if, like the father in Auschwitz you are confronted with the choice of saving your child only by destroying another person's child?

There are three basic talmudic texts and many commentaries that deal with the dilemmas of weighing one life against another. Two of them may have grown out of the persecutions and sufferings that Jews faced during talmudic and later periods. All of them came to bear on the trials and torments of Jews of the Holocaust. These texts do not provide clearcut answers to the overwhelming decisions people had to make in those dark days and in other periods of history. Actually, each of the texts contains ambiguities that allow for various interpretations. Together, however, they do provide both a set of principles and a framework within which such dilemmas may be considered. It is important to be aware that a framework exists when evaluating the past and when facing the choices that constantly confront us in contemporary life.

The following passage comes from the Babylonian Talmud and poses a cryptic puzzle. The ensuing discussion involves interpretations of the biblical phrase: "That your brother may live with you" (Leviticus 25:36).

> Two men are traveling through the desert, and one of them has a flask of water. If both of them drink, they will die. But if one drinks, he will be able to reach civilization.
>
> Ben Petura taught that they should both drink and die, rather than have one witness the death of his companion.
>
> Until Rabbi Akiva came and taught: It is written "That your brother may live with you." This means that your life comes before the life of your fellow man.[11]

There have been many heated arguments centered on this text. Many scholars side with Ben Patura, but Rabbi Akiva was a much greater scholar and his words carry more authority. What Rabbi Akiva is saying is that, all things being equal, if you face a choice between losing two lives or saving one, even at the cost of the other, you must save the one. And if you happen to be the "man with the water" you must save your own life rather than sacrifice it for the life of the other person. The noted British scholar Louis Jacobs has written extensively on this subject, questioning Akiva's position, or at least reinterpreting it. He points out that nobody says the man with the water is obligated to turn it over to the other man and thus sacrifice himself, for if such an obligation exists, the other man would be obligated to turn it back again. However, he insists, nothing in Jewish law and nothing Akiva is saying prevents the man with the water from turning it over to the other man if he wants to, as an act of special piety or a great act of heroism.[12] The question of whether such an act of self sacrifice is in fact heroic or is a form of suicide is still being argued among scholars.

But if there is disagreement about sacrificing your life to save another person, there is no disagreement among Jewish authorities about sacrificing another person's life to save your own. You are forbidden to actively kill someone or steal that person's sustenance in order to save your own life. If you must act in self-defense because someone has come to kill you, you are obliged to try to defend yourself by maiming the other person rather than by killing, if that is possible.[13]

Consider the second text:

> A man came to Rava and said: The governor of my town has ordered me to kill a certain man. And if I don't do as he says, he will have me killed. What shall I do?
>
> Rava answered him: Let him kill you rather than commit murder yourself. How do you know that your blood is redder than his? Perhaps his blood is redder.[14]

What makes you think that your life is more precious than the life of the next person? This text declares that all life is precious and all life has equal value — the life of an old man is no less valuable than the life of a new baby. Your life is no less important than the next person's, nor is his or hers less important than your own.

The third text is closely related. It deals not with murdering someone personally, but with handing someone over to be murdered. Part of the discussion revolves around Sheba ben Bichri, a man who rebelled against King David and then fled to the city of Abel. As told in the second book of Samuel, chapter 20, David's commander Joab surrounded the city and threatened to destroy it, until a "clever woman" convinced the townspeople to cut off Sheba's head and throw it to Joab, and in that way save the city. Here is the text:

> A group of people are walking along a road when they are stopped by heathen who say to them, "Give us one of you and we will kill him. If not, we will kill all of you."
>
> Let them all be killed, and let them not surrender one soul from Israel. But if the heathen single out one person, as was the case with Sheba ben Bichri, that person may be surrendered to them, so that the others may be saved.
>
> Rabbi Simeon ben Lakish said: Only someone who is under sentence of death, the way Sheba ben Bichri was, may be turned over. But Rabbi Johanan said: Even someone who is not under sentence of death like Sheba ben Bichri [but has been specified, may be turned over].[15]

Rabbi Simeon takes a narrow view of the ruling, maintaining that a group may be saved at the expense of one person only if that person is guilty of a crime punishable by death. Rabbi Johanan is more lenient, allowing a group to be saved simply if one person has been singled out for death by the enemy. The difference between Rabbi Simeon and Rabbi Johanan has not been resolved, but Maimonides later accepted the stricter view of Rabbi Simeon, saying, "If the individual specified has not incurred capital punishment, they should all suffer death rather than hand over a single Jew to them."[16]

Although written more than two thousand years ago, the talmudic passages cited above deal with issues that crushed upon community after community of Jews in Germany and Eastern Europe during the days of the Nazi terror. For the Jew from Oberland described in the opening account from Auschwitz, the question was, whose blood was redder — his son's or another youngster's. Rabbi Meisels, whom the man consulted, surely knew the texts we have just discussed, and their many commentaries. Another description of the incident, related by a witness and a survivor, says that the rabbi did murmur, "How do you know that your son's blood is redder than that of another child?"[17] Whether this was the case or the rabbi remained silent, as he described the incident himself, the man correctly inferred that Jewish law forbade him to redeem his son at the expense of another child's life.

On a much broader scale, the awesome quandary of whether to destroy some lives in order to save others became one of the prime practical as well as ethical dilemmas of the Jewish councils (*Judenräte*) that governed Jewish communities throughout Europe. The Jewish councils were successors of the kehillas, the democratically elected organizations that handled Jewish community affairs before the Nazi takeover. As the Nazis marched into cities throughout Europe, the *kehillas* were abolished and in their place were formed the *Judenräte*; councils subject to Nazi orders, which sometimes became the arms of Nazi terrorism and brutality. In some communities, Jewish leaders who agreed to serve on the *Judenräte* did so with great reservations. Some ran away to avoid being pressed into service. A few committed suicide. Others saw themselves as suffering servants, as it were, accepting odious responsibilities in order to help their fellow Jews.[18]

Truly dedicated members of the Jewish councils in some areas continued to enforce the most horrible of Nazi orders out of the conviction that if they did not and were replaced by other appointees of the Nazis, the lot of the Jews would be even worse than it was. Szmul Zygielbojm set an example of such reasoning. In the early days of the Nazi occupation,

Zygielbojm, who later committed suicide in an attempt to draw world attention to the plight of the Jews, suggested that the *Judenrate* be responsible for recruiting forced laborers for the Germans to avoid the terror of having Germans haphazardly pull Jews off the streets to be pressed into labor.[19]

Unfortunately, there were scoundrels and opportunists among *Judenrate* members who tried to save themselves and protect their families at the cost of other people. There were also Jewish leaders who became dictators in their own right: Jacob Gens of Vilna, Moshe Merin of Sosnowiec, Mordecai Chaim Rumkowski of Lodz and others ruled their ghettos with iron hands, and were as hated among many Jews as the Nazi rulers themselves.[20]

Rounding up people for forced labor was only the beginning of the selections the Jewish councils were required to make. Very soon the assignments became far more ominous, and the councils had the reponsibility to select people for resettlement and deportation, to provide lists of people judged fit or unfit for work, to hand out work cards to people whose jobs were deemed essential or unessential. On a scale previously unknown in Jewish history, the "heathen," as the talmudic passage put it, were demanding that some lives be destroyed in order to save others. In most communities, the talmudic ruling that forbade this was not unknown. Sometimes it was discussed, and sometimes it was ignored in the hope that some lives, indeed, could be saved.

In some communities, the elderly were the first selected for deportation. In others, criminals, beggars, and the retarded or mentally ill were selected. Eventually, the selections moved deeper and deeper into the heart of the communities.[21] And then the ethical dilemmas were brought into the open. In Vilna, in 1941, for example, the Germans issued about 3,000 yellow work permits that protected a worker and his family members. All others were to be deported, and the selection was left to the *Judenrate* and the Jewish police. The rabbis in the community protested to the Jewish leaders that their actions defied Jewish law, and it would be better not to distribute any cards than to select some among them to be saved. Jacob Gens, head of the Jewish police, ignored their objections. Later, at a public meeting, he gave this rationale for his actions: "When they ask me for a thousand Jews, I hand them over; for if Jews will not give on our own, the Germans will come and take them by force. Then they will take not one thousand, but thousands . . . With hundreds, I save a thousand. With the thousands that I hand over, I save ten thousand."[22]

A similar situation occurred in the ghetto of Kovno in Lithuania in the fall of 1941, but there the rabbi's reaction was different. The Germans gave the Jewish council about 5,000 white cards to be distributed to "artisans" or skilled workers and their families. At first the people suspected nothing, but soon word leaked out that the cards were actually "life permits," and whoever did not possess one would be deported and destroyed. The ghetto went wild, with people pushing their way into the council offices demanding cards, and grabbing cards from one another. Inexplicably, the Germans did not carry out their action at that time, but about a month later the Nazis ordered the Jewish council to round up all the ghetto inhabitants in the square to have their work papers inspected. Members of the council, knowing that this meant the selection and destruction of a major portion of the ghetto population, met to decide whether to obey the order or ignore it and take a chance on the consequences. They decided to consult the chief rabbi of Kovno, Rabbi Abraham Duber Cahana Shapiro. According to reports, Shapiro, weakened by illness, fainted when asked to rule on the matter. After he recovered, he spent the entire night studying his texts, and then ruled that if a community as a whole is threatened, and some way can be found to save some of its members, community leaders must take on the responsibility of doing everything they can to save those members. In this case, then, the community leaders must carry out German orders and gather all the people in the square.[23] As a result of that roundup, almost 9,000 people were sent to their death.

Rabbi Shapiro's ruling seems to contradict directly both the talmudic rulings about terrorists and Maimonides codification of those rules. Although he did not explain his rationale, it is possible that he felt that the council was not in itself selecting people for death. Perhaps he assumed that the council was simply rounding up people and the actual selections would be made by the Nazis. Or, he may have considered the text of the two men in the desert and decided that under any circumstances, it was more important to save one life than to lose two lives.

In any event, many rabbis of that time and later disagreed with his opinion, and in some areas, as in Upper East Silesia, the rabbis argued that the Jewish councils should not carry out the selections.[24] In several communities, council members refused to participate in the selections on moral grounds and were themselves shot or deported for their refusal.[25] Later, the councils were to be sharply criticized for their actions. Hannah Arendt,[26] among others, accused them of collaborating with the Nazis. After the war, a Jewish court held in Holland tried several members of the Dutch *Joodse Raade* (Jewish Council), but none was condemned as a traitor against his people.

Closely related to the issue of selecting people for deportation and

death was the moral and ethical responsibility incumbent upon community leaders to tell their people the real purpose of the selections and
deportations. It was, of course, to the benefit of the Nazis for Jews to be
under the illusion that deportation simply meant resettlement. Much has
been written about the so-called "passivity" of the victims, but in large
measure Jews who were deported did not rebel because they had no
knowledge of what they were destined to suffer. Sometimes that lack of
knowledge stemmed from deliberate deception on the part of Jewish community leaders, who did in fact know the truth.

In *The Politics of Genocide,* Randolph Braham describes "the conspiracy of silence" among Jewish and non-Jewish leaders in Hungary and
elsewhere. One of those leaders was (Rezso) Kasztner. Some people
allege that he made a deal with Adolf Eichmann; in exchange for silence
about deportations, Kasztner could choose and rescue about 20,000
"prominent" Hungarian Jewish leaders. After the war Kasztner was involved in a libel suit in Israel concerning his alleged collaboration with the
Nazi that led to the deportation of large numbers of Hungarian Jews with
little resistance. Although convicted by the Jerusalem District Court, he
was acquitted by the Supreme Court of Israel. The defense argued that
Kasztner believed there was no hope for the Jews of Hungary and that
warning them of the fate that awaited them would do no good and would
only endanger the few who might possibly be saved. By his actions, it was
maintained, he did manage to save some.[27]

Although never formally accused in the same way, the eminent German Jewish rabbi and scholar Leo Baeck followed a similar practice of
silence when he was interned in Theresienstadt. Baeck had been deported
to the camp in January, 1943. In August of that year, he learned from a
man named Grünberg, a Czech engineer, the truth about the transports
that carried people away from the camp and delivered them to Auschwitz.
He struggled with the question of whether to tell the council of Elders at
Theresienstadt what he knew, and finally decided not to because word
would spread through the camp. Since there was no hope of being saved,
he reasoned, "living in the expectation of death by gassing would only be
the harder."[28] Baeck argued that this situation was similar to that of
doctors dealing with a hopeless case of illness. It might be noted that
nothing in Jewish law forbids doctors from telling the truth to dying patients; emphasis is placed on the manner in which the truth is told. The
Shulhan Arukh (Code of Jewish Law) permits a physician to tell a dying
patient to set his or her affairs in order and to confess. The patient must be
assured that such action does not necessarily mean that death is im-
minent.[29]

Baeck has been criticized for his silence. By not speaking out, he was, in some ways, violating the talmudic law forbidding some people to be selected for death while others are saved. He also prevented people from actively fighting deportation, and, in an existential way, from having control of their own lives. It is easy, of course, to pass judgment with the benefit of hindsight. But given the traumas of those days, I do not believe we have the right, any of us, at this time, to judge or condemn the actions of humans forced to make superhuman decisions. Nor, as Lucy Dawidowicz points out,[30] do we know that had the Jewish leaders acted differently they could have saved more lives or even saved as many as they did. As Kasztner wrote, "Was it grace or fate if, under these circumstances, we were not always able to prevail in these endeavors?"[31]

Nevertheless, within the context of Judaism, we do need to acknowledge that principles of moral behavior exist even for the most extreme situations. The concept of the "redness" of all blood and of the immorality of choosing one person to be killed in order to save others stand as ideal guidelines for ethical conduct. The Jew from Oberland chose to live by those principles even though the rabbi whom he consulted strove to ease his situation by not telling him the actual laws. Within their circumstances, Jewish leaders were not always able to meet the standards set by those ideals. Their inability, however, does not detract from the validity of the laws and traditions, which remain now, as they always have been, absolutes toward which to strive.

The issues of weighing one life against another and of saving lives at the cost of others were community issues during the Holocaust. On an individual basis men and women were faced with sickening choices, often having to balance their own lives against the lives of others. Like the two men in the wilderness in the talmudic puzzle struggling with the question of who should have the water, so European Jews struggled in their everyday lives with decisions about how far to go in protecting themselves or in risking themselves for others. The Bible commands, "neither shall you stand idly by the blood of your neighbor",[32] and this commandment has been taken to mean that if you see someone in danger and you are in a position to help, you are obligated to do so. But to what extent should you endanger your own life to help someone else?

Questions of this sort were posed to Rabbi Ephraim Oshry, a Lithuanian rabbi of Kovno, during World War II. After the war, Oshry published several volumes of responsa to religious questions which he said had been brought to him throughout the war years. One of those responsa dealt with an incident that happened early in the war. Soon after the occupation of Lithuania, the Germans began rounding up Jews and holding them captive. Lithuanians, with a history of anti–Semitism, joined in the attacks and actions against the Jews. Among the Jews taken captive in one of the roundups were a number of yeshiva students. The dean of the yeshiva asked Rabbi David Itzkowitz, a prominent Jewish leader, if he would negotiate with the Lithuanians to free the students. Doing so would place the rabbi in grave danger because he might then be held captive along with the others.

Rabbi Oshry was asked whether Rabbi Itzkowitz could, according to Jewish law, endanger his own life in order to rescue the others. Many commentators and codifiers, although not all, interpret the biblical law about not standing idly by the blood of your neighbor to mean that a person might risk "possible danger" to himself or herself in order to save someone else from "certain danger." Accordingly, as in the case of the two men with the water, Rabbi Oshry ruled that because Rabbi Itzkowitz was certainly risking possible danger, the law would not demand that he approach the Lithuanians. But in keeping with the spirit of the law, such an action on his part was permitted, and would be looked upon as an act of great piety.[33] Rabbi Itzkowitz carried out his mission and survived it, although he later died in a concentration camp.

We have discussed the value of every life in Judaism as well as the issues of weighing one life against another. A third and final area of importance is the subject of giving up one's life for a value that may even be higher than life itself — the subject of martyrdom in the name of a cause or ideal.

In Judaism, martyrdom for religious beliefs, or simply for being a Jew, is called kiddush ha–shem, the sanctification of God's name. While martyrs have been greatly honored in Jewish tradition, martyrdom has not been held up as either an ideal or a state to seek out. Maimonides codified Jewish attitudes toward martyrdom, emphasizing that in order to save his or her life, a Jew may break any law except for committing murder, sexual unchastity (such as incest or adultery) or idolatry. However, he stressed, that if a Jew is made to transgress a law in public or at a time of great religious persecution, when the purpose of the persecution is to abolish Judaism itself, he is required to suffer martyrdom rather than transgress. On the other hand, Maimonides made a point of saying that a person who suffered death when it was not required — when he or she could have broken a law instead — is not to be considered a martyr but an ordinary suicide.[34]

This last view of Maimonides aroused enormous criticism by later French and German commentators, who felt that people who sacrificed themselves even when not required were, indeed, martyrs and that the choice is left with the individual.

The difference between Maimonides' approach and that of his critics reflects a difference in attitudes between the Spanish or Sephardic tradition and the Germanic or Ashkenazic tradition. These differences are discussed by Gerson Cohen in his classic paper, "Messianic Postures of Ashkenazim and Sephardim."[35] In brief, Spanish medieval Jews, living in a more rationalistic and sophisticated milieu than the Ashkenazim, had a tradition of conversion rather than martyrdom. They did not hold strong belief in physical resurrection, but through their philosophic and geometric studies, they predicted the advent of the Messiah, perhaps in their lifetime. For them, conversion was a way of being physically present when the Messiah arrived, with their bodies whole and their souls intact because although they had converted they continued to practice Judaism secretly.

Ashkenazic Jews had a firm, fundamentalist belief in physical resurrection after death, and a belief in the more distant advent of the Messiah at an unspecified time far in the future. Entire communities suffered martyrdom rather than violate a single precept of their religion, maintaining that they would be resurrected after they had died; their bodies and souls joined together again. Accounts of martyrs of the past were part of the everyday existence of East European Jews, and people who died for their religion were revered as great saints.

I believe that this Ashkenazic attitude toward martyrdom influenced the thinking of many Holocaust victims. That is not to say that they went meekly to their deaths, but that when faced with death, believing, traditionalist Jews were able to see themselves as part of that long line of martyrs who marched out of centuries of Jewish history.

Martyrdom was understood and accepted by pious East European Jews. Rabbi Oshry writes of one man, Reb Elyah, who asked to learn the correct form of the benediction for dying as a martyr and then went among the crowds that had been rounded up in Kovno teaching that benediction to the people.[36] And there are a number of descriptions in Holocaust literature of Hasidic rabbis and ordinary people who went to their deaths with great dignity singing the "Ani Ma'amin," affirming their belief in God and praising God as they walked along, wrapped in their prayer shawls.[37]

Perhaps the finest summary of Jewish attitudes toward martyrdom and toward life is embodied in the words of a rabbi of the Warsaw ghetto, delivered in January, 1943, several months before the uprising in April.

Rabbi Menahem Zemba of Praga, a well-known rabbi and scholar in this Warsaw suburb, who was later killed, spoke during a meeting of communal leaders:

> Sanctification of the Divine Name manifests itself in varied ways. Indeed, its special form is a product of the times we live in. During the First Crusade, at the end of the eleventh century, *Halakha* — as an echo of political events of the time — had determined one way of reacting to the distress of the Franco-German Jews, whereas in the middle of the twentieth century, during the rapid liquidation of the Jews in Poland, *Halakha* prompts us to react in an entirely different manner. In the past during religious persecutions, we were required by the law 'to give up our lives even for the least essential practice.' In the present, however, when we are faced by an arch-foe, whose unparalleled ruthlessness and total annihilation purposes know no bounds, *Halakha* demands that we fight and resist to the very end with unequalled determination and valor for the sake of sanctification of the Divine Name.[38]

His definition of *kiddush ha-shem* as an activist struggle to stay alive or die fighting was in the tradition of Masada, the Bar Kokhba rebellion, and the fighters for the State of Israel.

Throughout this discussion on the value of each life, on the dilemmas of choosing one life over another, and on the meaning of martyrdom in Judaism, one theme recurs. That is, that life is unique and invaluable, and it needs to be cherished and sustained at almost any cost. Ironically, in our open society today, those special lessons of Judaism, so vital during hundreds of years of persecutions and sufferings, have become submerged into a larger culture that seems to glorify violence, and in which life often becomes trivialized and devalued.

This anti-Jewish viewpoint about life was epitomized in a book that received a great deal of publicity, called *Exit House*.[39] The book was published shortly after the suicide of its author, Jo Roman, a New York artist. *Exit House* describes in great detail why she chose to take her own life and how she planned to go about doing it.

Roman had decided long ago that she would end her life at the age of seventy because she wanted always to live life to its fullest, never to be in any way held back by infirmity or old age. In her early 60s she developed breast cancer, and rather than undergo mastectomy, she decided to push her deadline with death up and end her life. In a letter that she instructed be sent to the *New York Times* after her death, and which hit the front page of the *Times,* Roman analyzed her choice of death and advocated "rational suicide" for others. A long videotape was made and shown on educational television of conversations she had with friends and of a party held on the last evening of her life. "I don't want to have a day of pain," she said. "I don't want to have a minute of pain." After the party, Roman took a fatal overdose of pills, which she swallowed with champagne.

Somehow the broad publicity and sympathetic presentation of her suicide made Jo Roman a heroine, a pioneer, an avant–garde thinker who had something significant to tell us about life and death. The fact that she was not in the final throes of a deathly illness, that she could have lived probably a normal life span and a normal life had she accepted an operation that thousands of women choose to accept, was forgotten in the midst of the attention given her case.

In Jewish thinking, Jo Roman would be considered an ordinary suicide, who, according to law, would not be accorded traditional burial rites.[40] That is not to say that Judaism shows no sympathy for desperately ill people for whom suicide seems the only solution.[41] Such sympathy does exist, and some rabbinic scholars have made a substantial case for permitting terminal patients to die in peace without using heroic measures to save them.[42] But there is no place in Jewish thought for the concept of "rational suicide," in order to avoid the pains and heartaches of life.

Jo Roman's idea of "rational suicide" stands in direct contrast to the survival struggle of thousands upon thousands of Holocaust victims. I believe that the Jews need to pay attention once again to what is probably one of the greatest teachings in the Jewish culture. That is, that "Man was created as a single individual to teach us that anyone who destroys a single life is as though he destroyed an entire world."

In contrast to "rational suicide" is a legend that surrounds the death of Moses, the great teacher and lawgiver of Israel. When God told Moses that his life was drawing to a close, Moses would not accept the verdict. With one hour of his life left, he pleaded, "Lord of the Universe, let me become like the beasts of the field that eat grass and drink water, but let me live and see the world." But God refused. Again he prayed, "If not, then let me become like a bird that flies in every direction, gathers its food every day and returns to its nest every evening." Once more, God refused. Seeing that he could not be saved through prayer, Moses sat down and occupied himself by writing God's name on a scroll. When Samael, the angel of death, approached and saw Moses writing, his face radiant with holiness, the angel withdrew in fear. God sent Samael back again, however, and this time, Moses fought with him until he blinded the bearer of death with his staff. Then a heavenly voice declared, "Enough, Moses, the time of your death has come." Now Moses obeyed God's command. He lay down, closed his eyes, and folded his hands across his chest. But in one final burst of rebellion, his soul refused to leave his body. Then, the legend concludes: "God kissed Moses and took away his soul with a kiss of the mouth. And God wept."[43]

Holocaust victims did not die gently with a kiss of God on their lips. Some died cursing God and some in silence. But the large majority of them, like Moses, did all that they could to hold onto the last breaths of life, until that final moment when the heavenly voice cried, "Enough!"

"I set before you life and death, blessing and curse," says the book of Deuteronomy. "Choose life . . ."[44] This is the Jewish ethic of living.

Notes

1. Meisels, Zevi Hirsch. *Responsa M'Kadeshe Hashem.* vol 1, no. 3 (in Hebrew). Chicago: Published by the author, 1955, p. 8.

2. Genesis. Chapter 1, verses 26–27. For a discussion of the unique relationship of humans to God, see Francine Klagsbrun, *Voices of Wisdom — Jewish Ideals and Ethics for Everyday Living.* New York: Pantheon Books, 1980, pp. 391–402.

3. Mishnah, tractate Sanhedrin. Chapter 4, paragraph 5.

4. Ibid

5. Leviticus. 24:17

6. Greenberg, Moshe, "Some Postulates of Biblical Criminal Law." In: *The Jewish Expression.* Edited by Judah Goldin. New York: Bantam Books, 1970, pp. 18–37.

7. Babylonian Talmud. Tractate Sanhedrin, p. 37b.

8. Mishnah, Makkot. 1:10.

9. *Mekhilta of Rabbi Ishmael.* Tractate Shabbata, chapter 1; Babylonian Talmud. Yoma, p. 85b.

10. Babylonian Talmud. Yoma, p. 84b.

11. Babylonian Talmud. Bava Mezia, p. 62a.

12. Jacobs, Louis. Greater Love Hath No Man . . . The Jewish Point of View of Self–Sacrifice. *Judaism.* New York vol. 6, 1957, pp. 41–47.

13. Babylonian Talmud. Sanhedrin, p. 74a.

14. Ibid

15. Jerusalem Talmud. Terumot, 8:12.

16. Maimonides. *Code (Mishne Torah).* "Basic Principles of the Torah," chapter 5, section 5.

17. Rozman, Shlomo. *Zikhron Kedoshim.* Rehovot: (Published by the author), 1968, pp. 380ff.

18. For a discussion of the councils and their dilemmas, see Jacob Robinson, "Introduction: Some Basic Issues that Faced the Jewish Councils." In: Isaiah Trunk, *Judenrät.* New York: Macmillan, 1972, pp. xxv–xxxv.

19. Robinson, Jacob. "Some Basic Issues that Faced the Jewish Councils." p. xxviii.

20. Dawidowicz, Lucy. *The War Against the Jews.* New York: Holt, Rinehart and Winston, 1975, p. 226 and pp. 240–241.

21. Trunk. *Judenrät,* pp. 420–424.

22. Dawidowicz. *The War Against the Jews.* p. 289.

23. Ibid., pp. 282–283.

24. Ibid., p. 299.

25. Trunk. *Judenrät*. pp. 437–438.

26. Arendt, Hannah. *Eichmann in Jerusalem; A Report on the Banality of Evil*. New York: Viking, 1963, pp. 117–118.

27. Braham, Randolph L. *The Politics of Genocide: The Holocaust in Hungary*. vol. 2. New York: Columbia University Press, 1981, pp. 719–722.

28. Boehm, Erich H., ed. *We Survived: The Stories of Fourteen of the Hidden and Hunted of Nazi Germany*. New Haven: Yale University Press, 1949, p. 293.

29. Caro, Joseph. *Code of Jewish Law (Shulhan Arukh)*. "Yoreh De'ah," chapter 335, section 7; chapter 338, section 1.

30. Dawidowicz, *"The War Against the Jews,"* p. 350.

31. Cited in Robinson, Jacob. "Some Basic Issues that Faced the Jewish Councils," p. xxxiv.

32. *Leviticus*. 19:16

33. Oshry, Ephraim. *Mi Ma'amakin*. 3 vols. New York: (Published by the author), 1949, 1963, 1969. vol. 2, p. 7.

34. Maimonides, *Code*. "Basic Principles of the Torah," chapter 5, sections 1–4.

35. Cohen, Gerson D. "Messianic Postures of Ashkenazim and Sephardim." Leo Baeck Memorial Lecture number 9. New York: Leo Baeck Institute, 1967, pp. 33–42.

36. Oshry. *Mi Ma'amakin,* vol 2, p. 28.

37. For further reference see Schindler, Pesach. The Holocaust and Kiddush Ha–Shem in Hassidic Thought. *Tradition*. New York, vol. 13–14, 1973, pp. 88–104.

38. Quoted in H. J. Zimmels, *The Echo of the Nazi Holocaust in Rabbinic Literature*. New York: Ktan, 1977, p. 63.

39. Roman, Jo. *Exit House*. New York: Seaview Books, 1980.

40. Tractate *Mourning*. 2:1–4.

41. See Cohen, Gerson, "Messianic Postures," p. 37 and footnote 48.

42. See Klagsbrun, Francine, *Voices of Wisdom*. pp. 505–509.

43. This is a shortened version of the legend as told in *Deuteronomy Rabbah*. Vilna: Romm, 1921, chapter 11, section 10.

44. *Deuteronomy* 30:19.

II THE ALLIES AND THE HOLOCAUST

2 THE HORTHY OFFER
A Missed Opportunity for Rescuing Jews in 1944

Bela Vago

A wealth of essays and books have been published, mostly during and since the sixties, about the role of the Allies in helping and rescuing Jews during the Holocaust. Those among the historians who strove for objectivity did not hesitate to emphasize the lack of objective conditions. These conditions in many cases jeopardized or altogether precluded rescue actions, even when the Allies' readiness and goodwill were unquestionable. An example of the juxtaposition of sympathetic attitudes with unfavorable objective conditions is the controversy concerning the bombing of Auschwitz; technicalities and military factors are invoked by some historians to account for the Allies' reluctance to carry out air strikes over the death camps.

The controversies over missed Allied rescue opportunities were particularly heated when the initiative came from the Nazis or their satellites and the Allies were expected to react positively. The most publicized case in this category of controversies is the so-called "blood for trucks" mission of Joel Brand in 1944. Perhaps the most striking case of an unheeded opportunity, however, was the Hungarian move in the summer of 1944 known as the Horthy Offer. Irrespective of its real motives and feasibility, this offer put the Allies into a position where responsiveness and concrete actions were expected as proof of their readiness to help and rescue Jewish lives. The negotiations between the Allies and their reaction to the offer made by Miklós Horthy, the Regent of Hungary, constitute a test case that has led to conclusions which discredit the goodwill of the Allies, mainly the British. This episode is labelled a "lost opportunity," without the excuse of logistical considerations or other kinds of objective, hindering circumstances.

After the German occupation of Hungary on March 19, 1944, the concentration and later deportation to Auschwitz of the country's Jewish population was carried out at an unprecedented pace, with an efficiency unparalleled in the short history of the annihilation of European Jewry. By July 9, 1944 the "dejewification" of the country had partly been achieved. By that date almost 440,000 Jews had been deported from the countryside and the suburbs of Budapest.[1] All that remained was the capital's Jewish population and the Jews stranded in Budapest after the entry of the Germans—some 200,000 to 250,000 persons.[2] In addition, tens of thousands of young men, most of them in the 20 to 45 age bracket and enrolled in forced labor service companies, were scattered throughout the country and on the Eastern front. At that time thousands of former members of the labor service companies were already in Soviet POW camps, and tens of thousands had perished on the Ukrainian front. The decimated Hungarian Jewry, already reduced to about thirty percent of its 1941 size, was to be liquidated sometime in July 1944 with the deportation of the Budapest Jews. When Hitler's plenipotentiary in Budapest reported on July 11th that the deportation of the Jews from the provinces had been completed, he also informed his government about the next step: the deportation of the Jewish population of Budapest.[3] These were the fateful days when Admiral Horthy stepped in to halt the deportations.

Horthy did not resign after the German occupation of Hungary. He consented to the installation of the pro–Nazi Döme Sztójay administration. He did not lessen the Hungarian military involvement in the war on Hitler's side. He also automatically sanctioned the deportation of the Jews from the provinces. However, from the very moment of the German occupation, he was looking for opportunities to free himself from Hitler's clutches. Long before the occupation, he had agreed to Prime Minister Miklós Kállay's secret peace feelers, and gave a free hand to his son, Miklós Horthy, Jr., to run an underground office preparing the *volte face*. When incomplete news reached him about the fate of the deportees, he disapproved of the German–Hungarian measures and turned against his most extremist officials who were responsible for the Jewish tragedy. The developments on the military map, especially the success of the Allied invasion in Normandy, convinced Horthy that the time was ripe for the extrication of his country from the war.

A number of internal events hastened Horthy's efforts to implement radical change in the Hungarian government. The public was in a defeatist mood, the behavior of the German troops after the occupation strengthened anti-German feelings, the economic spoliation of the country revolted the man in the street, and the military leaders were bitterly disappointed because of Hitler's failure to provide the promised military aid against the rapidly advancing Soviet armies. Moreover, the end of June and the beginning of July brought the first effective air bombardments of Budapest, creating a mood of panic.[4] In the second half of June, Horthy became alarmed by news of a right radical conspiracy against him.[5]

It seems clear that Horthy was sensitive to the Allies' warnings about the responsibility of those who sanctioned anti-Jewish actions.[6] The response to the telegram sent him by Gustav V, King of Sweden, on 30 June, 1944, protesting Hungary's anti–Jewish crimes, should be seen against this background.[7] The conjuncture of military and economic situations, the despondent mood and the right-extremist conspiracy can explain Horthy's reaction to the Swedish appeal and the Western warnings. Around July 10th, Horthy decided to dismiss the Sztójay government, appoint a military government led by General Géza Lakatos, and — as a gesture toward the Allies — stop the deportations.[8]

On July 15, 1944, Horthy informed Edmund Veesenmayer, the German plenipotentiary in Budapest, of his plans to appoint the General Lakatos cabinet. Veesenmayer drew the correct conclusions: the change of government would not only entail the suspension of the deportations, but would also have detrimental effects upon the German war economy and Hitler's conduct of the war.[9]

Horthy took another step to indicate his determination to change Hungary's attitude towards the Jews. He initiated or approved the elimination from the administration of those who were responsible for the deportations, and went so far as to punish some of them — in particular, the two pro-Nazi, extreme anti-Semitic under-secretaries in the Ministry of the Interior, László Baky and László Endre.[10]

Hitler's reaction was a mixture of offense and menace. He instructed Veesenmayer through Ribbentrop to protest against the planned dismissal of Sztójay, and especially warned Horthy not to hurt those who had carried out the anti-Jewish measures. Moreover, Hitler demanded the immediate deportation of the Budapest Jews, with the exception of a tiny minority of exempted persons, but warned the Hungarians that he would desist from his agreement to these exceptions if there were any delay to the deportation.[11]

Surprisingly, Horthy did not yield to Hitler and threatened to resign and thereby cause disarray in the country, since ninety percent of the population was behind him.[12]

The Horthy papers, part of which were published in 1965 in Budapest, contained a letter drafted by the Regent on July 17 to be sent to Hitler through Veesenmayer. Apparently, the letter was never received by the Führer. In addition to bitter complaints against the German occupation troops and especially the Gestapo, which constituted a "heavy load on German–Hungarian friendship," Horthy brought up the Jewish question as a reason for the need to change the administration. The further solution of the Jewish problem, wrote Horthy, "will be realized without the often unnecessary brutal and inhuman methods. The former government has applied methods which have been applied by no other nation, and have produced the disapproving criticism even of the German authorities in the country."[13]

The complaint against the inhuman treatment of the Jews sounded strange coming from the Regent, who two months earlier had sanctioned the deportation to Auschwitz of some 430,000 persons. But the condemnation of the atrocious measures should be appreciated since it was addressed to Hitler at a time when Hungary was still at the mercy of the German army. One can assume that Horthy was ill-informed or misinformed; actually, he pretended after the war that until August 1944 he had not been aware of the real fate of the deportees.[14]

Although Horthy's assertion sounds implausible, contradicting his own positive decisions at the beginning of July, one cannot overlook the fact that from March 19 to early July Horthy kept or was kept at a low profile in the country's political life. The sudden indignation and revulsion of the veteran anti-Semite against the brutality of the Nazis and the local extremists was a combination of political opportunism influenced by Horthy's moderate, anti-Nazi friends and his gentry mentality which approved of "humane," "conventional" anti-Jewish steps but opposed physical annihilation.

On July 17, the day Horthy showed courage in his talk with Veesenmayer, the Jewish question was raised in an interview granted by Sztójay to Maximilian Jäger, the Swiss Minister in Budapest. Jäger warned the Hungarian Prime Minister that because of Hungary's anti-Jewish measures his government was considering the severance of diplomatic relations with Budapest — doing so under the pressure of indignant public opinion.[15] This intervention may have prompted Horthy's decision to turn to the International Red Cross Committee (ICRC) and to the Swiss government with his proposal, which became known as the Horthy Offer.

On July 18, 1944 the Hungarian Foreign Ministry, still in Sztójay's hands, sent a letter to the Swiss legation in Budapest, indirectly replying to an American inquiry and protest about the fate of Hungarian Jewry.[16] The Hungarian note included a short survey of the Jewish problem, justifying the anti-Jewish measures and legislation as a means of national self-defense. The note emphasized the need to neutralize Jewish defeatism as the Soviet armies were advancing towards the Hungarian borders. Confirming the deportations, it stated that the Jews were being sent to work, inside the country and abroad. The Foreign Ministry stressed the fact that the rules of humanity and justice were always respected in the implementation of these measures. The "sporadic" incidents contravening the "humane" principles were ascribed to low-ranking officials who would be called to account for their acts. Decent living conditions ensured by the Hungarians to the Jews were described in detail. Only in the last paragraph of the entirely deceptive note was there mention of the turning point in Hungary's handling of the Jewish problem. This paragraph related the government's willingness to react positively to the interventions of "some organizations from abroad;" to allow material help to the Jews, and to permit "a very considerable number of Jews to emigrate to neutral countries, respectively to Palestine."[17]

The discrepancy between the blatant lies about the "humane" treatment of the Jews and Horthy's repugnance at the "inhumanity" of his subordinates reflects the deep rift between Sztójay and those around Horthy who decided to get rid of the Nazi puppet government and prepare the *volte face*.[18] In the meantime, Imre Tahy, the Hungarian Chargé d'Affaires *ad interim* in Bern, saw the leaders of the ICRC (on July 17) and informed them of the shift in Hungary's policy toward Jews. Tahy replied to the Red Cross' inquiry of July 7. He notified Carl J. Burckhardt about

1. Hungary's consent to Red Cross aid for the inmates of ghettos and concentration camps;
2. Hungary's agreement to the evacuation of Jewish children younger than ten years ("if possible to Palestine"), and Germany's agreement to the evacuation;
3. Hungary's willingness to allow the emigration of all Jews in possession of a Palestine visa (and also about Germany's agreement to their evacuation);
4. Hungary's agreement to the emigration of those Jews who had parents in Sweden or business relations with Swedish citizens to leave for Sweden or Palestine — likewise with Germany's consent.

Tahy also informed the Red Cross of Hungary's willingness to allow the visit of a War Refugee Board commission. He seemed anxious to shift the responsibility for the fate of the Jews onto Germany.[19]

As a result of this meeting, the ICRC released a communiqué mentioning the halting of the deportation, the Hungarian agreement to the Red Cross to help the interned and "marked" Jews, and the invitation to the Red Cross to be instrumental in the emigration of visa-holding children under ten years of age. Finally, the ICRC informed the Allies and the free world about the Hungarian consent to the emigration to Palestine of those who were in possession of proper visas.[20] On July 21, the ICRC sent its special delegate to Budapest to hasten the implementation of the offer. Dr. Robert Schirmer, the Chief ICRC representative in Berlin was instructed by Professor Max Huber, the President of the ICRC, to act in Budapest.[21]

On the day the Swiss government was approached by the Hungarian Foreign Ministry, the British Minister in Bern was informed of the Hungarian government's approval of the emigration from Hungary of all Jews possessing entry visas for various countries, including Palestine. The Swiss authorities also reported that the "German government will give transit permits for occupied territories. Necessary arrangements for this evacuation are to be made as soon as possible (by the Swiss Legation in Budapest) in collaboration with the Palestine Office in Budapest. Hungarian police passports will probably be used as travel documents."[22]

At the same time (July 20) the ICRC informed the Allies that it had received "official Hungarian assurances" that the deportation had ceased and the ICRC was authorized to provide relief to the surviving Jews in Hungary. Furthermore, the Committee was empowered by the Hungarians to cooperate in the evacuation of Jewish children under ten years of age in possession of visas to "reception countries," and "all Jews . . . holding entrance visas to Palestine."[23]

It is surprising that in his memoirs Horthy downgraded this important step. After mentioning that he ordered one of his armored divisions to Budapest to hinder the deportation of the Budapest Jews, he only briefly chronicles the actions by the ICRC and King Gustav of Sweden through Raoul Wallenberg to induce the Germans to consent to the free emigration of the Jews to Palestine. He, the Regent, fully endorsed these interventions, although, "unfortunately, without any success" wrote Horthy.[24]

As early as July 20 the British Foreign Office informed some of its diplomatic representatives that it was engaged in consultation with both the United States government and the Jewish Agency about Hungarian intentions. The Foreign Office, though, still questioned whether "the Germans, or the Hungarians, who are credited with having made offers to the International Red Cross in regard to exit-visas for refugees . . . are serious."[25]

The new situation, namely the Hungarian willingness to allow thousands of Jews to leave Budapest, and the presumed German agreement to Horthy's decision, faced the Allies with a delicate and unforeseen dilemma. They were now required to either respond with an immediate and unreserved agreement to collaborate in the evacuation of the Jews from Budapest and in providing for their accommodation, or to wait until the logistical details of the action could be solved and territories of refuge found. On July 21 the Foreign Office opined that "a limited number of visa-holding Jews should be manageable, but there will no doubt be heavy pressure on United States and United Kingdom governments to grant fresh visas in numbers far beyond the transport possibilities."[26] Simultaneously, the British suggested a reliance on the Intergovernmental Committee on Political Refugees (IGC) to find solutions to the challenge.

From the very beginning two contradictory factors caused uneasiness in London: among the released persons a very high percentage were to be children requiring immediate consideration; on the other hand, the prospect of a flow of Jews with Palestinian permits must have contributed to a dilatory attitude from the first hours. In the summer of 1944, the Colonial Office and the High Commissioner in Jerusalem were already worried about the possibility of a massive immigration to Palestine of survivors from the liberated territories. "It is clear that the floodgates of Eastern Europe are now going to be opened," wrote R. M. A. Hankey, a junior official in the Eastern Department of the Foreign Office in his minutes, "and that we shall in a very short time have masses of Eastern European Jews on our hands." He was worried about the Arab implications of the flow of survivors to Palestine, and basing his apprehensions on previous analyses by the Foreign Office, feared that "a serious political situation would arise throughout the Arab world as soon as the Palestine quotas were filled."[27]

In order to avoid such a situation, Hankey suggested that a distinction be made between refugees and immigrants, stating that "it is not reasonable that all refugees from Europe should automatically be regarded as suitable for immigration to Palestine because they are of Jewish race or persuasion." The suggestion to set up camps in the Mediterranean area was raised in the Foreign Office with the specification that these should not be established in Palestine, "and preferably not too near to Palestine." The Foreign Office, according to Hankey, "must at all costs protect the Colonial Office from unreasonable pressure to receive in Palestine all Jewish refugees . . ." In his view, "this is a matter of the highest political importance, affecting our relations with the whole Arab world, including Egypt."[28]

Although the quoted sentences were written by a middle-echelon official of the Foreign Office, they faithfully reflected the prevailing mood of the policymakers, and constituted the crux of the dilemma of the British government in handling the Horthy offer. Obviously, the "blood for trucks" offer cast its shadow on the Horthy offer. The skepticism which characterized the Allied reaction to the Brand mission, and eventually their categoric refusal to consider the Gestapo deal, indirectly influenced the cautious and hesitant response to the Horthy offer, especially on the part of the British. There was, however, no connection whatsoever between the two offers.[29]

The Swiss authorities and the ICRC informed the Jewish Agency almost immediately about the Horthy offer. Essentially, the Jewish Agency was told about four main issues involved in the offer:

1. The deportations would stop;
2. The ICRC would be provided with facilities to help the interned Jews in Hungary itself;
3. Those holding Palestinian certificates would be allowed to leave;
4. Children under ten years of age in possession of visas for any neutral or Allied country would be allowed to leave.[30]

Although issue number two had no practical implications, the Jewish Agency pressed for prompt action, primarily in order to promote emigration. A fruitless search began for the proper body to be entrusted with the responsibility for implementing the offer. The Jewish Agency leaders suggested in London that the IGC send a representative to Budapest, but the idea was rejected by the Allies.[31] The Jewish leaders accepted the suggestion that the ICRC be the mediator, and consequently asked that a Red Cross delegate be sent to Budapest. In fact, with the dispatch of Dr. Schirmer to Budapest this demand materialized even before the Jews had an opportunity to raise the suggestion.

From the start, however, Jewish representatives in London were warned about the difficulties which would cause delay in carrying out the rescue operations: financing, transportation and accommodation.[32] On their part the Jewish Agency delegates in London pressed for an urgent and positive response "not necessarily . . . involving big commitments, but one which would show that the American and British governments . . . were taking the offer seriously, and were not putting it in the same category as the Brandt (sic) affair."[33] At the same time, the Jewish

Agency initiated concrete steps in order to foster immigration to Palestine. The Jewish Agency representatives in Istanbul took the Hungarian offer at face value and sent instructions to Budapest through underground channels about organizing the emigration to Palestine.[34] The optimism of the Jewish Agency was strengthened by bits of information such as those received by its Istanbul representatives from Hungarian and Red Cross sources.[35]

Optimistic views on the feasibility of the Horthy offer, including transit through the Balkans, were aired in different Allied circles.[36] But again and again the British fear of having Palestine as final destination for the rescued cast its shadow on the negotiations between the Allies. As early as July 22 the Foreign Office was looking for alternative destinations, including Tripolitania and Algeria. The Foreign Office also suggested a joint approach with the United States government to various Latin American republics and to Portugal (with regard to Angola) appealing for asylum for the rescued. London also hoped that the United States would accept a considerable number of Jews.[37]

The British fear was augmented by Red Cross opinions that "the facilities granted (by Hungary) will only allow Jewish emigration from Hungary to take place if (the British government) is prepared to accept within the British Empire a considerably larger number of Jewish emigrants than has been the case hitherto."[38] The ICRC also proposed that the public statement published by the British and the Americans about the acceptance of the offer should mention the number of British visas granted to the Hungarian Jews.[39] Presumably Horthy's decision was not influenced at all by the number of British visas. On the other hand, the Red Cross and above all the United States emphasized the importance accorded by those involved in the rescue operations to London's willingness to open the gates of Palestine.[40]

The ICRC representatives were "extremely anxious" that there be a positive answer to the offer as soon as possible, and accurately evaluated the psychological and political corollaries of the Allied reaction: unless a positive answer was forthcoming "there is a danger that it will be withdrawn or, at any rate, whittled down, on the excuse that other countries, and especially the United Kingdom and the United States of America are not really interested in the matter."[41] Apparently, the IGC was also waiting for the appropriate instructions from the two Allied governments in order to implement the rescue operations, in coordination with the War Refugee Board.[42]

Had the British government acted promptly it would probably have enjoyed massive public support in Great Britain. On July 26, the Archbishop of Canterbury, representing the National Committee for Rescue from the Nazi Terror, led a delegation to the Foreign Office and suggested that Horthy be taken at his word by saying, "let as many of these people go as possible; we can take them all."[43] Sympathetic questions were raised in the House of Commons expressing great interest in the Hungarian offer and solicitude to ease the emigration.[44]

The United States reaction to the Horthy offer was unreservedly positive. In the second half of July, Washington asked the British several times to agree on joint efforts in order to convert the offer into deeds, namely to foster the emigration, particularly of the children, with the help of neutral countries, and provide the necessary material means for the implementation of the rescue activities.[45] The Americans considered the offer to be genuine and insisted that it "*must* be accepted as quickly as possible in order to save the largest number of lives possible."[46] Anticipating the British objections they asked that the reply "not be couched in terms of numbers for whom refuge can be found . . . nor should acceptance await calculation of other possible places in specified countries of asylum."[47] The Americans suggested that the two governments act immediately without waiting to consult or enlist the aid of other governments, and refused to shift the burden of the action onto the IGC, since such a solution would delay decisions and would be interpreted by Hungary as a virtual refusal of the offer.[48] The Americans agreed with the ICRC that a public statement to accept the offer was desirable. They also concurred with the ICRC on the point that the possibility of a withdrawal of the offer would lessen if a public declaration were forthcoming and that such a declaration would also forestall an attempt on the part of the Axis countries "to throw the blame for an eventual failure on the countries of immigration."[49] Consequently Washington proposed to the British that the ICRC should be informed about the acceptance of the offer no later than August 7.[50]

The Americans refuted some British concerns and excuses, including one asserting that the released Jews would leave Hungary in such numbers or with such speed that the Allies could not cope with the situation, and insisted that the two governments should commit themselves to take care of all the Jews who would be permitted to leave Hungary.[51] An impressive memorandum summing up the American views about the solution to these problems reached London on July 31. Earlier the Americans had made it clear to the British that "it might prove tragic if the fullest advantage of the present opportunity were not taken."[52]

In spite of the American deadline, August 7th, the British remained hesitant and undecided, even after the deadline date. The fear of a massive influx of Jews into Palestine haunted the British during the whole period which preceded the joint declaration. A meeting of the War Cabinet Committee on Refugees held on August 4 was inconclusive, because of the following dilemma:

a) The refusal to accept the Horthy offer might arouse hostile public opinion in Britain and in the United States,

but

b) Acceptance of the offer might risk civil war in Palestine owing to an inroad of Jews from Hungary into the Levant.[53]

At this meeting of the War Cabinet Committee on Refugees, the Secretary of State for the Colonies strongly objected to the Red Cross suggestions for the emigration of 41,000 Jews to Turkey via Romania. The meeting refused to join the United States in "signing a blank check" which the British could not honor. The participants were presented with a most improbable possibility; that the offer might have been inspired by Hitler in order "to create difficulties for the Allies in the Near East by allowing an exodus of Jews."[54]

As one of the War Cabinet Ministers bluntly put it: he was not sure at all if the Horthy offer "is not inspired or approved by Hitler as a plan to get rid of Jews and plant them on us or others." Sir Frank Newsam, the Home Minister, speculated that the offer might have been mounted by the Gestapo.[55] One of his remarks was characteristic of the outlook of those in charge of the Palestine policy: ". . . whatever happens we should not be maneuvered into a position in Palestine which breaks faith with the Arabs, and the agreed quota should not be exceeded."[56] A consensus was reached at the War Cabinet meeting of August 8 to accept the Horthy offer merely "as a gesture," informing the Americans at the same time "that they must not face us with the impossible in the question of providing accommodation."

One day earlier, on August 7, the Americans had agreed to the British request to postpone the joint decision until August 10.[57] The few days that remained before the new deadline were used by the British to convince the Americans that the IGC should be entrusted with the action; further, they were feverishly looking for refuge centers in the Mediterranean area, including Sicily, in order to exclude the Palestine alternative.

The second deadline for the joint declaration, August 10, was also not adhered to, because of the differences between the American wording and the British suggestions for semantic changes which in fact concealed essential problems. The British objected to accepting responsibility for "all Jews" permitted to leave Hungary, fearing that the number of rescued persons could amount to 60 to 70,000. They also insisted that cooperation with the Americans should be restricted to "the extent of (the British) resources,"[58] and asked explicitly for an American assurance that they "would take any balance" for which London could not provide.

The positive American attitude was met with little empathy by quite a number of leading personalities and high-ranking officials in London. Henry Morgenthau, Jr., was most instrumental during the negotiations with the British in favor of the joint declaration. Insinuations were voiced, however, linking the American policy to electioneering interests, especially Roosevelt's endeavor to assure Jewish votes. "Jewish votes . . . are being eagerly sought by both the political parties," noted N. Butler on August 2, adding "that Congress will not dare to be obstructive as regards receiving Jewish refugees."[59] "There may be pressure from the United States for electioneering reasons" sounded the warning to Eden on August 8 from inside his government.[60] The Cabinet Committee on Refugees expected American support for the Brand mission to be extended to the Horthy offer too: They reasoned that in Washington the "electoral necessities and the War Refugee Board backed by Mr. Morgenthau dictate a willingness to play with any scheme, however objectionable, which can be represented as rescuing European Jews."[61]

The joint declaration was finally published, after repeated delays, on August 17. The two governments informed Hungary through the International Red Cross that in spite of the "heavy difficulties and responsibilities involved," they would accept the Hungarian offer for the release of Jews, and would make arrangements for the care of those who reached neutral or United Nations territory as well as temporary havens of refuge.[62] Such assurances were to be given by the two governments to the neutral countries that permitted the entry of the rescued Jews. The declaration, which reached Budapest on August 18, ended with the warning that the two governments "do not in any way condone the action of the Hungarian government in forcing the emigration of Jews as an alternative to persecution and death."[63]

It should be mentioned that the Soviets were not involved in the Horthy offer. The first official British information about the proposal reached the Soviet government as late as August 13 at a time when the British–American negotiations for the acceptance of the offer were almost finalized. The British Ambassador in Moscow informed Andrei J. Vishinsky that the Western Allies believed the offer to be genuine and that arrangements to accept it were in process. The Ambassador noted that a public statement was under urgent consideration between London and Washington.[64] No word was said about a possible Soviet role in carrying out the operation. (There are no official documents to prove Soviet interest or involvement in the issue.) One or two days before the publication of the joint Anglo–American declaration, Vyacheslav M. Molotov sent a personal message to Eden in connection with an earlier Western suggestion that the Soviet Union should warn Germany and Hungary about their responsibility for the crimes committed against Hungarian Jewry. Molotov assured Eden that the Soviet government "are applying and will continue to apply all measures within their power in order that the bloody crimes of the Hitlerites shall not fail to bring . . . merciless punishment."[65] The Horthy offer was not mentioned by Molotov, and apparently the Soviets treated it as the concern of the Western powers alone.

While the Hungarians were waiting for a reply from the Allies, Horthy sent a handwritten letter to Max Huber, President of the International Red Cross. The apologetic tone of the letter reflected a propitious atmosphere in Budapest, conducive to the carrying out of the offer. Horthy wrote that he deplored the anti-Jewish measures, emphasized his awareness of the gravity of the problem, i.e., the deportation and liquidation of the greater part of the Jews, and added that he was unable to prevent the "inhumane acts," which no one could condemn more than his "chivalrous–minded and sensitive race." He repeated that he ordered his government to take the fate of the Budapest Jews in its hands, and hoped that this change would not lead to any serious complications — a hint at his hope for the German compliance with his decision and declaration.[66]

After August 18 the way was cleared, in principle, for the implementation of the Horthy offer.[67] There remains to ascertain whether the two essential conditions for the successful carrying out of the rescue operations were present at this crucial juncture: the consent of the Germans to the exit or transit through German territory of the rescued Jews, and the agreement of certain satellite or neutral countries to grant transit visas or temporary asylum.

Any scrutiny of the German agreement to the transit of Jews from Hungary to neutral countries, or to the Romanian and Bulgarian Black Sea ports, must take into account the absolute unreliability of the Nazi assurances. However, there is ample documentary evidence that at the time when Horthy made his offer the Germans indeed agreed, at least formally, to the emigration of a limited number of Jews. In a letter sent to Rolf Günther in the *Reichssicherheitshauptampt* (Reich Security Main Office) on July 24, Adolf Eichmann indirectly confirmed such German commitments. He deplored the fact that the German consent, communicated to the Sztójay government, did not make adequately clear the

German opposition to the emigration to Palestine. Instead of an unequivocal interdiction, the document asked only that, if possible, emigration to Palestine should be avoided.[68] By the end of July, Veesenmayer
confirmed that the Swiss and Swedish Legations in Budapest were informed about the German consent to the emigration of a certain number
of Jews. Talking to Prime Minister Sztójay, he emphasized that the German authorities agreed to the release of 7,000 persons and not of 7,000
families (about 40,000 persons), as erroneously thought by the Swiss diplomats in Budapest. He also conceded the German consent to the release
of a further 400 Jews on a Swedish scheme.[69] At the same time Himmler's
office indirectly confirmed the release from Hungary of a number of "exempted Jews," who were to leave Hungary through German territory to
Western Europe.[70] On August 15, SS sources again confirmed the Nazi
consent to the release of 7,400 Jews, with the stipulation that they were
only to go to Switzerland or Sweden and not to Romania, which could be
a springboard for Palestine.[71]

The conditional and questionable German consent to release a limited
number of Jews, mainly those who were on Horthy's so-called "exemp-
tion list," should be understood in the context of the July–August conjuncture: in its policy towards Hungary, Berlin was interested in
appeasing Horthy, while on the international scene the German Foreign
Office and even Himmler were engaged in a process of improving their
image in the eyes of the neutrals, above all Switzerland and Sweden.

The question of the feasibility of transporting the Jews to and through
certain satellite countries, and their emigration to other destinations, was
less problematic than the German transit consent. For, while the Horthy
offer was being discussed, thousands of Jews were leaving Romania and
Bulgaria for the Middle East, although a small number of refugees were
allowed to stay in Romania.

The Romanian authorities did not hinder the emigration of Jews
through Constanţa in the spring and summer of 1944. According to British
data, more than 1,200 Jewish refugees reached Palestine via Constanţa
and Instanbul between March 30 and May 15, 1944. The chances that the
Romanians would allow the emigration of some 1,300 Jewish children by
the end of June 1944 were good and in August the transit of 2,000 Jews
seemed assured.[72] Dr. Judah Magnes, President of the Hebrew University
of Jerusalem, who was familiar with the prevailing conditions in the area
during that summer, opined that Romania was helpful in easing the emigration from the country.[73]

At the same time the Turkish authorities eased their transit policy. The
Turkish consular officers in the Balkans were empowered to grant transit

visas to Jewish refugees, and in June they "even allowed the passage through Turkey by rail of more then 1,200 refugees, most of whom had no Turkish transit visas." The Turkish consular officers were helpful in Budapest in granting entry and transit visas,[74] and arrangements were progressing in August in Ankara for easing the admission into Turkey of more refugees from Hungary, Romania and Bulgaria.[75]

As to the security aspects of the transportation of the refugees from the Balkans to Palestine or some other destination in the area, conditions were quite safe. A few days before the Horthy offer reached the Western capitals, the British Air Ministry informed the Foreign Office that the chances of safe travel from Romanian ports to the Middle East were quite good. "We are not in a position to give any 'safe conduct' in the sense of an absolute guarantee against the hazards of war" — wrote an official from the Air Ministry — but "there are already . . . relief ships operating in the Aegean and we take every step in our power to see that these ships do not suffer damage by air action on our part."[76] Relevant to the security question was the Air Ministry's assurance that the safety measures "could also be applied to any ship bringing Jews from the Dardanelles to Palestine, if it is the policy of His Majesty's Government to encourage this evacuation."[77] The same assurances were communicated by the Foreign Office to the British Legation in Bern on the day the Horthy offer reached the Swiss capital.[78]

In the second half of July the Jewish Agency felt that the problem of the transportation of the refugees through the Balkans (Romania, Bulgaria, Turkey) was "apparently largely solved."[79] In the first days of August news came of the consent of the Romanian authorities to the emigration of some 2,000 Jews from Constanţa.[80] Optimism among the Red Cross people was so great that at the beginning of August, according to Western sources, the ICRC "had already made arrangements for the sending to Palestine via Constanţa (of) some 40,000 (Hungarian) Jewish refugees"[81] — information which eventually proved to be inaccurate. However, the news reflected the optimistic view prevailing in the free world of the feasibility of the release and rescue across the German lines of some 40,000 Hungarian Jews.

During the four weeks between the announcement of the offer and the joint declaration, a wealth of data were gathered in London and Washington about the Swiss and Swedish readiness to accommodate thousands of refugees and the possibilities of finding asylum for them in Spain and in Portugal. Switzerland was ready to accept 5,000 children already by the end of July,[82] and the Swiss authorities were willing to accord temporary asylum for more refugees.[83] There was no doubt about Sweden's willingness to accept a considerable number of refugees, mostly children. Wallenberg's first weeks in Budapest, which coincided with the launching of the Horthy offer, made it clear that Sweden would accept thousands of released persons.[84] There were good chances that the United States would finance the absorption of children from Hungary by Portugal,[85] and the IGC was busy during August enlisting the necessary funds for the maintenance of refugees from Hungary who were to reach neutral countries.[86] Thousands of Hungarian Jews were expected by Western Jewish representatives to be allowed to enter Spain,[87] and several hundreds were expected to be accepted by other Western countries.[88]

Since the objective conditions appear to have existed for the extrication of up to 40 to 42,000 Jews within the framework of the Horthy offer, a survey of the actual, concrete measures taken by the Western Allies after the publication of their joint declaration is in order.

On August 21, an interdepartmental meeting was held in London, with the participation of delegates of the IGC. It was agreed that the Swiss government and the International Red Cross should be asked to implement the rescue operation inside Hungary and that the IGC should organize the transportation, "if it proved possible to remove these people from Hungary."[89] The British and the United States Legations in Bern were entrusted to get the Red Cross involved. They were also to promote the acceptance by Switzerland of 8,000 refugees in addition to those who had already been accepted for admission to Palestine.

However, instructions relating to the possible activation of the Red Cross reached the United States consul of Geneva only by the end of August or the beginning of September, and the Red Cross was not approached until September 5.[90] Thus, beyond the month that elapsed from the Horthy offer until the joint Anglo–American declaration, another nineteen days passed before the Allies approached the Red Cross in Geneva. Even at that date no practical measures were taken to start the extrication of at least a few thousand Jews from Budapest. In the meantime, during August and the first days of September, important internal events had altered the political constellation in Hungary and consequently Hungary's relations with Germany, while the Romanian volte-face of August 23 and Bulgaria's move to join the Allied side on September 9 had completely changed the military and political situation on the Danubian scene.

Horthy's slowly moving anti-German scheme brought tardy results. On August 24 the Hungarian government — in fact Horthy — rejected renewed Nazi requests for the deportation of the Budapest Jews.[91] Horthy's almost two-month-old plan to dismiss Sztójay and to appoint General Géza Lakatos at the head of a military government finally materialized on August 30, after the Romanian anti-German coup had created a new situation which proved paradoxically unpropitious for the implementation of the rescue operation. Immediately after the announcement of the Romanian coup, war broke out between the Reich and its former satellite, and Hungary foolhardily declared war on Romania, crossing the South-Transylvanian border on September 4. Thus, the emigration and rescue routes through Romania and the so-called Danube route became blocked.

In spite of the collapse of the German front in Southeast Europe as well as Romania's and Bulgaria's decisions to join the anti–German war, in the first two weeks of September the release of some 2,000 Jews for Palestine, down the Danube waterway, was still being considered. The transportation was to have been from Budapest to the Bulgarian frontier by Danube steamers, and from there to Istanbul by rail. The Swiss Legation in Budapest was entrusted to obtain safe conduct from the Germans and the Allies.[92] Surprisingly enough, the Germans were still willing to permit the departure of 2,000 Jews, but the British dissuaded the Swiss authorities from going on with the preparations for the journey because the Danube "had been thoroughly mined by Allied Air forces."[93] On September 16, the American military authorities informed the Swiss government that owing to "the extensive Allied mining operations in the Danube River, safe conduct could not be provided."[94] In the last days of September the Joint Chiefs of Staff decided — probably rightly — that it was impracticable for the United States to grant safe conduct for the travel of the 2,000 Budapest Jews, and thus this final extrication plan developed through the Horthy offer was shelved.

During the last days of September and the first half of October, after the liberation of Northern Transylvania, when fighting started on Hungarian territory, Horthy was feverishly preparing for his unsuccessful *volte face*. October 15, the day of the utter failure of Horthy's anti–German move and the installation of Szálasi's Arrow Cross regime, marked the end of Horthy's twenty-five year rule and of the offer as well.

A number of involved contemporaries commented on the fact that the reluctance of the British and the inefficiency of both the British and the American governments to handle the Horthy offer contradicted their apparent good intentions. In London, Eleanor F. Rathbone, M.P., Vice President of the National Committee for Rescue from Nazi Terror wrote to Eden and to his deputy, George Hall, on July 31. She was perturbed by the fact that almost three weeks after the Horthy offer appeared in the press, Hungary had not yet been informed about the British declaration to find transport and accommodation for all who could get out. "Hence the International Red Cross and the neutral powers who had representation in

Hungary lack the encouragement to make every effort which such an assurance would certainly have given them," wrote Miss Rathbone. "Also, Horthy may well feel that the Great Powers (at least our Government) have ignored his offer, and if pressed by the Gestapo may yield to them." She also accused the American State Department of being "notoriously slow in replying."[95]

At about the same time Alfred Zollinger, the ICRC delegate in the United States, "bitterly complained about the attitude of the British and American Governments" in a meeting with Dr. A. Kubowitzky (Kubovy), one of the World Jewish Congress leaders. Zollinger threatened that unless the Red Cross received real help from the British and the Americans in the near future regarding the rescue of the Budapest Jews, they (the Red Cross) would publish their incriminating material.[96] Even such bitter complaints against the inactivity and inefficiency of the Western Allies proved useless in speeding up the rescue operation, which as we have seen completely failed to materialize.

As a matter of fact, while a large part of the Budapest Jews managed to survive the Szálasi era, tens of thousands were deported, killed or perished between the time the Horthy offer was made public and Budapest was liberated in February 1945. This number could have been substantially reduced, and the ordeal of the potential beneficiaries of the scheme could have been prevented, by an early implementation of the Horthy offer.

The failure of the Horthy offer meant not only a missed opportunity to rescue Jewish lives in 1944: The response to the offer proved that America, in spite of intended goodwill, was too slow to react effectively and not resolute enough to act without the British. America proved incapable of exerting pressure on the British authorities who sacrificed the entire rescue scheme on the altar of their Arab policy. The specter of a Jewish influx to Palestine precluded any humanitarian enterprise on the part of an administration which in any case lacked resolve to help and rescue Jews during the Holocaust.

Notes

1. Veesenmayer informed the *Auswärtiges* Amt (German Foreign Office) on July 11 that the deportation of the Jews from the provinces had been accomplished on July 9, 1944. The total number of deportees was 437,402. *A Wilhelmstrasse és Magyarország. Német diplomáciai iratok Magyarországról, 1933–1944* (The Wilhelmstrasse and Hungary. German Diplomatic Papers on Hungary. ed. by György Ránki et al. (Budapest: Kossuth, 1968), Doc. 697. (Cited hereafter as *Wilhelmstrasse*).

2. The Hungarian authorities put the number of the Jews in Budapest, including those

who were in hiding and converted Jews, at 280,000. *Vádirat a nácizmus ellen* (Indictment Against Nazism), Vol. III. ed. by Elek Karsai. (Budapest: Magyar Izraeliták Országos Képviselete, 1967), Doc. 157. (Cited hereafter as *Vádirat*). As against this exaggerated estimate the Jewish Council knew about 200,000 Jews in Budapest. Jenö Lévai, *Zsidósors Magyarországon* (Jewish Fate in Hungary). (Budapest: Magyar Téka, 1948), pp. 260–261. (Cited hereafter as Lévai, *Zsidósors*). Veesenmayer wrote on July 17 about barely more than 200,000 Jews. Randolph L. Braham, *The Destruction of Hungarian Jewry. A Documentary Account*. (New York: World Federation of Hungarian Jews, 1963), Vol. II, Doc. 200. (Cited hereafter as *Braham*). For reliable statistical data, consult the only comprehensive scholarly work about the Holocaust of Hungarian Jewry: Randolph L. Braham, *The Politics of Genocide. The Holocaust in Hungary*. (New York: Columbia University Press, 1981), 2 vols. (Cited hereafter as Braham, *Genocide*).

3. *Wilhelmstrasse*, Doc. 697.

4. Major air raids against Hungary began on April 17. The raid on July 2 was carried out by some 700 aircraft. On July 14 a major raid hit the industrial areas of Budapest.

5. Around July 7 László Baky, one of the Under Secretaries in the Ministry of the Interior, led an unsuccessful anti–Horthy Arrow Cross plot, aimed also at the deportation of the Budapest Jews.

6. In addition to a strong warning by Roosevelt on March 24, 1944, and another American warning on June 12, the United States warned the Hungarian government on July 14 that it stood "condemned before history" and "cannot escape inexorable punishment." (*Department of State, Bulletin*, vol. XI, p. 59; see also *Documents on American Foreign Relations*, Vol. 7, 1944–45, New York, 1976, p. 251).

7. *Vádirat*, Vol. III, Doc. 25-1; Horthy's reply in Doc. 25-2. About the echo of the King's intervention see telegram no. 2503 from Stockholm to Washington, July 6. (National Archives, Department of State, War Refugee Board, 840.48. Refugees/7–644). (Cited hereafter as *NA*.) There are indications that the King's intervention was promoted by Chief Rabbi Marcus Ehrenpreis and by Professor Hugo Valentin. Miriam Kubovy, *Ultimate Rescue Efforts. The Year 1944*. Collection of Documents from the World Jewish Congress Archives in New York, Vol. III, Meeting of the Advisory Council of European Jewish Affairs, October 17, 1944, New York, Dr. Kubowitzky's report. (Cited hereafter as *M. Kubovy*). For a British reaction to the King's intervention see Public Record Office, Foreign Office, 371. (Cited hereafter as *P.R.O., F.O. 371*.) Sir V. Mallet from Stockholm, telegram no. 744, July 1, 1944.

8. His own version in Horthy Miklós, *Emlékirataim* (My Memoirs), (Buenos Aires: Talleres Graficos Cagnasso y cia, 1953), pp. 260, 263. Early German reports about the change in Horthy's policy in *Braham*, Doc. nos. 188, 190. On July 8, Horthy informed Veesenmayer about the Baky conspiracy (*Wilhelmstrasse*, Doc. 695).

9. *Wilhelmstrasse*, Doc. 699.

10. Ibid., Doc. 700, 706, 707.

11. Ibid., Doc. 700 (par. 5).

12. Ibid., Doc. 701.

13. *The Confidential Papers of Admiral Horthy*. ed. by Miklós Szinai and László Szücs, (Budapest: Corvina Press, 1965), Doc. 65.

14. Horthy, *Emlékirataim*, p. 259. For the government's knowledge of the fate of the deportees and for the reports of Deputy Foreign Minister Mihály Arnóthy Jungerth, see Jenö Lévai, *Fehér könyv. Külföldi akciók zsidók megmentésére* (White Book. Rescue Activities Abroad on Behalf of Jews). Budapest: Officina, n.d., pp. 48–49, and Karsai, *Vádirat*, Vol. III, Docs. 7 and 28.

15. *Wilhelmstrasse*, Doc. 702. (Veesenmayer to Ribbentrop on July 17.)

16. *P.R.O., F.O. 371*, WR 814/3/48. On July 18, the Hungarian Foreign Ministry sent a note to the neutral diplomatic representations in Budapest about its new policy towards the Jews (Lévai, *Zsidósors*, pp. 233–234.) About the "salutary effects" of the later American warnings, see Kelley to State Department, telegram no. 1472, Ankara, August 11 (*NA*, 840.48 Refugees/8–1144).

17. *P.R.O., F.O. 371*, WR 814/3/48.

18. Count István Bethlen, Baron Gyula Ambrózy, Horthy's Chief of Cabinet, and quite a number of conservative and liberal anti-Nazi personalities as well as high-ranking generals were pressing Horthy for the *volte face*. Lists of alternative governments were in circulation long before Sztójay's dismissal.

19. Burckhardt's note in Yad Vashem Archives, P–10/172 (Dr. Dworzetzky's collection). About the change in Hungary's policy and the Horthy offer see Braham, *Genocide*, pp. 752–759, 762–769.

20. Karsai, *Vádirat*, Vol. III, Doc. 110a. Tahy's report in Jenö Lévai, *Abscheu und Grauen vor dem Genocid in aller Welt*. (New York–Toronto–London: Diplomatic Press, 1968), pp. 232–235. See also Harrison to State Department, tel. no. 5040 from Bern (*NA*, 840. Refugees/8–544).

21. Karsai, *Vádirat*, Vol. III, Doc, 210b.

22. Norton to Foreign Office, telegram no. 3328 from Bern on July 18 (*P.R.O., F.O. 371*, WR 285/3/48).

23. Intercroixrouge telegram no. D9217 (*P.R.O., F.O. 371*, Vol. 42811). Among the first informations which reached the State Department (see *NA*, 840.48 Refugees/7–2444). See also Ibid., 840.48 Refugees/8–544. For an early British reaction see *P.R.O., F.O. 371*, WR 915/3/48.

24. Horthy, *Emlékirataim*, p. 260.

25. F.O. telegram no. 886 to Madrid on July 20 (*P.R.O., F.O. 371*, WR 311/3/48).

26. F.O. telegram no. 6509 to Washington on July 21 (*P.R.O., F.O. 371*, Vol. 42809, p. 155).

27. Minutes by R. M. A. Hankey, July 20 (Ibid., Vol. 42810, p. 57).

28. Ibid.

29. Ibid., WR 540/3/48 (August 3) and WR 556/3/48 (August 5).

30. Memorandum of a discussion with Shertok and Linton (of the Jewish Agency), July 21, signed by H. W. Emerson, Director of the IGC (Ibid., Vol. 42810, pp. 200–202).

31. Ibid.

32. Ibid. The problem of financing, transportation and accommodation was raised on several occasions (E.g. F.O. to Washington, telegram no. 7062 on August 9, Ibid., WR 536/3/48).

33. See note 30 (par. 4).

34. *Archives of the Yishuv Rescue Board in Istanbul, Vol. I: Catalogue of the Hungarian Files* (in Hebrew), Institute for Research of the Holocaust Period, The University of Haifa and the Ghetto Fighters' House, 1977, Doc. nos. 237, 239.

35. Chaim Barlas, *Hatzala Bi'mei Shoa* (Rescue During the Holocaust). (Tel Aviv: Ghetto Fighters' House, 1975), pp. 277–78, 325–27).

36. E.g., the British Embassy in Ankara to the Refugee Department of the F.O., July 24, (*P.R.O., F.O. 371*, WR 505/3/48).

37. Eden to Sir R. I. Campbell (Washington), telegram no. 6588 on July 22 (Ibid., Annex III. to WR 682/3/48).

38. Memorandum by the ICRC on July 31 (Ibid., Vol. 42812, pp. 126–127).

39. Communication of Alfred E. Zollinger, the ICRC delegate in the United States (transmitted from Washington to F.O. on August 1, Ibid., WR 536/3/48).

40. E.g., a memorandum by the Counsellor of the U.S. Embassy in London (Ibid., July 31, WR 520/3/48).

41. Emerson to Walker on July 27 (Ibid., WR 484/3/48).

42. Ibid.

43. Meeting between the Secretary of State (F.O.) and a delegation led by the Archbishop of Canterbury (Ibid., July 27, WR 500/3/48).

44. See for example Ibid., WR 528/3/48 (July 29), WR 551/3/48 (August 1), and WR 571/3/48 (August 2).

45. Ibid., WR 524/3/48 and WR 525/3/48 (July 31 and August 1).

46. A State Department memorandum (July 31) transmitted by Sir R. I. Campbell to F.O., telegram no. 4118, August 1 (Ibid., WR 536/3/48).

47. Ibid.

48. Ibid.

49. See note 39.

50. Among other documents see Campbell's telegram on August 1 (note 46). For a well-documented short description of the Anglo–American negotiation, see Henry L. Feingold, *The Politics of Rescue. The Roosevelt Administration and the Holocaust, 1938–1945.* (New Brunswick: Rutgers University Press, 1970), pp. 266 ff.

51. See note 46, par. 2.d.

52. Summary Report of the Activities of the War Refugee Board With Respect to the Jews in Hungary (*M. Kubovy*, Vol. III, p. 513).

53. P.R.O., War Cabinet Committee on Refugees, August 4 (J.R. (44) 21) About the fear of "influx" of Jewish refugees into Palestine see also Ibid., July 28, WR 453/3/48.

54. Ibid., W.P. (44)434, August 8, par. 4. See also F.O. 371, WR 556/3/48 (F.O. telegram no. 991 to Ankara on August 8).

55. "Sir Frank Newsam expressed some doubt whether the offer was genuine. It seemed more likely to have emanated from the Gestapo." (P.R.O., War Cabinet Committee on the Reception and Accommodation of Refugees, Minutes, August 4, J.R. (44)4th Meeting).

56. *P.R.O., F.O. 371*, WR 607/3/48. About British fears of German maneuvers see *NA*, 840.48 Refugees/9–1144 OMM.

57. P.R.O., War Cabinet, August 8, W.P. (44)434. About the Anglo–American negotiations in August see, *inter alia, P.R.O., F.O. 371*, WR 536/3/48 (F.O. to Washington, telegram no. 7103 on August 11).

58. P.R.O., War Cabinet Conclusions 107(44), par. 2a and 2b (August 16). "The Swiss should be kept strictly to 5,000 . . . and not more" — demanded Sir H. MacMichael (telegram no. 943 from Palestine to C.O. on August 4, *P.R.O., F.O. 371*, WR 561/3/48).

59. *P.R.O., F.O. 371*, WR 536/3/48.

60. Ibid., WR 607/3/48.

61. Conclusions of the Cabinet Committee on Refugees (Eden to Churchill on July 13, P.R.O., P.M./44/530). Cf. Ibid., CAB. 95/15 (July 13).

62. There were some mistakes in the first version of the joint declaration released on August 17. The correct wording is in E. A. Walker's text (*P.R.O., F.O. 371*, WR 705/3/48, August 22). See also Ibid., WR 770/3/48.

63. Ibid., WR 705/3/48.

64. Sir Archibald Clark Kerr to A. J. Vishinsky on August 13, no. 35/77/44 (Ibid., Vol. 42816, p. 113).

65. Personal message of Molotov to Eden on August 16 (Ibid., Vol. 42815, p. 64).

66. Horthy's handwritten letter to Dr. Max Huber on August 12 /G51/4/G85/ (Yad Vashem Archives, Dr. Chaim Posner Collection); about the German attitude regarding the partial evacuation, see Karsai, *Vádirat*, Vol. III, Docs. 102–1, 120, 121b, 157, 185b, and: A

German condition to their agreement — the start of the deportation from Budapest. Ibid., Doc. 157 (August 2, 1944).

67. Strangely enough, at the beginning of September the head of the Political Department of the Hungarian Foreign Ministry denied that the "offer" had been a Hungarian one; he noted that the Hungarians merely complied with the offer of different (non–Hungarian) organizations. He added that the plan had not failed because of the Hungarians (however, without hinting at those who had foiled it). Dénes Csopey to Károly Bothmer, September 2, 1944 (Karsai, *Vádirat*, Vol. III, Doc. 232b).

68. Yad Vashem Archives, JM/2214 (K 209321).

69. Veesenmayer to Ribbentrop on July 29 (*Wilhelmstrasse*, Doc. 707).

70. See Ref. 68.

71. Minutes by Th. H. Grell in Berlin on August 15 (*Wilhelmstrasse*, Doc. 708). About the German attitude see Harrison, telegram no. 5043 (*NA*, 840.48 Refugees/7–2144). See also *P.R.O., F.O. 371*, WR 520/3/48 (July 27).

72. War Cabinet Committee on the Reception and Accommodation of Refugees, June 29, Annex, par. 3 and 10 (P.R.O., JR (44)16).

73. Sir H. MacMichael to Secretary of State, Colonies, telegram no. 881 on July 17 (*P.R.O., F.O. 371*, WR 315/3/48). About the Romanian attitude see also Kelley to State Department, telegram no. 1321 from Ankara on July 20 (*NA*, 840.40 Refugees/7–2044).

74. See Ref. 72.

75. *Inter alia*, Sir H. Knatchbull–Hugessen's telegram no. 1249 (August 3) and no. 1291 (August 9) from Ankara to F.O. (*P.R.O., F.O. 371*, WR 558/3/48 and WR 644/3/48). Cf. F.O. telegram no. 1068 to Ankara (August 21), Ibid., WR 556/3/48. For the Turkish attitude see also Ibid., WR 556/3/48 (F.O. to Ankara, telegram no. 1068 on August 21). About emigration from Bulgaria see *M. Kubovy*, Vol. II, p. 285 (J. W. Pehle to Dr. A. L. Kubowitzki on July 27).

76. Mackenzie (Air Ministry) to Henderson (F.O., Refugee Department), C.S. 23230/S.6 on July 11 (*P.R.O., F.O. 371*, WR 223/3/48).

77. Ibid.

78. F.O. to Bern, telegram no. 2358 on July 19 (Ibid).

79. Eliezer Kaplan to Shertok, transmitted by Sir H. MacMichael on August 28 (no. 937, WR 555/3/48).

80. Sir H. MacMichael to Secretary of State, Colonies, no. 977 on August 7 (Ibid., WR 643/3/48). See also WR 888/3/48 (September 4).

81. Harrison from Bern to State Department, telegram no. 4972 on August 3 (*NA*, 840.48 Refugees/8–344).

82. Norton to F.O. from Bern, telegram no. 3566 on July 31 (*P.R.O., F.O. 371*, WR 523/3/48).

83. F.O. (draft) telegram to Bern on August 29 (Ibid., WR 906/3/48). About the Swedish attitude see also Ibid. WR 556/3/48 (telegram no. 1248 from Ankara on August 3).

84. Among a great number of relevant documents see F.O. to Stockholm, telegram no. 638 on August 4 (Ibid., WR 556/3/48). On a late German information about Sweden's intervention for the emigration of 8,000 Jews to Palestine see Yad Vashem Archives, JM/2214 (K 209276 and 209279). For a survey about the Swedish role in P.R.O., see CAB/95/15 (J.R.(44)25, Annex II, November 30).

85. Telegram no. 1413 from Lisbon to F.O. on August 8 (*P.R.O., F.O. 371*, WR 674/3/48).

86. Draft of a letter by E. A. Walker to Treasury on August 19 (Ibid., WR 526/3/48).

87. Carlton J. H. Hayes from Madrid to Washington on September 26 (*NA*, 840.48 Refugees/9–2644).

88. E.g. Ireland (Sidney H. Browne, Second Secretary of the U.S. Embassy in London to P. Mason (F.O.) on October 4 (*P.R.O., F.O. 371*, WR 1306/3/48). About Cuba's attitude see Garret G. Ackerson, First Secretary of the U.S. Embassy in Cuba, telegram no. 7845 on September 7 (*NA*, Department of State, WRB).

89. War Cabinet Committee on Refugees, September 29 (J.R.(44)23) / P.R.O., CAB. 95/15, par. A./. Cf. S.H. Browne to Walker on August 29 (*P.R.O., F.O. 371*, WR 943/3/48).

90. Ibid., WR 943/3/48.

91. Horthy got rid of Baky (September 2) and of Endre (September 8); the internal scene was cleared for the dismissal of Sztójay in the second half of August. For Horthy's opposition to the deportation see *Wilhelmstrasse*, Doc. 711 and Yad Vashem Archives, JM/2214 (K 209122). On August 25 SS *Obergruppenführer* Winkelmann (in Budapest) received Himmler's order to stop the deportations (*Wilhelmstrasse,* Doc. 712).

92. F.O. to Bern, telegram no. 2824 on August 29 (*P.R.O., F.O. 371*, WR 906/3/48).

93. Cordell Hull to Admiral Leahy, September 16, Appendix C to Enclosure B (*NA*, Department of State, B 98836). See also *NA*, 840 Refugees/9–844.

94. Admiral Leahy to Cordell Hull, September 28 (*NA*, Department of State, B 101208). See also Appendix to Enclosure "A" (Ibid., B 98835).

95. *P.R.O., F.O. 371*, WR 521/3/48.

96. *M. Kubovy*, Vol. I., p. 176 (Meeting between Zollinger and Kubovy in Washington on August 4).

3 THE STRUGGLE FOR AN ALLIED JEWISH FIGHTING FORCE DURING WORLD WAR II

Monty Noam Penkower

Two days before Adolf Hitler issued the decisive order that was to inaugurate history's bloodiest conflagration, the first victims of the Führer's blueprint for global conquest offered their services unconditionally to the future Allied cause. On August 29, 1939, immediately upon his return to London from the twenty–first Zionist Congress in Geneva, Chaim Weizmann pledged to Britain's Neville Chamberlain the fullest active support of Jews in Palestine and throughout the world "in this hour of supreme crisis." Repeating one theme of his poignant farewell to the Congress's delegates, the president of the World Zionist Organization (WZO) and the Jewish Agency asserted that Jews "stand by Great Britain and will fight on the side of the democracies." The Agency placed itself in all matters under the "coordinating direction" of His Majesty's Government (HMG); it stood ready to undertake arrangements forthwith for the utilization of Jewish manpower, technical ability, and sundry resources. Weizmann did not gloss over the Zionist movement's political differences with the Mandatory power in the Promised Land, but he concluded the official communiqué with an appeal that these give way "before the greater and more pressing necessities of the time."[1]

Weizmann actually could entertain little hope that the policy of HMG towards the Zionist cause might take a turn for the better with the outbreak of World War II. Only the previous February, Jewish delegates to a conference in London's St. James Palace had been informed by Colonial Secretary Malcolm MacDonald that considerations of imperial strategy required the sacrifice of Zionism in the event of war: The Moslem world might endanger British interests in the Middle East, Northern Africa, and India, and since the weaker Jews perforce wished a British victory, they had to approve political concessions to the Arab position in Palestine. The subsequent White Paper of May, limiting Jewish immigration to 75,000 for the next five years — thereafter with Arab consent — bore the stamp of these arguments. It also suggested Britain's decision to conclude all commitments to the Jewish national home promised by Lord Balfour's cabinet in November, 1917.[2]

Nor did the official Zionist leadership, with the exception of Jewish Agency Executive chairman David Ben Gurion, advocate on the eve of world war armed revolt to counter the White Paper. An acrimonious battle in the Congress's political committee made it evident that Ben Gurion's alternative had few supporters; the formal resolution which followed these deliberations limited itself to the vague statement that "the Jewish people will not acquiesce" in the Mandatory's new policy for Palestine.[3]

Not surprisingly, Britain's prime minister replied to Weizmann's letter in noncommittal fashion. Expressing his warm appreciation for the contents and spirit of the communication, Chamberlain noted "with pleasure" the Jewish Agency's promise of "wholehearted cooperation" regarding manpower, technical ability, and sundry resources. "You will not expect me to say more at this stage," he ended, "than that your public–spirited assurances are welcome and will be kept in mind."[4]

The following day, upon hearing that Great Britain had declared war against Germany in accordance with her treaty obligations to Poland, the Jewish Agency Executive and the *Va'ad Leumi* (National Council) rallied to the Allied standard. The two Jewish organizations jointly announced a census of all people in the Palestinian *Yishuv* (Jewish community) between the ages of 18 and 50 for economic and military purposes to serve the Jewish homeland and to aid the British army in Palestine. Shortly thereafter, Ben Gurion met the commanders of the Hagana defense force and insisted: "We must help the British in their war against Hitler as if there were no White Paper; we must resist the White Paper as if there were no war."[5]

The Zionist Executive, in taking this step, already knew that British military circles in the Middle East, as opposed to London, had strong reservations about accepting military assistance from the Jews. One War Department official informed Moshe Shertok (later Sharett), chief of the Agency's political department, that the offer of 20,000 to 40,000 Palestinian Jews to defend Palestine was indeed welcome but raised the primary difficulty of military equipment. Chief of the Imperial Staff Edmund Ironside expressed strong sympathy for the Agency's two–pronged proposal of mobilization for Palestine's defense and a unit of volunteers from Jewry in the free world to serve wherever needed, even speaking of a Jewish presence of ten million in Palestine and the adjacent countries as a real positive force in the world of the future. But General Wavell, commander of British forces in the Middle East, candidly told Shertok that he opposed the formation of a Jewish army owing to its inevitable clash with the Arabs of the area. Michael Barker, general officer commanding in Palestine, confidently turned to the map hanging on his office wall to show Jewish Agency spokesmen that with no immediate likelihood of Italy joining Germany at the front, the British had no need of a large army in the Holy Land. Syria, to the north, had a substantial French force which would fight with the British; the British controlled Transjordan on the east and maintained a substantial force in Egypt to the south. Iraq and Saudi Arabia would not assault HMG, at least for the present. But the formation of a specifically Jewish force there, he concluded along the imperial line taken at the London Conference, would immediately lead to a widespread Arab revolt.[6]

The undaunted Agency Executive pressed on with its recruitment program, confident that the exigencies of war would prove the intrinsic worth of its case and halt the White Paper's implementation. Over 136,000 men and women from a total Jewish population of slightly less than half a million registered for service. Around 60,000 Jewish recruits (as against 63 Arabs) quickly made up shortages in British army technical units operating in Palestine.

Negotiations with Barker's assistants regarding Palestinian units went along concurrently on the mutual understanding that these would be, in effect, if not in name, Jewish units. The Agency thought that the government might also wish to enlist Arabs on a separate basis, but doubted that the Palestinian Arabs, having spent the last three years in armed revolt against the Mandatory authorities, would rally in large numbers to the Union Jack. This cooperation ground to a halt, however, with Barker's sudden announcement that the Palestinian units under discussion would have to be mixed on the basis of numerical parity between Arabs and Jews. His proposals indicated that the White Paper would govern war mobilization in Palestine as well, forcing the Jewish national home, as Shertok put it in early October, "into the position of any diaspora community." In the Agency's view, the composition of such units would also invite mutual sabotage and recrimination between the two peoples in Palestine, thereby harming an *ésprit de corps* and the attainment of even a minimum level of efficiency by the unit as a whole.[7]

Quickly realizing that political considerations were their major stumbling block, the Zionist authorities began a diplomatic offensive in London to obtain an Allied Jewish fighting force. Receiving little tangible support for the idea from Foreign Secretary Lord Halifax, Weizmann found a ready ear in Winston S. Churchill, his longtime acquaintance who had just been appointed First Lord of the Admiralty. In a brief conversation on September 19, Churchill had assured the WZO president that he would arm the Palestinian Jews registered for national service, convinced that this would thereby allow British troops to leave Palestine for the western front and lead the Arabs to come to terms with the Jews. Encouraged, Weizmann began to urge on various British government departments the development of the industrial and scientific potentialities of Jewish Palestine, especially as the Mediterranean route was still open. The Agency also advanced the name of Orde Wingate, former commander of the Hagana's "special night squads" during the Arab revolt (and its current, confidential advisor on military strategy), to take command of the training of Jewish officers for the future military unit.[8]

The recruitment of Jews in the free world in tandem with the *Yishuv*'s effort proceeded apace elsewhere in Europe and across the Atlantic. Nahum Goldmann, representing the Agency at the League of Nations in Geneva, obtained the approval in principle of French Colonial Minister Georges Mandel for raising 10,000 American Jewish volunteers in order to create a Jewish Legion within the French army; Czech and Polish Jewish refugees in Europe could join this corps as well.[9] The Zionist Organization of America (ZOA), asked by Ben Gurion a day after the war began to offer a Jewish Legion to the British as it had done during World War I, heard from the British ambassador that he would advise them of HMG's policy regarding an oath of allegiance to King George VI for the duration of the war without forfeiting U.S. citizenship.[10]

The British cabinet appeared disinclined to alter its prewar position, however. In cables to the colonial secretary, Palestine High Commissioner Harold MacMichael discounted the Jewish war effort as self–seeking, and he soon informed Ben Gurion and Shertok that HMG would proceed to effect the immigration and land clauses of the White Paper despite the war and the Agency's recruitment drive.[11] At a meeting of the cabinet in mid–October, the colonial secretary checked Churchill's support of Wingate's memorandum for the large enlistment of Palestine's Jews by raising alarms about renewed Arab–Jewish conflict. Churchill's wishing "an outlet for the more adventurous spirits" among Jews and Arabs, along with his assertion in cabinet that the White Paper could not be regarded as a satisfactory solution for the Middle East, was not sufficient to move MacDonald.[12]

At that very moment, the British authorities in Palestine also attempted to break the power of the Hagana. Forty–three participants in a secret officers' training course were surprised with arms in their possession by a British patrol and received harsh sentences. The Mandatory had worked openly with the Hagana to suppress the Arab rebellion, and Palestine's history clearly indicated the Jewish need for arms in self–defense against the Arabs, yet the British authorities now purported to be shocked at the existence of this military organization. General Barker insisted to Ben Gurion that the organization's proper name was *Hatkafa* (attack). Systematic searches for Jewish arms should be undertaken, Barker proposed to his superiors, and if the Hagana and similar organizations would not hand over their arms, the government should drastically reduce the strength of the Jewish police and discharge those who had joined British military units. MacDonald gave no comfort to Shertok in the matter, while a confidential Colonial Office memorandum dismissed the effect of potential Jewish propaganda on American opinion as carrying "little weight." General Ironside took a sharply different view, cabling Barker to reduce the "stupid sentence" on the 43. "Fancy," the chief of the Imperial Staff told Weizmann, "they had condemned one of Wingate's lads to life imprisonment; he ought to have been given the D.S.O." The Jewish army would come despite the Colonial Office, he went on, and "besides, if it is to be a better world after the war, the Jews must get Palestine."[13]

The Jewish Agency Executive in London arrived at a final decision on the Jewish fighting force in the middle of November. Following Wingate's advice, it proposed a Jewish force for Palestine's defense; a Jewish division composed of volunteers from abroad and a Palestinian nucleus; and a cadre of 500 officers to be trained in Britain for the 15,000 man division. Only a division, Wingate convinced a group assembled at Weizmann's suite in the Dorchester Hotel, could act on its own, include all arms of the forces, and not be easily demobilized. (As for Shertok's and Ben Gurion's fears of 15,000 young men being taken out of Palestine, Wingate argued that by the time the proposal was implemented by the slow moving British, the war would reach the Middle East, and HMG would employ the division there.) Ironside's aide, Colonel MacLeod, informed Shertok of Ironside's insistence that the Jewish offer be unconditional as to place of service and that the negotiations be kept secret. Weizmann wrote to Ironside on December 1, transmitting the Agency's confidential memorandum for the Jewish division and officers' cadre (no mention made of a Palestine defense force). A positive reply under MacLeod's signature arrived three days later.[14]

Matters inched forward, however, as Wingate had predicted, and nothing conclusive transpired by the time 1939 ran out. "M. M. (Malcolm MacDonald) stands by his betrayal . . . the White Paper policy is to continue," wrote Ben Gurion, on his way home from London, to a member of the Hagana executive. Wavell cautioned Weizmann, about to depart for the United States, that a Jewish force might incite the Arabs of Egypt and Iraq. To make the Agency's position even more difficult, the French Minister of War turned down the establishment of Jewish units under the tricolor, while United States Ambassador William Bullitt in Paris informed Goldmann that the American neutrality laws foreclosed any such help from across the ocean. The Agency Executive turned down HMG's request for the enlistment of trench diggers (Pioneer Corps) for the Western front as a "Palestinian" unit; Ben Gurion explaining to Barker in the course of a stormy interview that the Jews wished to be accorded the same honorable recognition given any other nation: only thus could they play their proper part in the war. Left to themselves, the British raised the unit in part from the unemployed; the group, mostly Jews, later aided in the Allied retreat from St. Malo harbor and then in important battles in Eritrea.[15]

Churchill's taking the reins of British power after the Nazi invasion of the Low Lands and the fall of France in May, 1940, together with Italy's entry into the war as an Axis belligerent a month later, saved the volatile situation for the *Yishuv*. The new Colonial Secretary, Lord Lloyd, and Secretary of War Anthony Eden at first opposed a Jewish force on the grounds of British security in the Middle East, but Churchill pressed both to free eleven battalions of regular British troops in Palestine and to arm and organize the Jews in their own defense. Weizmann's official request of Churchill for mobilizing the full resources of the Jewish people in Palestine and elsewhere, including the raising in Palestine of "several divisions," an air force squadron, and a military intelligence unit, fell on sympathetic ears. In June, Lloyd agreed to larger enlistments of Jewish Palestinians and their formation into distinctive Jewish units. With the appointment of a new British military commander over Palestine, arms seizures came to a halt. While the plan for a Jewish division was still being negotiated, Ben Gurion urged Lloyd in early July and Weizmann again wrote Churchill a month later to arm the Jews of Palestine in self–defense. American Zionists, on their end, exerted themselves to enlist advocates in Washington for the idea. The prime minister's influence proved decisive, and Eden informed Parliament on August 6 of the cabinet's decision to recruit separate Arab and Jewish units as battalions of the veteran Royal Kentish Fusiliers (the "Buffs").[16]

In the ensuing months, the Agency's quiet negotiations with the cabinet and the War Office brought the Jewish division to the edge of realization. But the sudden death of Lord Lloyd, recognized patron of the Jewish division, spelled the demise of the project. His successor, the anti–Zionist Lord Moyne, chose to accept the advice of Britain's military and political representatives in the Middle East, who looked askance at the idea of any Jewish force. Such officials took no comfort in the fact that Jews constituted over 72 percent of the roughly 9,000 recruits from Palestine up to the beginning of 1941. British ambassador Miles Lampson in Cairo, High Commissioner MacMichael, and General Haining of the War Office all insisted that at least the constitutional clauses of the White Paper be carried out without delay as a *quid pro quo*.[17]

Moyne, Eden (now heading the Foreign Office), and the new Secretary of War sought Wavell's views. He obliged by favoring implementation of the White Paper and opposing the Jewish contingent on the grounds of Arab hostility and especially the shortage of military equipment. Churchill brushed aside Wavell's fears of the Arabs, recalling that he had recently got the Jewish refugee survivors aboard the *Patria* admitted into Palestine despite the general's worries on that score, "and not a dog barked." Yet, wishing Wavell to approve HMG's strategy regarding the defense of Greece against the German onslaught, he told Moyne in early March to inform Weizmann that lack of equipment alone required postponing the plan for six months. Never to know that Churchill gave up the military program temporarily in exchange for no implementation of the White Paper's constitutional clause, Weizmann called the decision a "sore blow." Repulsed, he again set out for the United States seeking new political leverage with which to strengthen the Zionist cause.[18]

The Jewish Agency could not move the cabinet. The pro–Nazi revolt in Iraq; the Hagana's help in Britain's invasion of Vichy Syria; the conspiracy of army officers Anwar el–Sadat, Gamal Abdul Nasser, and the Egyptian chief of staff, and the Muslim Brotherhood to support Adolf Hitler in return for their country's independence from British rule — all did not count in the balance. Nothing transpired regarding a Jewish force until Weizmann came back to London in August, where he received

Moyne's letter announcing the need to leave the matter in "cold storage" for another three months. Equipment scarcity (a defense suggested earlier to Eden by the British Minister Resident Middle East, Oliver Lyttleton) and the new factor of Russia's entry on the Allied side precluded a favorable decision at this time, advised the Colonial Secretary. Weizmann's letter to Churchill on September 10, particularly noting the keenness of America's Jewish citizens to support Great Britain if only given the Jewish fighting force, failed to bear fruit.[19]

A definite reply from Moyne — not Churchill — in mid–October, citing the previous reservations against the Jewish division, dashed the Agency's hopes of September, 1940, for good. Rather than endorse "most alarming" talk from Ben Gurion and Weizmann of securing three million Jews and sovereignty in Palestine, the Colonial Secretary added to a Parliamentary pro–Zionist delegation of Victor Cazalet, Josiah Wedgwood, and Percival Harris that the "best course was to keep things as steady as possible for the present." On November 9, 1941, Weizmann informed the public for the first time about both HMG's concealment of the distinctive service given on various fronts by 10,000 Jewish recruits under the anonymous rubric Palestinians and Britain's failure to live up to its promise of the Jewish division. Newspaper editorials and a heated debate in the House of Lords decried the government's decision as continued appeasement of the unreliable Arabs. (At that same moment, Hitler confidentially assured former Mufti of Jerusalem Haj Amin el–Husseini that he would continue the war "until the complete destruction of the Judeo–Bolshevik rule had been accomplished," and appointed his foreign guest to lead the Arab forces against Palestinian Jewry as soon as the *Wehrmacht* reached the Southern Caucasus.) But Churchill could do nothing more than promise, in a public letter to the London *Jewish Chronicle* on the occasion of its centenary, that on the day of Allied victory the sufferings of the Jews and their part in the struggle against the German *Führer* would not be forgotten.[20] The first phase of the Jewish Agency's effort had ended in complete failure.

The inability after two years to secure HMG's approval for a Jewish force led the Agency's leadership to view the United States as its new political center of gravity. Already in March, 1941, Ben Gurion had proposed a twofold program of action to the Agency Executive regarding the future of Palestine: strengthen the Hagana to form a Jewish army, and demand Jewish rule in Palestine after the war as a means of bringing millions of Jews to the national homeland with all speed. HMG's continuation of the White Paper, despite the presence of some strong pro–Zionists in the war cabinet, led the Agency Executive chairman to despair of a change from the British. He knew, at the same time, that American Zionist pressure had helped persuade London in May and June to strengthen Jewish self–defense in Palestine. Accordingly, Ben Gurion suggested in a memorandum that autumn to Weizmann and others at Agency headquarters in 77 Great Russell Street that it would be easier to win public opinion in America for such a "radical and maximum solution" than in England. Much more disinterested in Palestine than the Mandatory, and therefore able to take a more objective view, the United States also possessed the largest Jewish community in the world. That great mass of Jews, Ben Gurion argued on the basis of previous visits to America, supported the *Yishuv*'s effort in principle. The general American public, he thought, could also be won to support the establishment of "Palestine as a Jewish Commonwealth immediately after the war." He would leave for the United States to undertake this mission.[21]

Ben Gurion's novel thesis that the achievement of a maximalist Zionist program depended upon capturing American public opinion had been adopted much earlier by his arch rival, Vladimir Jabotinsky. The president of the Revisionist New Zionist Organization had called a truce in his movement's armed struggle with the British immediately after the German invasion of Poland. On September 4, 1939, the former lieutenant in the Jewish 38th Battalion of Royal Fusiliers which fought under Allenby to capture Palestine from the Turks wrote to Neville Chamberlain: extend the precedent of the World War I Jewish Legion and create a Jewish army prior to the establishment of Palestine as a Jewish state. When Colonial Secretary MacDonald refused to consider his request that HMG give tacit or open encouragement to Jewish immigration to Palestine beyond the White Paper, the Revisionists' charismatic leader decided to bring his appeal to the American people.

Jews and non-Jews began to answer Jabotinsky's call, first made publicly in June, 1940, at New York's Manhattan Center, for a Jewish army of 100,000 to rally to England's side against Hitler. Important contacts were established with the aid of influential Americans like Mr. and Mrs. John Gunther and British Colonel John Patterson, former commander of the World War I Jewish Legion. A memorandum, explaining that such a project, by "placing the Jewish people on the map," would diminish the "inevitable pressure" of Europe's Jews escaping "zones of distress," went to various statesmen that summer. Suddenly, Jabotinsky died in early August, 1940, and the New Zionist Organization's ship floundered in search of a helmsman.[22]

Members of an *Irgun Tzva'i Leumi* (National Military Organization) delegation to the United States moved to fill the vacuum. Even before reaching the New World in 1939–1940, they had clashed with Jabotinsky over a more militant anti–British policy in Palestine and the diaspora. Once on these shores, the small band decided to fight the White Paper and secure the full boundaries of historic Palestine with a more aggressive style of propaganda than Jabotinsky, their mentor, desired. Led by the dynamic Hillel Kook (alias Peter Bergson), the young group vainly appealed to United Palestine Appeal chairman Abba Hillel Silver to take the reins from those supporting what they termed the "Weizmann spirit" of defeatist anglophilism; Stephen Wise, chairman of the umbrella–type Emergency Committee for Zionist Affairs (ECZA), received a request for substantial funds so that the militant *Irgun* could continue to combat Arab terrorism in Palestine. Upon Weizmann's public admission of the Agency's failure to attain a limited Jewish division, the "Bergson boys" then organized the nonsectarian Committee for a Jewish Army to raise a combined force of 200,000 Palestinian and stateless Jews for Allied service in Palestine and its environs. Their opening drive in Washington, D.C., on December 4, 1941, with special messages of support from Secretary of War Henry Stimson, Senators Claude Pepper, Edwin Johnson and Guy Gillette, and other notables, drew much coverage and inspired *PM*'s editorial advice to employ United States Lend Lease equipment for the projected Jewish army.[23]

The Committee's slogan — "Jews Fight for the Right to Fight" — had particular power, coming exactly on the eve of America's entry into the war. Thousands of sympathizers, including many Jews far removed from Zionism, joined the fledgling group and its national chairman, the celebrated Dutch author Pierre Van Paassen. Americans preferred to think in large terms, and a Jewish army of 200,000, whatever its logistic problems, possessed greater attraction for many than the Agency's call for a Jewish division numbering 20,000 to 40,000. For the first time, as Kook gauged the revolutionary step years later, Jews appeared on the front pages with a dramatic appeal instead of in the back covers listing religious services and obituaries. Senators Johnson and Elbert Thomas proved especially effective in voicing the Committee's position in Washington, while Captain Jeremiah Halpern and Lord Strabolgi gained numerous supporters in Parliament and captured the front pages of the London *Jewish Chronicle*.[24]

Ben Gurion and Weizmann, for their part, chose to concentrate on winning over the White House and influential Jewish organizations in the first months of 1942, and on uniting American Zionists behind a public manifesto for Jewish statehood and a Jewish army for Palestine. Certain members of the ECZA sought to co–opt the Committee for a Jewish

Army's resourceful leadership, but in Ben Gurion's eyes, the covert association of the Committee's organizers with the independent *Irgun* in Palestine made any partnership impossible. Ultimately, the first comprehensive conference of the country's established Zionist organizations took place at the Biltmore Hotel in New York on May 9–11, 1942, where they agreed upon the establishment of Palestine as a Jewish commonwealth in the new world order. Until the realization of that achievement, the Biltmore resolutions proclaimed, the Jewish Agency should control immigration and development, and the Jews of Palestine should be given a "Jewish military force fighting under its own flag and under the high command of the United Nations."[25]

While the idea of a Jewish army made headway in the United States, the British felt compelled to cooperate with the *Yishuv* in an effort to halt Field Marshal Erwin Rommel's advance on the gates of Alexandria. During the summer of 1940, and again a year later, the British had turned to the Jews of Palestine and received valuable help in underground operations to meet the danger of a Nazi invasion in the Middle East. Intelligence work, sabotage, "Arabist" agents, and the training of Hagana members for a radio network for Palestine in case of a German takeover had all received British sanction during those months of crisis. The rule of Arab–Jewish parity in the Buffs had also been discarded in mid–1941 when the British Army required additional Jewish enlistment. In early 1942, the British, enjoying the flush of a recent victory in the western desert, approved of a Hagana plan for guerrilla activities in northern Palestine in case of a Nazi conquest of the country. The Palmach, the mobile striking force which had been organized by the Hagana command in May, 1941, after Rommel first reached Egypt's borders, received the command's assignment to execute this plan. Unknown to the British, their support of a large–scale training program at this time saved the Palmach from disintegration. Courses began in mid–April, 1942, at Mishmar Ha'Emek; they provided the *Yishuv* with the nucleus of its future professional army.[26]

Still, the Agency's request that HMG immediately mobilize all available Jewish manpower to defend Palestine against Rommel's *Afrika Korps* met with a limited response. Ben Gurion cabled the British Minister Resident Middle East, Richard Casey, on April 15 that the 10,000 Jews now dispersed in the single, defense companies of the Buffs should be prepared for war service at the battalion level; another 10,000 should be similarly mobilized, together with a 6,000 Supernumerary Police Force; and an additional 40,000 to 50,000 should be equipped for home guard duty. Field Marshal Dill, then in Washington, approved Ben Gurion's pro-

posals, and so cabled London. Shertok wrote to General Claude Auchin-
leck, British commander–in–chief for the entire region, in like vein two
days later, adding ominously that "an even swifter destruction" would
overtake the Jews of Palestine if the Nazis overran the country than had
fallen on "hundreds of thousands" *(sic)* of their fellow Jews who had
perished to date in Hitler's Europe. Weizmann carried the plea to the
sympathetic United States Under Secretary of State, Sumner Welles, and
also wrote Ambassador John Winant in England to that effect. After the
fall of Tobruk to the Germans on June 21, he again sent a letter to Churchill calling for a large fighting force of Jews in Palestine. But Auchin-
leck's immediate need for all available arms, the bulk coming from the
United States, to be rushed to the front at El Alamein did not permit the
fulfillment of the Agency's desperate hopes.[27]

The Agency also failed in its attempt to obtain Wingate's services as
the leader of a large Jewish military force in Palestine at this eleventh
hour. On July 7, President Franklin D. Roosevelt received Weizmann (but
expressly not Ben Gurion), only to tell the chief architect of the Balfour
Declaration that he wished to wait about ten days before issuing a statement regarding the Jewish force. The British feared that the Egyptian
Army might turn against them, he explained. "You might as well try and
appease a rattlesnake," Weizmann retorted. The President's thoughts,
smacking of what Weizmann termed Britain's traditional placating of the
Arabs, dissatisfied the WZO leader. But Roosevelt insisted to Secretary
of the Treasury Henry Morgenthau, Jr., that the first consideration was to
make sure the British would keep Cairo and Alexandria from falling. If
this were done, and if 50,000 rifles and 10,000 machine guns could then be
gotten to the Jews, Wingate would be his choice to lead them.[28]

Churchill, too, favored Wingate's appointment, but did not get his
way. In the end, the British military authorities refused to free Wingate
from commando preparations in India against the Japanese forces holding
Burma. The prime minister had to content himself once again with a
message of faith to the beleagured Jews. A demonstration in Madison
Square Garden, convened on July 21, 1942, to protest the Nazi massacre
of Jews, heard Churchill's message of special tribute to the Jewish war
effort in Palestine. Official British silence on this contribution had been
broken for the first time, but the Jewish division had still not come to
pass. Wingate lost his last hope of again leading the Jews in battle; he
would die two years later in an air crash in the Burma jungle.[29]

The British authorities finally made some concessions to the mounting
pressure for a Jewish military force, but these hardly met the Agency's
demands. At Colonial Secretary Lord Cranborne's urging, the Secretary

for War announced in Parliament on August 6 HMG's decision to create a Palestine regiment consisting of separate Jewish and Arab battalions for general service in the Middle East; to expand the Supernumerary Police Force to a maximum of 2,000; and to complete the establishment of a Jewish Rural Special Police by enrolling 2,500 additional recruits with all necessary training and arms. The Colonial and War Secretaries took this limited step specifically to check "extreme Zionists" like Shertok who sought, according to the secretaries' confidential cabinet memoranda, to use the Jewish army as "a valuable bargaining counter at the peace table" or to achieve a Jewish state by force after the war. Accordingly, the battalions would not depart from the Buffs' static mission of guarding military installations without modern arms or new training. The 1,500 new men of the Supernumerary Police Force also received inferior training and equipment within the framework of the temporary village police. In sum, the battalions, strengthened by over 4,600 new recruits from June to the end of September, 1942, made only small progress to the goal of a Jewish fighting unit.[30]

Following HMG's major victory at El Alamein (October 23–November 4, 1942), the British reverted to their traditional position of no military cooperation with the *Yishuv*. Receiving no further support from HMG, the Palmach had to go back underground. Shertok insisted that the Jewish battalions did not wish to remain "hewers of wood and drawers of water" while European Jewry was being decimated in Germany's Final Solution — to no avail. General Alexander of Middle East Command fell back on the problem of limited equipment and the value attached by the British government to defensive duties against Arab sabotage. At most, the British cabinet decided to have the Secretary of War announce in Commons on December 15, 1942, that the defensive role of the Jewish battalions might be different if and when "equipment and circumstances" permitted.[31]

Thus, at the very moment that the Anglo–American Alliance first acknowledged Hitler's calculated plan to kill all of European Jewry, the Jews of Palestine had the bitter lot of fighting "nameless and scattered." Almost 20,000 Palestinian Jewish recruits were serving in the British armed forces by the end of 1942, with over 7,000 in internal defense, and 1,000 in various Allied armies. Another 60,000 could be found meeting direct British needs in factories, camps and workshops, and in army transport. Laboratories of the Hebrew University, the Daniel Sieff Research Institute, and the Haifa Technical Institute contributed precision instruments and valuable chemical products to the Allied forces. British Army orders for Jewish goods totalled close to 14 million pounds between

1941–1942. The Jewish Agency forwarded important information from refugees about current industrial and other conditions in Nazi–occupied Europe to HMG's military branches. The record of support by Palestine's Arab population for the Allied cause hardly approximated this British–censored record of performance, while the governments of Iraq, Syria, and Egypt favored the Nazi invader, and the former Mufti of Jerusalem used the Axis airwaves to herald the Third Reich in the Moslem world and recruited thousands from the Balkans into Moslem *Wehrmacht* units. Yet the demand for a distinctive Jewish fighting force, which could strike a blow against Hitler and avenge the more than 2,000,000 Jews already dead in the unyielding onslaught of the Holocaust, continued to go unanswered.[32]

With the danger of Rommel's invasion over, the British administration in Palestine did all it could in the first half of 1943 to weaken the *Yishuv*'s recruitment effort. A company from one of the Jewish battalions was sent abroad, negating a British promise of September, 1940, to avoid such an action. In April, 1943, the Jewish Agency was also denied access to the Sarafand training camp, and British detectives, seeking evidence for the existence of a secret military organization and coercion to obtain Jews for HMG's forces, ransacked the *Yishuv*'s recruitment center in Tel Aviv. The Agency responded by closing all its recruitment offices. Although these quarters were opened two months later after the British realized that enlistment could occur only with the Agency's cooperation, the Mandatory power offered no apologies. Jewish recruitment never regained its previous momentum. The British further weakened Jewish military strength by shipping out the second Palestinian battalion in early July without assurances that it would be used for actual duty.[33]

Such maneuvers reflected British fears of a Jewish revolt, suspicions which also drove the war cabinet to try and dampen Zionist agitation through a diplomatic offensive with Washington. Anxious about reports of impending Arab–Jewish conflict over Palestine and its potentially adverse effect on the Allied campaign in North Africa, the U.S. State Department found the Foreign Office receptive to issuing a joint Anglo-American statement on Palestine. That declaration, maintaining in effect the White Paper policy until the war's end, contained a specific injunction at Whitehall's request against any solution for Palestine based on armed force. The British Middle East military and political authorities, having met earlier in Cairo to discuss the subject, recommended that all hidden arms in Palestine be seized and Mandatory strength increased by one infantry division, including armor. By also bringing the British police force up to full strength, a British gendarmerie in Palestine would thus be created in the Promised Land.[34]

Minister of Production Oliver Lyttleton proved especially adamant. As British Minister Resident, Middle East, he had provided the War Office in August, 1941, with the rationale of equipment scarcity as the answer to Weizmann's request for a Jewish fighting force. Now Lyttleton refused to have HMG "surrender to Jewish chauvinism," which he considered inimical to "our imperial interest." (The minister and colleagues did not know that Egypt's King Farouk, who informed the Third Reich of his continued hope for an Axis victory, had recently been involved in negotiations via the ex–Mufti to be spirited to the German Lines.)[35]

Only Minister for India Leopold Amery and Winston Churchill markedly supported the *Yishuv* as Britain's only reliable ally in the Middle East and, hence, the Agency's demand for a Jewish state. Owing to Churchill's insistence, the Cabinet decided not to approve the seizure of illegal Jewish arms in Palestine. Otherwise, the joint declaration appeared headed for issue. At the last minute, pressure from various American Jewish quarters in August halted its promulgation.[36]

What the two governments failed to achieve behind closed doors, the British authorities in Palestine attempted to secure by a public arms trial that same month. Determined to sully the name of Zionism in American public opinion particularly and to end the contraband sale of British arms into Jewish hands, the Mandatory tried two members of the Hagana, Eliyahu Syrkin and Eliyahu Reichlin, for illegally transferring to Haifa 105,000 rounds of ammunition and 300 rifles from British stores in Egypt. An earlier trial of two British deserters, engaged in selling stolen goods and arms to Arabs and Jews alike, had heard their attorney slander the Jewish soldiers then fighting with the British Eighth Army in North Africa. The court heard no mention of the widespread Arab trafficking in arms throughout the Middle East, mass desertion from the Palestinian Arab units, or the refusal of HMG's Transjordanian Force to take up arms against Rashid Ali's pro-Nazi revolt in Iraq. Only in such a circumstance, Ben Gurion riposted, did HMG permit Jewish soldiers to be listed as other than "Palestinians." The British went further immediately thereafter at the Syrkin–Reichlin trial, staged in the presence of the invited American press, aiming to discredit the *Histadrut* (Jewish trade union organization) and the Jewish Agency.

The prosecutor sought to portray the Hagana as a secret organization whose real purpose, described as "stealing Allied arms," was "a cancer" in the body of the democracies' war effort. Golda Meyerson (later Meir), called to the stand, confronted HMG by publicly revealing for the first time the "secret" of past British cooperation with the Hagana and Palmach. After sixty sessions which stretched the credibility of the prosecution's witnesses, Reichlin received seven years in jail and Syrkin ten.

Even more ominous was the seven–year sentence given by the military court to Avraham Sacharov, a member of Hagana's secret acquisitions unit *(Rechesh)* and known as "Weizmann's bodyguard," for possessing two rifle bullets without a permit. Shortly afterwards, a magistrate's court sentenced one Arab in Hebron to six months' imprisonment for possessing a British rifle and 86 rounds of ammunition.[37]

A large-scale arms search at Hulda and a particularly forceful one at Ramat Ha'Kovesh that fall left no doubt that the British authorities sought to liquidate the Hagana. Shertok met High Commissioner Mac-Michael on November 17 and warned that "our arms are intended to be used for defense, and any attempt to take them away from us will touch the *Yishuv* to the quick." "Extreme acts" might follow, he added, resulting in much bloodshed on both sides. This grave warning and protests by Zionists in Washington and London had the desired effect. The last thing HMG desired was to provoke a Jewish revolt throughout Palestine; Mac-Michael convinced the military to halt the anti–Hagana actions. The Hagana emerged from this crisis with its power intact, and the open tension of the past few months subsided.[38]

The British realized that they also had to compromise on the question of the Jewish flag. Palestinian Jews serving in British transport units managed from the beginning to mark the Star of David on their trucks, but those in the Palestinian regiments had to don the neutral badge of an olive branch surrounded by the word "Palestine" in English, Arabic, and Hebrew. Unfurling their individual flag alongside the Union Jack in a hall of worship to celebrate the Jewish New Year in October, 1943, the second battalion's third unit was supported the following day by all the other Jewish sections in the Bengazi area in remonstrating against the discriminatory order. Some time after this attempt to restore Jewish pride in place of Palestinian anonymity, the British removed the punishment meted out to the battalion for its insubordination, and provided some up-to-date equipment and combat training. HMG thus acknowledged for the first time, albeit in a limited fashion, the *Yishuv*'s insistence that the emerging Jewish nation on the soil of the Holy Land be recognized as a fellow member in the war against Hitlerism.[39]

Precisely at this juncture, the Jewish Agency renewed its demand for a separate fighting force. Shertok's last request, in January, 1943, for a division or, as a first step, a brigade group based upon the 22,000 Palestinian Jews then serving in the British Army, had been turned down on that occasion by the Secretary of War. But by now the front had receded from the Middle East, and with the Allied invasions of Sicily and Italy, such a military arm could fight in Europe free from British and Arab fears about its appearance in Palestine and the Middle East. In addition, it would be difficult, as Shertok wrote a colleague during the arms trials, to deny the *Yishuv* its "holy task" in the campaign to conquer the Jewish "Valley of Slaughter" and to save the remnants of its people. Those serving in the British army, in particular, did not wish to have it said that only the heroic resistance movements of the Warsaw Ghetto and elsewhere in Hitler's Europe could take up arms to the death as Jews.

The time seemed most propitious for a successful conclusion to the long campaign. Churchill confirmed this at a private luncheon with Weizmann on October 25, and promised his guest that he would fulfill Balfour's inheritance and "establish the Jews in the position where they belong."[40]

Weizmann picked up the thread the following month, but more than half a year passed without any results. On November 23, 1943, he and colleague Lewis Namier met with British War Secretary James Grigg, who promised to transmit their request to the cabinet. Lengthy negotiations ensued. The British chiefs of staff cabled the War Office their fears of Jewish designs, and warned that the partition of Palestine recommended by a special cabinet committee would so jeopardize British security interests in the Middle East as to require: three divisions in Palestine alone, two to three divisions in Syria, Iraq and Lebanon; two in Egypt; two-thirds of a division in Libya; two fighter squadrons; seven fighter bomber squadrons; and two PT boat squadrons after the war. In early 1944, the United States War Department put an end to congressional resolutions favoring Palestine as a Jewish state after the end of hostilities on the ground that Moslem unrest could yet hamper the Allied war effort. Given this perspective, the department decided not to press the British even concerning a Jewish force for the liberation of Europe itself. The resumption of active warfare in Palestine against the Mandatory administration by the *Irgun* and the Stern group during these same months gave added strength to the anxiety of the British and American military, and thus threatened further to demolish the Agency's quest for this particular objective.[41]

Grigg dug in his heels against all entreaties from Weizmann and Shertok. Weizmann sat down with the Secretary of War in March, 1944, and in a letter at the month's end officially asked that the Allies, who had failed to save Jewry, include in the invasion of Europe a "force of free, fighting, Jews . . . to uphold the honour of their people, avenge its martyrs and help to liberate the survivors"; the existing Jewish Palestinian units should be grouped into a division or a brigade, with new Jewish recruits to come from Palestine, liberated Italy and North Africa, and other countries. Shertok reiterated the demand in early April, but it took until June 21 for

Weizmann to receive Grigg's evasive reply: he had submitted his own judgment to the war cabinet, where the matter now rested. The British commanders–in–chief committee had, in fact, called for binationalism under British rule as the best solution for Palestine; it continued to insist on retention of all the necessary facilities in Palestine to secure British military interests in the Middle East, whatever the cabinet committee's final decision. Grigg remained suspicious that the Hagana intended to train at Britain's expense either to resist an anti–Zionist Mandatory policy after the war, or to present HMG with the *fait accompli* of a Jewish state when Britain's main effort would be directed to the defeat of Japan. Accordingly, he recommended to his cabinet colleagues that they turn down a Jewish force of any size.[42]

As a last resort, Weizmann turned to the one individual in whom he had placed his faith since the 1917 pledge of Arthur Balfour. On July 4, 1944, he addressed a personal communication to Churchill. Recalling Britain's promise four years earlier of an Allied Jewish fighting force and noting the war service of Palestinian Jewry's volunteers, now numbering 24,000, the Zionist leader requested that these men form a division of their own and be permitted to carry the flag with the Star of David onto the battlefield of Europe. Grigg replied three days later, informing Weizmann that negotiations were taking place on the "limited plan" with the general officer commanding, Middle East, and expressing doubts that "your cracking the whip" would "make the horse move any faster." The elder Zionist statesman did not respond, for in the interim he had fallen into a deep depression over the Foreign Office's refusal to take up the so–called "blood for trucks" offer of the Nazis for the possible rescue of Hungarian Jewry, the last sizeable remnant of the Jewish people in Europe.

In his chief's absence, Shertok sharply cut off Grigg's reprimand. The Jewish Agency expected no favorable reaction from the supreme British military command in the Middle East, he retorted by official letter. Only the "highest political authorities" could take into account the considerations of fulfilling a promise once given and "the moral obligation to let at least a few thousand Jews fight as Jews at a time when millions of their people are doomed to death."[43]

Unknown to the Zionists, the catastrophe of Hungarian Jewry had deeply moved the prime minister, and he resolved to do something concrete for the Jewish people. Shocked at seeing a cable on June 27 about the gassing of some 400,000 Hungarian Jews in Auschwitz–Birkenau, and noting its suggestion to bomb the extermination centers, railway lines to the camps, and government buildings in Budapest, Churchill empowered Foreign Secretary Eden to act on his behalf in favor of the bombing proposals. Two days after receiving this telegram, he reminded Eden of his determination not to break Balfour's word to the Zionists. What the Jewish people were currently enduring in Europe, Churchill told his cabinet on July 3, made "a strong case" for sympathetic consideration of projects regarding the *Yishuv* after the war. (The prime minister evidently had in mind the proposal for a Jewish state, then pending before the Cabinet committee.)

As for Grigg's objections even to a brigade group, Churchill thought the formation of such a small force within the British army, as Weizmann suggested, from already existing Jewish units to be both capable of execution and morally proper. "I like the idea of the Jews trying to get at the murderers of their fellow countrymen in Central Europe," he argued in a memorandum to Grigg on July 12. "It is with the Germans that they have their quarrel. . . . I cannot conceive why this martyred race scattered about the world and suffering as no other race has done at this juncture should be denied the satisfaction of having a flag." When Grigg sought a stipulation that the brigade group be available for general service in any area, Churchill reiterated his agreement with the Agency's insistence on the European theatre.[44] That same month, the prime minister also gave his support to the Agency's plan for 100 Jewish men from Palestine to be parachuted into the Balkans, where they could join 31 others currently engaged in a British–Jewish Agency project of anti–Nazi sabotage, Jewish resistance, and rescue.[45]

Churchill's decisive intervention paved the way in August for the realization of the Agency's limited objective. He replied to Weizmann with the assurance of his personal attention and sympathy in the matter of a Jewish fighting force. The War Office would shortly be in a position to discuss actual proposals; in the meantime, he wished particulars about the flag before embarking on "this contentious ground." Weizmann answered that very day, sending a sketch of the symbol for Jewry the world over: two horizontal blue stripes on a white background with a blue Star of David in the center. At the same time, the prime minister acceded to a request from Grigg and Colonial Secretary Oliver Stanley that the brigade not be brought back intact to Palestine after service in Europe, so as not to create "wide disturbances." On August 17, 1944, Grigg informed Weizmann about the Cabinet's approval of the Jewish Brigade Group. The infantry brigade and ultimately the entire force would be transferred to Italy, "so that you may be granted your heart's desire — the chance to fight the Germans."[46]

The appearance of the Jewish flag on the European front remained a final obstacle, but Churchill also saw this through. Seeking Roosevelt's reaction, the prime minister informed his closest war ally that, "after much pressure from Weizmann," he had set up what in the United States would be called a "regimental combat team." The step would give great satisfaction to the Jews, and "surely the Jews, of all races, have the right to strike at the Germans as a recognized body" under their own standard. This would be "a message to go all over the world," he cabled FDR. On hearing that the American President raised no objection to the Jewish Brigade as suggested, the Cabinet agreed on September 4 to the entire proposal.[47]

The Jewish Brigade became a reality at the end of September, 1944. The War Office noted the Cabinet's decision in a public communiqué on the 19th, but Churchill chose to feature the news during his war survey in the House of Commons nine days later. Vast numbers of Jews were serving with the Anglo–American forces on all fronts, he pointed out, "but it seems to me indeed appropriate that a special Jewish unit, a unit of that race which has suffered indescribable torments from the Nazis, should be represented as a distinct formation among the forces gathered for their final overthrow." The prime minister was certain that its members "will not only take part in the struggle but also in the occupation which will follow."[48]

Although some members of the Agency Executive harbored grave doubts about the sincerity of British intentions, it officially expressed deep gratification with this acknowledgment of Jewish services rendered to the Allied war effort and of "the Jewish desire for national recognition." Suspicions lingered that service in the brigade would come too late for actual combat but as a future occupation force in Europe. The probability of this contact with the German people horrified some of the executive, who also worried that HMG planned such duties precisely to weaken the *Yishuv*'s military strength just when Palestine's future would be decided. Yet the political success achieved far outweighed these fears in the end. The Anglo–American press overwhelmingly applauded HMG's decision, as did Parliament. The only opposition came from a handful of Jewish anti–Zionists, the ex-mufti, some Arab leaders, and from the Nazi propaganda machine, which warned that the move would only strengthen Germany's will to resist her enemies to the utmost. The struggle for an Allied Jewish fighting force had come to an end.[49]

A Summary Overview

The Jewish Brigade owed its creation, in the first instance, to the Jewish Agency. With justice could Shertok cable the American Zionist Emer-

gency Committee "this Agency's achievement from beginning to end."
Certainly his untiring activities on behalf of a Jewish force, opposed at
times by different political factions in the *Yishuv*, entitled him to first
patrimony. Weizmann's diplomatic pressure in London, and notably his
strong influence on England's prime minister, played the other chief role.
Ben Gurion's crusade to capture Palestinian and American Jewry for an
independent Jewish army and state meant much to its success. The Agency's major champions in Great Britain, Wingate, Wedgwood and Cazalet,
used every opportunity to castigate their government's unwillingness to
establish such a force. And the *Yishuv*'s significant effort on behalf of the
Allied cause, especially when compared with that of the Arabs, could not
fail to make some mark.[50]

The Committee for a Jewish Army, the only organization committed
full-time to the idea in question, did yeoman work in galvanizing public
opinion for the Jewish combat force. Its full-page newspaper advertise-
ments, stirring stage productions like Ben Hecht's "We Shall Never
Die," and subsequent activity as the Emergency Committee to Save the
Jewish People of Europe and then the Hebrew Committee of National
Liberation all made a deep impression in the United States and Great
Britain. Indeed, Palestinian Jewry's true military contribution first came
to light with Van Paassen's *The Forgotten Ally*, a 1943 best seller in both
countries which he had written while chairing the Committee for a Jewish
Army. The Committee's resolute activities reached the point where the
established Zionist groups, upon failing to co-opt its leadership, attempted to discredit in government circles Peter Bergson and the other
mavericks of the *Irgun* delegation. Ambassador Halifax and the Colonial
Office wished to silence Bergson by drafting him into the British Army, a
plot which his supporters in Congress foiled at the last moment. The
committee's ability to capture the public imagination certainly allowed
the prime minister to assert in Cabinet that this cause enjoyed great support on both sides of the Atlantic. And in a way its founders never intended, the organization's large-scale, aggressively put demands made it
easier for Churchill and his colonial and foreign secretaries to deal with
the established Jewish Agency, its smaller requests for a Jewish division
and then a brigade, and with the more moderate Weizmann.[51]

Churchill's deep sympathy for the concept of an Allied Jewish force
overcame the major forces of opposition, and gave this proposal some
real form at last. Without the prime minister's support, evident at every
crucial stage since September, 1939, the Jewish Brigade would never have
gotten by the careerists in London and the Middle East. The United
States War and State Departments also rejected the idea, and a report in
mid-1943 from Roosevelt's personal emissary to the Middle East, which

did much to shape government opinion, omitted any mention of the *Yishuv*'s war record. The president never made the public commitment to the Jewish force which he had promised Weizmann in July, 1942, and his "platonic interest," to quote the Jewish Socialist leader Harold Laski, did not strengthen its cause until the prime minister pressed FDR in August, 1944. Churchill justified the Jewish Brigade on military grounds, on the basis of his firm views supporting a large Jewish state in Palestine, and on the conviction that the scourge of the Holocaust called for a redemptive response from HMG to let the Jews of the Promised Land confront the murderers of their people in battle. Its subsequent record drew the prime minister's public praise. The triumph belonged to him above all.[52]

The brigade did meet the demands of the Zionist leadership to some extent. It tore aside the mask of anonymity which the British had imposed on the Jewish volunteers from Palestine. Fighting under its own flag, its Jewish officers, and commanding officer, Brigadier Ernest F. Benjamin, the force of some 5,000 participated on the Adriatic front with distinction in early 1945. The effort "redeemed our honor in our own eyes and in the eyes of others," asserted Shertok after the war. The climax came when a contingent of the brigade, each man sporting its blue–white–blue shoulder patch bearing a yellow Star of David and the words "Jewish Brigade Group" with the equivalent Hebrew initials "Chativa Yehudit Lochemet" (Chayil), marched through London under the Jewish flag in the Allied Victory March on June 8, 1946. At last that yellow star could be worn with pride, replacing the yellow badge of shame which had marked Jewry's millions for martyrdom in World War II. The brigade, the first outside Jewish group to come in contact with the casualties of the Holocaust, served as "a living bridge" after the armistice to bring these scarred remnants of European Jewry to Palestine, in defiance of British immigration quotas. Finally, the excellent military training which its members received in the last months of the war proved invaluable to the *Yishuv*'s armed struggle against HMG until the creation of the State of Israel three years later.[53]

But the Zionists' rare and limited victory failed to achieve the political significance for which they had grappled with HMG on the diplomatic front those past five years. The British had radically altered their view of Palestinian Jewry since Malcolm MacDonald first dismissed the *Yishuv*'s strength during the conference which gave birth to the White Paper. Nor did that statement of policy serve, as London had first expected, to bring about Arab loyalty during the war. Yet precisely its new realization of increased, militant Jewish power in Palestine — even Wavell admitted that the Jews, left to themselves, would defeat the Arabs — led an anxious Middle East Command to insist that the White Paper still be maintained throughout World War II and to oppose a Jewish state thereafter. Palestinian Jewry, as a consequence, was damned for having either too little power or too much. The British and the *Yishuv*, even in time of shared crisis, treated each other with distrust. As soon as the military authorities in Palestine had no need for the Agency and the *Yishuv*'s military value, this co-operation ground to a halt. Discrimination against the Jewish volunteers of Palestine continued in the case of the brigade as well, the British disallowing any recruitment among Italian Jewry or physically fit Holocaust survivors to help the brigade attain its full strength of 6,000, and insisting on the unit's dispersion before its soldiers returned home. This last condition recalled the fate of the Jewish Legion after the last world war.

The assassination in Cairo of Minister Resident Lord Moyne, Churchill's close friend, by the Stern group on November 6, 1944, raised serious doubts even in the prime minister's mind, and sharpened HMG's antagonism to Zionist aspirations. This hostility also sowed the dragon's teeth of Jewish civil conflict in Palestine: the Stern group, followed by the *Irgun,* refused to accept the Jewish Agency's actual truce with HMG during the war; the Hagana mounted a *saison* of retaliation against the dissident "terrorists." World War II ended, as it had begun, with the White Paper in force, and the doors to their one available large refuge firmly bolted against the Jews.[54]

At the root of the difficulty lay the different assumptions of the two contending forces regarding their individual positions in Palestine. Because British colonial practice traditionally viewed all HMG's subjects as an integral part of the Empire, it followed, in the words of the Foreign Office, that "the right of racial minorities to be recruited into units other than the normal forces of the state" could not be tolerated. The British had recruited "since time immemorial" on the basis of territorial domicile, opposing "racial prejudice" as "alien to our national feelings and instincts." The *Yishuv* insisted, on the other hand, on an equal partnership in the Mandate's implementation, thus incurring the continued hostility of the administration in Palestine. And ultimately of greatest significance, as Weizmann told MacMichael's successor in October, 1944, the Jewish community there did believe that the Biblical mandate predated Britain's right to govern its Promised Land.[55] Thus the Agency's demand to fight as Jews during World War II, rather than as "Palestinians" for defensive duty alone. The two opposing stances were, fundamentally, irreconcilable.

In the end, the tragedy of Jewish statelessness had forced the *Yishuv* to serve as Great Britain's nameless ally during World War II. Its final contribution of more than 31,000 soldiers to the British Army and multifold activities in other areas counted for little in the international diplomatic arena, the Arabs' sorry military record notwithstanding. HMG, as MacMichael understood it at the outbreak of hostilities, could take the *Yishuv*'s support for granted: as long as no threat confronted the Jewish national home, the British needed no large combat force from Palestine; when Rommel drew near, Jewish recruitment logically climbed without a fighting force of its own. Still, in consequence of Britain's anti-Zionist policy, as Churchill charged, HMG had to maintain more than 20,000 troops in Palestine during the war.[56]

Having expressed the faith in August, 1940, that "moral factors as well as purely material ones" would bear on victory, Ben Gurion understandably castigated four years later the empty expressions of sympathy towards defenseless European Jewry from the self–professed guardians of democracy, who "stood aside and let it bleed to death." The people who, more than any other, had the strongest reasons for fighting in united fashion under its own flag against the Nazi moloch never received Allied approval to do so. In this respect, the Jews were *sui generis,* unlike the Poles, Czechs, and other victims of the Third Reich who were allowed and indeed encouraged to form military units of their own.[57]

The *Yishuv*'s role in the Allied victory, therefore, met with the same official silence which muffled the last cries of its European brothers and sisters for immediate rescue before being throttled by the Nazis and their accomplices. At a time when Jewry was fighting for its very life, only one combatant accorded the Jews recognition as openly engaged in conflict with Nazism. Adolf Hitler carried this conviction until his suicide in a Berlin bunker on April 30, 1945, having concluded his Political Testament for signature at 4 A.M. the previous day: "Above all I charge the leaders of the nation and those under them to scrupulous observance of the laws of race and to merciless opposition to the universal poisoner of all peoples, international Jewry." As a result, Europe became a Jewish graveyard rather than a battlefield commensurate with the honor of the Jewish people.[58] The *Yishuv* saw no choice but to take up arms for Jewish sovereign independence after the war. The time had come, it concluded, to end the curse of anonymity and to bring the stateless survivors of the Holocaust home.

Notes

1. Weizmann to Chamberlain, Aug. 29, 1939, *Weizmann Archives,* Rechovot, Israel (hereafter *WA*). The League of Nations mandate for Palestine, assigned by the major Allies

to Great Britain in 1920, recognized the Jewish Agency as representing the Jewish people on all matters concerning the Jewish homeland there.

2. Yehuda Bauer, *From Diplomacy to Resistance, A History of Jewish Palestine 1939–1945* (Philadelphia: Jewish Publication Society of America, 1970), p. 212.

3. Ibid., pp. 47–48; David Ben Gurion, "The British Have Set a Trap — Our Only Way Out," *Jewish Observer and Middle East Review* (hereafter JOMER), Aug. 30, 1963, 10–12; Goldman to Brandeis, Sept. 5, 1939, file 53, Robert Szold MSS., *Zionist Archives*, New York (hereafter *ZA*).

4. Chamberlain to Weizmann, Sept. 2, 1939. *WA*.

5. Ben Gurion. "The Yishuv Goes to War," *JOMER*, Nov. 1, 1963, 20–23. Ben Gurion quickly realized that only the reality of increased power, particularly expressed in immigration and Jewish armament in Palestine, might sway the British in the *Yishuv*'s favor. Ben Gurion diary, Sept. 22, 1939, *David Ben Gurion Archives*, Sde Boker, Israel (hereafter *BGA*).

6. Moshe Sharett, *Yoman Medini*, vol. 4 (Tel Aviv: Am Oved, 1974), pp. 331–38, 343; Bauer, *From Diplomacy to Resistance*, pp. 81–82; Bernard Joseph, "Memo on Palestine," Jan. 1941, Jewish Agency confidential 1939 files, *ZA*.

7. Ben Gurion, "The Yishuv Joins Up," *JOMER*, Dec. 20, 1963, p. 18; Jacob Lifschitz, *Sefer HaBrigada Ha Yehudit* (Tel Aviv: Yavneh, 1947), p. 20; Shertok report, Oct. 9, 1939, American Jewish Conference files, *Hadassah Archives*, New York (hereafter *HA*); Sharett, *Yoman Medini*, vol. 4, pp. 436–38; Yitschak Lamdan, ed. *Sefer HaHitnadvut* (Jerusalem, Mossad Bialik 1949), pp. 31, 41–42.

8. Weizmann–Halifax talk, Sept. 18, 1939, and Weizmann–Churchill talk, Sept. 19, 1939, *WA;* memo, Sept. 26, 1939, *Jewish Agency Executive London* (hereafter *JAEL*), *WA;* Oct. 22, 1939, *Jewish Agency Executive Jerusalem* (hereafter *JAEJ*), *Central Zionist Archives*, Jerusalem (hereafter *CZA*). For more on Wingate's stance, see Christopher Sykes, *Orde Wingate, A Biography* (Cleveland: World Publishing Company, 1959), pp. 206–209, 219–20; Weizmann notes, Oct. 24, 1939, *WA*.

9. Sharett, *Yoman Medini*, Vol. 4, pp. 364, 368; *The Autobiography of Nahum Goldmann, Sixty Years of Jewish Life* (N.Y.: Rinehart and Winston, 1969), pp. 187–88.

10. ZOA–Hadassah meeting, Sept. 9, 1939, Rose Jacobs MSS., *HA; ZOA* conference with Lothian, Sept. 11, 1939, file 112, R. Szold MSS.

11. MacMichael to MacDonald, in reply to Sept. 2, 1939, British Foreign Office files (hereafter *FO*) 371/23239, *Public Record Office* (hereafter *PRO*), Kew, England; MacMichael–Ben Gurion–Shertok talk, Sept. 26, 1939, Colonial Office papers (hereafter *CO*), 733/406/75872/12, *PRO*.

12. Oct. 19, 1939 meeting, Cabinet 65, *PRO;* Gabriel Cohen, *Churchill U'Sheailat Eretz Yisrael, 1939–1942* (Jerusalem, Yad Yitzchak Ben Tsvi, 1976), pp. 27–28.

13. Ben Gurion, "The Arrest of the 43," *JOMER*, Nov. 8, 1963, 16–19; Barker memo, Nov. 2, 1939, in Luke to Baggallay, Nov. 13, 1939, FO 371/23251, *PRO;* MacDonald–Shertok talk, Oct. 20, 1939, American Jewish Conference file, *HA;* Weizmann–Ironside interviews, Oct. 30, 1939, and Nov. 14, 1939, *WA*. The sentences were lowered to sixteen months imprisonment. Bauer, *From Diplomacy to Resistance*, p. 101.

14. Ben Gurion, "Ironside Supports Jewish Army," *JOMER*, Nov. 15, 1963, 19–20; Bauer, *From Diplomacy to Resistance*, pp. 85–86; Sharett, *Yoman Medini*, vol. 4, pp. 500, 523; Weizmann to Ironside, Dec. 1, 1939, *WA*.

15. Ben Gurion, "Ironside Supports Jewish Army," *JOMER*, Nov. 15, 1963, 22; Weizmann–Wavell talk, Dec. 8, 1939, *WA;* Sharett, *Yoman Medini*, vol. 4, pp. 535–36; Ben Gurion, "Why We Fought For Britain," *JOMER*, Nov. 22, 1963, 15–17; Lamdan, *Sefer*

HaHitnadvut, pp. 39–40, 53–96. Leading American Zionists also had decided to oppose a Jewish Legion, irrespective of their country's neutrality laws, out of fear of contributing to "tremendous agitation" then current against Jews as "war mongers." Schultz to Goldmann, Nov. 6, 1939, file 214A, *World Jewish Congress Archives*, New York.

16. Winston S. Churchill, *The Second World War, Their Finest Hour* (N.Y.: Bantam Books, Aug. 1977 ed.), pp. 541, 141, 149; Lloyd to Churchill, May 22, 1940, and June 27, 1940, FO 371/24566, *PRO;* Ben Gurion, "Table Talk With Lord Lloyd," *JOMER,* Dec. 13, 1963, 15–17; Bauer, *From Diplomacy to Resistance,* pp. 106, 87–89; Montor to Kaplan, June 25, 1940, Eliezer Kaplan MSS., *ZA; JAEL,* Aug. 9, 1940. At the same time, Churchill killed the Colonial and Foreign Offices' support of a secret offer from Iraqi Foreign Minister Nuri Said to have HMG begin implementing the White Paper's constitutional clause in exchange for Iraqi support for the Allied cause, with a public declaration for full implementation after the war. Cohen, *Churchill U'Sheilat Eretz Yisrael, 1939–1942,* pp. 63–73.

17. *JAEL,* Sept. 9 and 18, 1940, and Oct. 16, 1940, Z4/302/24, *CZA;* Lloyd to Weizmann, Oct. 17, 1940, *WA;* Thompson to Churchill, Jan. 23, 1941, and Churchill's note in PREMIER MSS. (hereafter PREM) 4, 52/5, II, *PRO;* Haining to Shuckburgh, Aug. 22, 1940, and Haining to Moyne, Feb. 8, 1941, War Office files (hereafter WO) 32/8502, *PRO;* MacMichael to Lloyd, Nov. 12, 1940, FO 371/24565, *PRO;* Ben Gurion, "The Yishuv Joins Up," *JOMER,* Dec. 20, 1963, 19.

18. Wavell to War Office, Feb. 26, 1941, PREM 5, 51/9/II, *PRO;* Churchill to Moyne, Mar. 1 and 4, 1941, Ibid.; Moyne to Weizmann, Mar. 4, 1941, and Weizmann to Moyne, Mar. 6, 1941, *WA;* Amitzur Ilan, "HaMinimax VeOrmat HaHistoria," in Y. Gorni and G. Yogev, eds. *Medina'i Beltot Mashber, Darko Shel Chaim Weizmann BaTenua HaTsiyonit, 1900–1948* (Tel Aviv, Ha Kibbutz HaMeuchad, 1977), p. 153, note 22.

19. Bauer, *From Diplomacy to Resistance,* pp. 153–62; Robert Stephens, *Nasser: A Political Biography* (N.Y.: Simon and Schuster, 1971), Ch. 2; Moyne to Weizmann, Aug. 28, 1941, *WA;* Lyttleton to Eden, Aug. 9, 1941, S 25/1555, *CZA;* Weizmann to Churchill, Sept. 10, 1941, *WA.*

20. Moyne to Weizmann, Oct. 15, 1941, *WA;* minutes of delegation's talk, Oct. 17, 1941, WO 32/9502, *PRO; Palcor,* Nov. 10, 1941; *Jewish Telegraphic Agency* (hereafter JTA), Nov. 26, 1941; Mufti diary entry, Nov. 26, 1941, Virginia Gildersleeve MSS., Special Collections, Columbia University, N.Y.: London, *Jewish Chronicle,* Nov. 14, 1941.

21. Meeting, Mar. 11, 1941, Minutes, *BGA;* Emergency Committee for Zionist Affairs minutes, May–June, 1941, *ZA;* Ben Gurion memo, "Outlines of Zionist Policy," Oct. 17, 1941, *WA.*

22. Jabotinsky to Chamberlain, Sept. 4, 1939, FO 371/23250, *PRO;* Jabotinsky–MacDonald talk, Sept. 6, 1939, FO 371/23242, *PRO;* Vladimir Jabotinsky, *The Jewish War Front* (London: Allen and Unwin, 1940) (later republished as *The War and the Jews,* in New York, Dial Press, 1942); FO 371/24566, *PRO;* Jabotinsky to Czech foreign minister, Aug. 1, 1940, Box 2, NZO U.S. files, *Metsudat Ze'ev,* Tel Aviv.

23. Interviews with the author: Hillel Kook, June 22, 1972, and Samuel Merlin, Mar. 27, 1972; Bergson to Silver, Apr. 10, 1941, and Bergson to Wise, May 7, 1941, Hebrew Committee of National Liberation MSS., *Metsudat Ze'ev;* Monty N. Penkower, "In Dramatic Dissent: The Bergson Boys," *American Jewish History,* 73 (Mar., 1981), 282–85.

24. Pierre Van Paassen, "World Destiny Pivots on Palestine," *New Palestine,* Dec. 12, 1941, 9–10; Bergson interview; Bergson to Halpern, Apr. 9, 1942, Box 26–40, Committee for a Jewish Army MSS., *Metsudat Ze'ev;* Committee for a Jewish Army–London MSS., *Metsudat Ze'ev.*

25. Ben Gurion, "U.S. Jewry on Threshold of Unity," *JOMER,* Apr. 3, 1964, 16–18,

and "Memo to the President," *JOMER*, Apr. 10, 1964, 18, and "From Basle to Biltmore," *JOMER*, Apr. 24, 1964, 17–19. For the deepening split between Weizmann and Ben Gurion on this and other issues, see Yosef Gorni, *Shutfut U'Ma'avak* (Tel Aviv, HaKibbutz HaMeuchad, 1976), Chs. 4–5. The rift actually began when Ben Gurion refused to accept the offer of a Jewish division, because its 3000 Palestinian Jews would have to leave to service anywhere at HMG's order. Diary Sept. 11, 1940, *BGA; JAEL*, Sept. 18, 1940, Z4/302/24, *CZA*.

    26. Bauer, *From Diplomacy to Resistance*, Chs. 3–5; Slutsky, *Sefer Toldot HaHagana*, 3, (Tel Aviv, Am Oved 1972), Chs. 20–21.

    27. Ben Gurion to Casey, Apr. 15, 1942, Z5/1361, *CZA;* Shertok to Auchinleck, Apr. 17, 1942, Jewish Agency files, 16/3, *ZA;* Weizmann to Winant, Apr. 25, 1942, Box 30, John Winant MSS., *Franklin D. Roosevelt Library* (hereafter *FDRL*), Hyde Park, N.Y.; Bauer, *From Diplomacy to Resistance*, pp. 219, 183–84.

    28. July 3, 4, and 7, 1942, vol. 5, Henry Morgenthau, Jr., Presidential Diaries, *FDRL;* July 7, 1942, vol. 547, Henry Morgenthau, Jr., Diaries, *FDRL;* Weizmann–Roosevelt talk, July 7, 1942, Z5/1378, *CZA*.

    29. Churchill to Cranborne, July 5, 1942, and Cranborne to Churchill, July 6, 1942, PREM 5, 51/9/II, *PRO;* Churchill message in *JTA*, July 23, 1942.

    30. Cranborne to Grigg, July 15, 1942, WO 32/10258, *PRO;* secretaries' memo, Aug. 1, 1942, WP 42 (332), Cabinet 66, *PRO;* Lamdan, *Sefer HaHitnadvut*, pp. 97–131; Bauer, *From Diplomacy to Resistance*, pp. 220–21.

    31. Ibid., p. 191; Shertok to Pinkerton, Nov. 23, 1942, Correspond. files, *BGA; JAEJ*, Dec. 13, 1942, *CZA; New Judea*, Dec. 1942, 48.

    32. Shertok statement, Dec. 21, 1942, Labor ZOA papers, Box 1, *YIVO Archives*, New York; ZOA Admin. Committee minutes, Feb. 21, 1943, *ZA;* I.S.O. Playfair, *The Mediterranean and the Middle East*, vol. 2 (London, H.M. Stationery Office, 1956); Joseph B. Schechtman, *The Mufti and the Fuehrer* (N.Y., T. Yosselof, 1965), Ch. 3–4. On Feb. 21, 1943, Shertok brought American Zionists the latest figures from Palestine; as against 21,000 Jews, about 8,000 Arabs had been recruited, while the proportion in the Palestinian population was then 1 Jew to 2 Arabs. The 8,000 Arab total included Arabs from Transjordan and Syria, with about half of this figure evaluated as "came and went." ZOA Admin. Committee minutes, *ZA*. For an exhaustive analysis of the subject under discussion up to this point, focusing on events in Palestine and London, see Yoav Gelber, *Toldot HaHitnadvut*, 1, *HaHitnadvut U'Mekoma BaMediniyut HaTsiyonit VeHaYishuvit, 1939–1942* (Jerusalem, Yad Yitzchak Ben Tsvi, 1979).

    33. Shertok report, Feb. 23, 1943, Jewish Agency files, *ZA;* Bauer, *From Diplomacy to Resistance*, pp. 268–68; Lamdan, *Sefer HaHitnadvut*, pp. 50–51; *JAEJ*, June 13, 1943, *CZA*.

    34. Monty N. Penkower, "The 1943 Joint Anglo–American Statement on Palestine," *Herzl Yearbook* 8 (1978), 212–21; Middle East Conference memo, May 19, 1943, FO 371/ 34975, *PRO*.

    35. Lyttleton memo, Cabinet 66, *PRO;* Ettel memo, Mar. 24, 1943, and addendum, reprinted in *Nation Associates* memo, June, 1948, in Clark Clifford MSS., *Harry S. Truman Library*, Independence, Mo., Box 14.

    36. Penkower, "1943 Joint Statement," 221–33. Amery first broached the idea of a generous partition of Palestine for the Jews in a much earlier memo to Churchill. Amery to Churchill, Oct. 4, 1941, PREM 4, 52/5, *PRO*.

    37. Ben Gurion, "The Birth of the Jewish Brigade," *JOMER*, Jan. 10, 1964, 18–19; Golda Meir, *My Life* (N.Y., Putnam, 1975), pp. 184–89; Shertok to Goldmann, Aug. 30,

1943, S 25/73, *CZA;* Slutsky, *Sefer Toldot HaHagana,* vol. 3, pp. 176–80; *New York Times,* Oct. 7, and 8, 1943.

38. Jessie Lurie, "Guns in Palestine," *Nation,* Jan. 22, 1944, 92–94; Shertok–MacMichael talk, Nov. 17, 1943, Jewish Agency 1939 files, *ZA; JAEL* minutes, Nov. 26, 1943, and Dec. 3, 1943, Z4/302/28, *CZA.*

39. Slutsky, *Sefer Toldot HaHagana,* vol. 3, pp. 730–32, 774–76: Yoav Gelber, *Toldot HaHitnadvut,* vol. 2, *HaMa'avak LeTsava Ivri* (Jerusalem, Yad Yitzchak Ben Tsvi, 1981), Ch. 3. The last–named concessions proved shortlived, however. Lamdan, *Sefer HaHitnadvut,* pp. 136–42.

40. *Political Report of the London Office of the Executive of the Jewish Agency, Submitted to the Twenty–Second Zionist Congress at Basle, Dec. 1946* (London, n.p., 1946), pp. 37–38; Shertok to Locker, Sept. 13, 1943, Z5/1217, *CZA; JAEL,* Oct. 1943 meetings, Z4/302/27, *CZA;* Churchill–Weizmann talk, Oct. 25, 1943, *WA.*

41. Bauer, *From Diplomacy to Resistance,* pp. 348, 311–23; chiefs to staff memo, Jan. 22, 1944. Cabinet 95/14, *PRO;* Goldmann to Shertok, Apr. 4, 1944, Z5/778, *CZA;* Joseph to Weizmann, Mar. 31, 1944, S 25/560, *CZA.*

42. Lifschitz, *Sefer HaBrigada,* p. 42; Weizmann to Grigg, Mar. 28, 1944, Correspond. files, *BGA;* Shertok report, May 8, 1944, *JAEL, CZA;* Grigg to Weizmann, June 21, 1944, *WA;* commanders–in–chief memo, May 2, 1944, CO 733/461/75872/II, *PRO;* Grigg memo, June 26, 1944, Cabinet 66, *PRO.*

43. Weizmann to Churchill, July 4, 1944, and Grigg to Weizmann, July 7, 1944, *WA;* Abba Eban, "Tragedy and Triumph, 1939–1949," in Meyer Weisgal and Joel Carmichael, eds. *Chaim Wezimann, A Biography by Several Hands* (London, Wiedenfeld and Nicolson, 1962), pp. 272–73; Lamdan, *Sefer HaHitnadvut,* p. 146.

44. Churchill to Eden, June 29, 1944, PREM 4, 52/5/II, *PRO;* July 3, 1944 discussion (86/44/1), Cabinet 66, *PRO;* Churchill, *The Second World War, Triumph and Tragedy* (N.Y., Bantam Books, 1962 ed.), pp. 590–591n.

45. British fears of Zionist political aims limited the entire program's potential ever since the idea of Jewish parachutists had been raised by the Jewish Agency in early 1943. Again, Churchill's sympathies went counter to those British authorities ultimately responsible for the decision, and the large–scale program failed to materialize. Bauer, *From Diplomacy to Resistance,* pp. 274–86; Zerubavel Gilad, ed. *Magen BeSeter* (Jerusalem: Jerusalem Post, 1952), pp. 193–97, 211–67; Slutsky, *Sefer Toldot HaHagana,* vol. 3, Ch. 32.

46. Churchill to Weizmann, Aug. 5, 1944, and Weizmann to Churchill, same date, *WA;* Grigg to Churchill, Aug. 6, 1944, PREM 5, 51/9, *PRO;* Grigg to Weizmann, Aug. 17, 1944, *WA.*

47. Churchill to Roosevelt, Aug. 23, 1944, and Roosevelt to Churchill, Aug. 28, 1944, PREM 4, 51/9/I, *PRO;* Sept. 4, 1944 decision (116/44/6), Cabinet 65, *PRO.*

48. *Political Report . . . Basle,* p. 39; *Great Britain, Parliamentary Debates* (Commons), Sept. 28, 1944, vol. 403, Col. 474.

49. Gelber, *Toldot HaHitnadvut,* vol. 2, pp. 422–423, 431–432, 436–448; Lamdan, *Sefer HaHitnadvut,* pp. 148–49; *JTA,* Oct. 1, 1944.

50. Shertok to Silver, in American Zionist Emergency Committee, executive committee minutes, Oct. 12, 1944, *ZA.* The debate regarding the possibility of a Jewish force to serve outside Palestine's borders began immediately within the Yishuv and its leadership. *JAEJ,* Sept. 24, 1939, *CZA;* Bauer, *From Diplomacy to Resistance,* pp. 94–96, 174–78, 211–18; Gelber, *Toldot HaHitnadvut,* vol. 1, *passim.*

51. Penkower, "Bergon Boys," 297–309; Halifax to FO, Aug. 24, 1944, and Sept. 11, 1944, FO 371/40145, *PRO;* CO memo, Sept. 8, 1944, CO 733/461/75872, 14A, *PRO;* Pierre

Van Paassen, *The Forgotten Ally* (N.Y., Dial Press, 1943). And HMG's spokesman in Parliament, in ridiculing Strabolgi's continued insistence on a large Jewish army, could intimate publicly for the first time that a Jewish brigade might be in the offing. Strabolgi and Croft statements in Commons, July 4, 1944, quoted in *New Judea*, June–July 1944, 157–58.

52. Hoskins Apr. 20, 1943 report, PSF, Confidential files, State Dept., Box 5, *FDRL;* Laski's remarks in *JAEL* meeting, Oct. 13, 1943, *WA;* Churchill to Bridges, Oct. 1, 1944, PREM 4, 52/5, *PRO;* Churchill, *The Second World War, Triumph and Tragedy*, p. 453; *Great Britain, Parliamentary Debates* (Commons), May 2, 1945, vol. 410, col. 1509.

53. Slutsky, *Sefer Toldot HaHagana*, vol. 3, pp. 668–69, 797, and Ch. 39; Lamdan, *Sefer HaHitnadvut*, pp. 950, and 675–794; Lifschitz, *Sefer HaBrigada, passim.*

54. Churchill to Ismay, Jan. 25, 1944, PREM 4, 51/11, *PRO;* Slutsky, *Sefer Toldot HaHagana*, vol. 3, p. 729; Eban, "Tragedy and Triumph," pp. 274–75, 277–79. According to the British official record, the total strength of the Jewish Brigade at the war's end stood at 4,021, of whom 3,170 were serving in Europe. The casualties: 33 killed, 157 wounded, and 4 missing in action. *Great Britain, Parliamentary Debates*, (Commons), July 1, 1947, vol. 439, col. 1125.

55. Baxter to Halifax, Mar. 9, 1943, FO 371/35032, *PRO;* Ben Gurion, "War and the Jewish People," *New Palestine*, Oct. 27, 1939, p. 5; JAEJ, Oct. 22, 1944, *CZA.*

56. MacMichael to Colonial Secretary, in reply to Sept. 2, 1939, FO 371/23239, *PRO;* I.S.O. Playfair, *The Mediterranean and the Middle East*, vol. 1 (London, H.M. Stationary Office, 1954), pp. 17, 93.

57. Ben Gurion, "Jewish Army," *New Judea*, Aug. 1940, 172–74; Ben Gurion, "To the Tribunal of Nations," *Palestine and Middle East* 17 (July, 1944), 123–24.

58. Facsimile in H.R. Trevor-Roper, *The Last Days of Hitler* (N.Y.: The Macmillan Co., 1947), p. 180. For Shertok's perception of this reality, see his incisive speech to the Jewish Brigade on the occasion of its disbandonment. Lamdan, *Sefer HaHitnadvut*, pp. 950–57. It is estimated that, apart from the contribution of the Yishuv, some one and a quarter million Jews served in the Allied armies during World War II. Lifschitz, *Sefer HaBrigada*, p. 58n.

III THE HOLOCAUST: SELECTED AREAS

4 THE JAPANESE IDEOLOGY OF ANTI-SEMITISM AND THE HOLOCAUST

David Kranzler

Japanese Attitudes Toward the Jews: An Overview

The Bolshevic Revolution is part of the Jewish plot; Zionism seems to be the goal of the Jews, but they actually want to control the world's economy, politics and diplomacy. Unless the Japanese realize this danger, Japan will be left behind in the struggle for world supremacy. The League of Nations, Freemasons, May Day celebrations, are (all) under Jewish control.[1]

The Jewish plot must be destroyed by force . . . The Jews are responsible for the American and European "control" of the Chinese Nationalist Government . . . The anti–Japanese activities in England are all instigated by Jewish freemasons . . . They are responsible for the immorality of the Japanese youth by showing their (Jewish) films . . . the Jews control the American press and thereby public opinion, turning it against Japan.[2]

These statements were made by two Japanese officers who became key factors in an extraordinary chapter in the history of the Holocaust: The haven offered by the Japanese in Shanghai to almost 18,000 Jewish ref-

The author thanks Ms. Gertrude Hirschler for her editorial assistance.

ugees from Germany, Austria and Poland who might otherwise have perished in Hitler's ghettos and gas chambers.

In one of the most ironic twists of the Holocaust we find the Axis powers not only permitting, but actually encouraging emigration of Jewish refugees. The small Jewish community of Shanghai as well as all the major Jewish organizations of America attempted to halt emigration to the only place in the world willing to accept Jews in 1938–1939 without any visas or papers of any kind.

Germany continued to press thousands of Jews to leave, even without visas. Italy permitted the use of its ports and shipping, and Japan — the real power in Shanghai since the Sino–Japanese hostilities of 1937 — maintained public silence for six months and permitted the refugees to settle in the city. The Japanese authorities did not impose restrictions on immigration until August 1939, after the refugee population had reached 14,000 or almost three–fourths the number of Shanghai's Japanese residents. Even then, they did not act without first requesting, and receiving, assurances from Sir Victor Sassoon, the merchant prince and influential leader of Shanghai's established Jewish community, that no protests would be forthcoming from the Jews of England and the United States. Notwithstanding these restrictions, the Japanese admitted to Shanghai another three to four thousand refugees, including one thousand from Poland, between the outbreak of World War II in September, 1939, and the entry of Japan into the war in December, 1941.

The victims of Nazi oppression took up residence primarily in Hongkew, the Japanese controlled sector of Shanghai's International Settlement. In February, 1943, under pressure from Nazi Germany, the Japanese government imposed a ghetto of sorts on the refugees, but this "restricted area" bore little resemblance to the inhuman Nazi prototype. Moreover, over 4,000 stateless Russian Jews and most of the Sephardic Jews of Baghdad who had come to Shanghai before 1937 did not have to move into the ghetto at all.

This study is an attempt to explain the individuals, the motivations, and above all the ideology that influenced Japanese policy toward the Jews during the Holocaust era, a policy which indirectly saved thousands of Jewish lives — a ray of light in a period of almost unrelieved darkness.

Paradoxically, the singular behavior of the Japanese, partners of the Rome–Berlin Axis, in dealing with the Jewish refugees in their sphere of dominion can only be explained by the influence on Japanese policy of certain Japanese "experts on Jewish affairs" and their peculiar type of anti–Semitism. What follows is the story of how these experts, middle-echelon officers in the Japanese army and navy, gained sufficient influence to shape the policies of the Japanese empire in apparent opposition to its ally, Nazi Germany. The cause advocated by this officer clique fitted into the intricate pattern of Japan's domestic and foreign affairs.

Among those responsible for formulating and implementing Japan's policy toward the Jews during that period were the two officers whose statements are quoted at the beginning of this study. The diatribe about the Bolshevik Revolution as part of the Jewish drive for world dominion came from Colonel Norihiro Yasue, who was to become chief of the Japanese military mission at Dairen, Manchuria. The portrayal of the Jews as manipulators of the West, instigating hostility against Japan in England and America and corrupting the morals of Japanese youth, was the brain–child of Yasue's naval colleague, Captain Koreshige Inuzuka.

Colonel Yasue, under the pseudonym of Hokoshi, translated into Japanese the *Protocols of the Elders of Zion* and wrote anti–Semitic tracts of his own bearing such titles as *The Jewish Control of the World*. Captain Inuzuka, using the pen–name Kiyo Utsunomiya, produced yet another Japanese version of the *Protocols,* along with translations of other anti–Jewish literature. Yet, Colonel Yasue was instrumental in closing down *Nash Put,* an anti–Semitic newspaper published by the White Russian community of Harbin, Manchuria.[3] He was responsible for the elimination of the letter *J* from the passports of Jews in Peking.[4] But in 1941 his name was to be inscribed in the Golden Book of the Jewish National Fund for his services to the Jewish people.[5]

In November 1940 Captain Inuzuka stunned his country's German allies with a broadcast assuring the Jews in Japan and in areas under Japanese domination that they would be treated "on the principles of equality" as long as they remained loyal to the Japanese authorities. In March 1941 Inuzuka received a silver cigarette case inscribed, "To Captain Inuzuka, Imperial Japanese Navy. In gratitude and appreciation for your service for (sic) the Jewish people (from the) Union of Orthodox Rabbis of the US" During the summer of 1941, two years after the restrictions on immigration into Shanghai were put into effect, it was Inuzuka who helped make it possible for over 1,000 Polish refugees stranded in Japan to enter Shanghai's Hongkew sector.[6]

The key to this official Japanese benign policy toward the Jews, and to the men behind it, lies in the particular interpretation which Yasue, Inuzuka and the other Japanese "experts on Jewish affairs" gave to modern anti–Semitic ideology. The manner in which this Japanese variant of anti–Semitism was implemented by the government of Japan is likewise considerable. Men such as Yasue and Inuzuka sincerely believed the canard — imported from Russia and the West — that the Jews wielded decisive financial and political power on the international scene. But instead of seeking to eliminate the Jews, the Japanese under the tutelage of the experts decided to harness what they perceived to be "Jewish power," whether in Asia, in Europe or in the United States, for the best interests of Japan: the development of Manchuria.

The intention was to form an industrious and intellectual class in Manchuria — Japan's hinterland — by creating a new Palestine or Jewish Homeland in Manchuria. The settlement would theoretically serve as both a counterweight to Russia's nearby Jewish state of Birobidjan, and the cultivation of the United States as a more friendly power through the "all powerful Jews" who surrounded President Roosevelt, such as Treasury Secretary Henry Morgenthau, Jr., Rabbi Stephen S. Wise and others.

The notions about the leverage of Jews in international affairs, as preached by the "experts on Jewish affairs," were reinforced by Japan's own experience with Jews. After Commodore Matthew C. Perry first opened Japan to the Western world in 1853, Jewish merchants and export–importers found their way to Japan and became effective promoters of Japanese products throughout the Western hemisphere.

Perhaps the most influential individual in shaping the Japanese image of the powerful international financier was an American–Jewish philanthropist, Jacob H. Schiff, the German born president of the New York banking firm of Kuhn, Loeb and Company. During the Russo–Japanese War of 1904–05 Schiff arranged the floating of important loans that helped finance about half the Japanese navy. This navy later routed Russia's Baltic fleet. To the Japanese, the loans negotiated by Schiff had significance far beyond their cash value. They seemed to demonstrate that European governments and financial circles which initially had been skeptical about Japan's viability as a modern nation were now willing to take a chance on her prospects. Actually, Schiff had arranged the initial loan even before Japan's first victory at the Yalu River.[6]

Japan had been represented in the loan transaction by Baron Korekiyo Takahashi, who was later to become Japan's finance minister and then prime minister. In his autobiography,[7] Takahashi wrote that Schiff's ready response to Japan's plight had been motivated by a personal consideration: Schiff had wanted to punish Tsarist Russia for her mistreatment of his fellow Jews in the Kishinev pogrom of 1903. Takahashi and other highly placed Japanese were undoubtedly also aware of Schiff's Jewish connections in Germany (such as M. M. Warburg and Co. in Hamburg) and in England (Sir Ernest Cassel); powerful friends who enabled him to arrange for the multinational second, third and fourth loans so badly needed by Japan.

The Japanese came to see Schiff as the epitome of the Jewish financier — powerful enough through personal wealth and international ties to help shape world affairs, and ready to use these assets on behalf of his fellow Jews. Three decades later, Japanese notions about the financial strength of the Jews and their worldwide solidarity were to be bolstered when Jewish importers in the democratic world launched a boycott against Nazi Germany. The boycott benefited Japanese trade. Clearly, said the Japanese "experts on Jewish affairs," the Germans were right: the Jews were indeed a potent force.[8] Therefore, they had to be treated judiciously. "(The Jews are) just like a shellfish dish," Captain Inuzuka was to write early in 1939, "It is a rare delicacy but unless one knows well how to prepare it properly, it may prove fatal."[9]

By the late 1920s the attitude of Inuzuka and other younger Japanese military men toward the Jews had been molded by a curious mix of influences that seemed to confirm each other. Recollections of what appeared to them as the role of "Jewish power" in recent Japanese history mingled with a crude form of anti–Semitism imported from Siberia. In 1918 and again in 1922, Japanese armed forces had entered Siberia to help the remnants of the White Russian forces prevent the advancing Bolshevik armies from reaching East Asia. Both expeditions proved a complete failure. A less known, unfortunate result of the contacts between White Russian and Japanese officers during the campaign in Siberia was that the Japanese absorbed an unhealthy dose of Russian anti–Semitic propaganda. Among those who responded to these White Russian teachings were two generals, Kiichiro Higuchi and Nobutaka Shioten, and also Colonel Norihiro Yasue and Captain Koreshige Inuzuka, all of whom were familiar with the Russian language.[10] The White Russian officers infected their Japanese counterparts with their hatred of Bolsheviks and Jews, who, in the minds of some, became synonymous. It was through their White Russian mentors, too, that Japanese officers such as Yasue and Inuzuka came to know anti–Semitic Russian literature in Japanese translation. Thus, they read *The Essence of Radicalism* (1919) and, of course, *The Protocols of the Elders of Zion,* which had been making the rounds for some time. During those years *The Protocols of the Elders of Zion* became the infamous bible of anti–Semitism throughout the world.[11]

Protocols had been proven by an astute reporter of the *London Times* to be a complete fabrication based upon a Frenchman's satire on Napoleon III. This exposure, however, did not lessen the book's widespread appeal to anti–Semites. The Japanese experts continued to believe that every syllable of the book was true, including the myth that the Jews were the secret fomentors of a world revolution under the guise of Bolshevism, a movement hated and feared by Japanese of every political and social persuasion. But while the Japanese were certain that the only way to remove the Bolshevik menace was through all out war (which Japan was not able to wage), they believed that the Jewish threat could be neutralized by turning the Jews, at home and abroad, into a tool serving the interests of Japan.

During the 1920s and 1930s anti–Semitic literature also reached Japan from France, Britain and the United States. But perhaps the greatest inspiration for the budding Japanese anti–Semitic ideology came from Germany, a country the Japanese had long admired for her efficiency and technical know–how. Following the Franco–Prussian War of 1870, Japan had adopted the structure and discipline of the victorious Prussian army as the model for her own military forces. The Japanese tendency to look to Germany for the latest scientific and technological advances persisted even after Germany's defeat in World War I. German became a required language for all aspiring young Japanese officers. As a result, they were able to read Nazi anti–Semitic literature in its original language long before Hitler's propaganda machine made it available in Japanese translation.

However, the anti–Semitic ideology which the Japanese evolved from these scurrilous writings and from their direct contacts with Nazi propagandists was different from that which inspired the Jew–haters in Europe. European anti–Semitism was based in large part on the age old Christian tradition of identifying the Jew with the Devil, the anti–Christ, to be hated and feared. Seen from that vantage point, the *Protocols* only reinforced the myth of the Jews seeking to take over the world for Satan's purposes, an image taken as a license for the pogroms and massacres over centuries that culminated in the Holocaust.

The Japanese, however, brought a totally different perspective to their reading of the *Protocols* and other European exposes of the Jews. Like the Europeans, they believed in the existence of a mighty Jewish power, but unlike the Europeans, the Japanese were not motivated by hatred or contempt. The Japanese anti–Semites regarded the Jews simply as a mighty force, like energy, which, if harnessed properly is a marvelous tool, but can be explosive if tampered with the wrong way.

As a result, their proposed solution of the Jewish problem, too, was at sharp variance with the "Final Solution" of Adolf Hitler and his cohorts. The Jews should not be killed or oppressed, these ideologues reasoned, but utilized intelligently for the welfare of the Japanese empire. This pragmatic approach, which was to determine Japan's treatment of the Jews during the Hitler era, was motivated by one of numerous Japanese ultranationalist militarist factions, of which Colonel Yasue and Captain Inuzuka played a prominent role. Ironically, this ultranationalism, which spelled disaster for militarist Japan, helped save thousands of Jews from the Holocaust. For this reason, its historical background and psychological motivations, and the place which it assigned to the Jews in its plans, merit examination in some detail.

Beginning with Japan's entry into the Western world in the 1850s until the early 1940s, when World War II came to the Pacific, the Japanese designs on the Asian mainland took the form of a two pronged policy: guarding the nation against attacks from without, and strengthening its economic base from within. Small in size, poor in natural resources, and burdened with an evergrowing population, Japan early cast hungry eyes upon Korea and China, and especially Manchuria, the "edge of Asia," as the solution to her problems. Manchuria held particular attraction because of her population and rich endowment of unexploited natural resources. Manchuria could also provide a buffer zone between Japan and ever-encroaching Russia, always the much feared enemy, and relieve Japan of her problems of overpopulation. As for China and Korea, which had become fair game in the international scramble for political and economic concessions, Japan saw them as a vast market for her manufactured goods.

Confronted with the Western power play on the Asian mainland and the opening of her islands to the West, Japan realized that in order to survive and become a strong power herself in the modern industrial world, it was imperative that she acquire Western skills and methods without delay. Young men were sent to Europe and the United States to study Western ways; to Germany for modern military science, to England for naval knowledge, and to the United States to observe the latest industrial advances.

In the wake of World War I, Western influences spread rapidly among the postwar Japanese youth, particularly in the urban areas, and the older generation became aware that Westernization was not an unmixed blessing. Modernism introduced into Japan American-style dancing, jazz, movies, and the hedonism and unfettered individualism which appeared to represent the destruction of traditional Japanese values.

Japanese society was built upon the premise of the family. The extended family was the nation, and the emperor above all was revered as demigod. The individual counted for relatively little; his comforts, his personal desires and aspirations had to be subordinated to the welfare and prestige of his family and of his country. But now, revolutionary ideologies from left to right, which had taken hold in Europe following the overturn of age old monarchical and social systems, had gripped the burgeoning student bodies at Japanese universities and infected even some of the young officers in Japan's armed forces. In the eyes of the conservatives, the labor strikes, rice riots, inflation and the failure of many small business establishments that marked the 1920s were symptoms of the negative influence of the modernism imported into Japan with American and English social and cultural patterns.

The ultranationalists in Japan's leadership now saw the West — which they primarily identified with the United States and Great Britain — as introducing into Japan not only modern science and technology, which Japan needed in order to survive, but also dangerous foreign ideas and ways that would end in the disintegration of the traditional Japanese order. Revulsion toward these "subversive" ideological imports led the conservatives to launch an active effort to eliminate them and to bring about a so-called Showa Restoration, with increased emphasis on the semi-divine power of the emperor and respect for old style authority in general. Western influences were to be restrained insofar as they were needed to promote the growth and power of Japan but Western evils had to be uprooted so that the pristine Japanese way of life could survive, undisturbed.

This brand of extreme Japanese nationalism was further spurred by the great Depression and the severe economic stress that followed. By the end of the 1930s, Japan's economic problems, including the systematic blocking of cheap Japanese exports by many countries, had created mass unemployment and stirred the unrest that laid dormant during the 1920s.

These disturbances intensified nationalist feelings against Western parliamentary democracy and unbridled capitalism.[12] Japan's troubles were blamed on the Western powers, especially the United States and Great Britain, which were denying Japan's right to great power status and were strangling her economically in order to strengthen their own bases of expansionism. Anxiety and dissatisfaction exploded in political assassinations and an abortive military coup in February 1936. Finally, in the outbreak of war between Japan and China in 1937, the ultranationalists stepped up their efforts to create a "patriotic unification movement." The government set up a comprehensive program of propaganda and thought control.

During the late 1920s and early 1930s two factions had emerged among ultranationalists in the army, with civilian sympathizers on both sides: a younger, more radical group, known as the Imperial Way included Colonel Yasue and a Control Group, consisting mostly of older officers. Both factions were critical of Japan's domestic and foreign policies, and both held in common the desire to eliminate Western style liberal and individualistic ideas and replace them with the principles of Nipponism. Also, both groups sought a bigger role for the military in Japanese politics and policy making.

The ultranationalist groups differed in important respects with regard to domestic and foreign policy. While the Control Group did not support drastic changes in the political system, the Imperial Way clique was ready to impose a form of state socialism by *coup d'etat,* if that would help restore the pristine values of Japanese society. In the view of the Control Group the only way for Japan to achieve economic self–sufficiency and political power was by moving into China, with the ultimate aim of securing the rich British and Dutch possessions of the Malay Peninsula and colonies such as the East Indies in Southeast Asia. Fully realizing the implications of such expansionist moves, the leaders of the Control Group aimed at preparing Japan politically, economically and, above all, militarily for an eventual war with the United States. The Imperial Way radicals, on the other hand, were firmly opposed to any action that would bring Japan into conflict with the United States and Britain. Instead, they focused on Manchuria as the solution for Japan's problems of overpopulation and lack of natural resources, and as a buffer area between Japan and the Soviet Union. The proponents of the Manchuria solution, who were known as the Manchuria faction envisioned Manchuria as an autonomous state, a haven for all its ethnic groups — Japanese, Manchurians, Chinese, Koreans, and White Russians,"[13] — and Jews. When the Imperial Way group gained ascendancy, its leadership sought to utilize Jews at home and abroad for the realization of both its aims: the industrial and economic development of a Japanese dominated Manchuria and the avoidance of armed conflict with the United States and Britain.

Among the most influential leaders of the Imperial Way clique which won the upper hand over the Control Group, were two middle–echelon staff officers of the Kwantung army, Colonel Kanji Ishiwara and his close friend, Colonel Seishiro Itagaki. In Japanese military tradition, the commander usually took the advice of his junior officers and assumed responsibility for the plans they, not he, had conceived. These two colonels, and their peers, had a greater personal influence on the destinies of the Kwantung army than did its commanding general. One of the Ishiwara's close friends was Colonel Norihiro Yasue, expert on the Jews and translator of the *Protocols of the Elders of Zion.* Overriding ineffectual opposition by the civilian government in Tokyo, Ishiwara and Itagaki were to be responsible for the eventual Japanese occupation of Manchuria in 1931–32.

Ishiwara was among those radical officers who sought a national, almost spiritual revolution in "Showa Restoration." His concept of Japan's goals was wider than that of the other ultranationalists; it was built on a sense of universal mission. He derived his beliefs from a combination of what he saw as Japan's essential spirit and his particular interpretation of Nichiren Buddhism, the main elements of which were patriotism and a belief in an apocalypse emerging into a golden age with Japan as the spiritual center of the universe.

Nichiren Buddhism possesses a dynamism and a proselytizing spirit unique among Japanese religions. Ishiwara sought, in essence, to apply the moral principles of his panAsian ideology first to East Asia and then to the world at large. Initially, he thought in terms of a battle with the United States because America was the prime source of the democratic ideas he considered inimical to Japanese ideals. But in the course of further study and his practical experience as Japan's chief of staff (1935–1937), he relegated the confrontation with the United States into the apocalyptic future and singled out the Soviet Union, and Communism, as the more immediate threat. Accordingly, Ishiwara, along with other members of the Imperial Way group, advocated an alliance with Nazi Germany in order to isolate the Soviet Union, and declared that "every effort had to be made to keep China, Britain and the United States from interceding on the side of the USSR."[14]

On the positive side, Ishiwara's ideology impelled him to press for the establishment of Japan as "the leader of East Asia" and to silence the opposition of the white race to this goal. It was he who first envisioned the centrality of Manchuria in that scheme. He saw his own Kwantung army occupying Manchuria and developing a fully planned economy there, out of reach of the bungling bureacrats in Tokyo. As already indicated, Ishiwara and his "Manchurian faction" asserted that Manchuria should not become a colony of the Japanese empire but an independent, multiracial nation which would have complete autonomy in its internal affairs. Only its defense and foreign relations would be entrusted to Japan.[15]

Ishiwara's doctrines of panAsianism found many adherents in the military establishment, but his influence was the greatest among the members of the powerful Kwantung army, which was to carry through the invasion and occupation of Manchuria in 1931–32. Many of the Kwantung army's officers were Ishiwara's peers and classmates — a relationship which in Japanese society was an extremely close one. Among the latter, in addition to Ishiwara's friend Seishiro Itagaki, were Colonel Hideo Iwakuro

and two of the Russian language experts from the Siberian expedition —
General Kiichiro Higuchi and Colonel Yasue. These officers were all
members of the *Toa Remnei,* the East Asian League led by Ishiwara and
dedicated to the dissemination of his panAsian philosophy.

The League included not only army officers but also an occasional
navy man; for instance, Yasue's colleague, Captain Inuzuka. Through the
League Ishiwara was able to win these and many other individuals over to
his views, particularly his vision of Manchuria as the cure for Japan's ills.
This group of officers were instrumental in planning the Manchurian Solution, and Ishiwara's friends like Yasue and Inuzuka, basing their concept
of the Jews as an "international power," made the Jews part of Ishiwara's
overall scheme. This meant that Jews were to be encouraged to settle in
the multiracial state which would be built under Japanese domination.

In the multiracial state, Jews would supply the skills needed to indus-
trialize Manchuria. Their presence, in turn, could be used to attract loans
from wealthy Jews abroad for the development of the area. Moreover, if
Jews were given a home in Manchuria — as we shall see, the Japanese
even had visions of a Jewish homeland there to counteract the Soviet
Jewish autonomous republic of Birobidjan — they could be utilized to
gain for Japan the friendship of Western Jews and, through the latter, the
goodwill of Western governments.

In 1936, four years after the Japanese occupied Manchuria, there was
to be a mutiny in which some leaders of the Imperial Way group were
purged. As a result, the role of the Imperial Way clique in Japanese affairs
was greatly diminished, but the clique remained influential particularly
in Manchuria, where its members were in complete control of the Kwantung army.

Japan's occupation of Manchuria incurred her condemnation by the
United States and the League of Nations. As a result, the Japanese withdrew from the League. The response of the West — represented by the
United States and the League of Nations — to Japan's outreach on the
Asian content, triggered an ultranationalist backlash against what was
considered a hypocritical, unjust and condescending attitude toward Japan, especially on the part of Britain and the United States. Increasingly
isolated, Japan sought new allies among the European powers, primarily
Nazi Germany. She needed German power to neutralize Russia. Germany, in turn, hoped that Japanese pressure would forestall incursions
by the Soviet Union. In addition, Germany needed Japan as an ally in
the inevitable conflict with Britain, possibly also to keep the United States
at bay.

The social, economic and political problems that beset Japan during the 1920s and 1930s generated an increasingly intense search for an overall solution. A small group of ultranationalists found what they thought to be the cause — and the answer — to their country's troubles: the Jews.

Nobutaka Shioten, Colonel Yasue and Captain Inuzuka had "learned" from the *Protocols of the Elders of Zion* that the Jews were wealthy and powerful enough to manipulate governments wherever they chose. The Jews had a monopoly on gold, control of the press, and they could foment immorality and economic crisis whenever and wherever they wished. Recollections of Jacob Schiff's financial arrangements for Japan only served to verify the ultranationalists' stereotype of the omnipotent Jewish financier and his ability to steer the course of world events. According to the *Protocols* and similar textbooks of anti–Semitism, the Jews controlled the political and financial destinies also of the two powers upon whom the wrath of many extreme nationalists in Japan now centered: the United States and Great Britain. According to another source, Jacob Schiff, Otto Kahn and Paul Warburg — all of them Jews — had controlled the American economy and the Congress of the United States in their day, while Bernard Baruch and Henry Morgenthau, Jr. still controlled President Franklin D. Roosevelt as they had President Wilson two decades earlier. Indeed, the Japanese extremists who believed these myths considered "American" synonymous with "Jewish."

They were also convinced that Britain had become a Jewish dependency and that the influence of the Jews reached out to many other countries including the Soviet Union.[16] Jews were master exporters of revolutions, especially in the form of Bolshevism, and used Russia as their base for such operations.[17] Zionist ideology was merely a coverup for a Jewish plot to gain control over the whole world.[18]

According to Kiyo Utsunomiya (Captain Koreshige Inuzuka), writing in *The Jewish Problem and Japan,* "The League of Nations was planned and is controlled by Jews . . . British and American Jews protested the Japanese occupation of Manchuria . . . (and) took retaliatory economic measures against Japan through the League of Nations." The Jews were planning the destruction of Japan's military power, encouraged defeatism by creating internal conflicts, and attempted to subvert the Japanese population by forming secret societies and spreading convincing propaganda.

To some Japanese ultranationalists, the Jew became the symbol *par excellence* of the white man, and he was condemned as the exploiter of Asia.[19] It goes without saying that the Japanese who believed such fairytales also believed the Jews to be the rulers of China, both economically and politically. In their version, Chiang Kai–shek's stubborn resistance to the Japanese in the Sino–Japanese War was all part of the Jewish intrigue. In 1937, the year the Japanese occupied Peking, Shanghai and Nanking, Utsunomiya wrote:

> . . . Jewish financiers . . . intend to drive the Japanese out of China . . . (moreover) the British, French and German Jews have given a loan of $200,000,000 to China for the development of Southwest China, in order to forestall a further advance of Japan southward . . . (as part of) an anti–Japanese plot by the Jews.

But even while he accused the Jews of collaborating with Chiang Kai–shek to the detriment of Japan, Inuzuka, under his real name, attempted to secure a loan of 200,000,000 yen from American Jews for a Jewish settlement in Shanghai. Also under his real name, Inuzuka, who would be responsible for saving thousands of Hitler's intended victims by permitting them to enter Shanghai, referred to the German persecution of Jews as an "unavoidable, imperative move."[20] What he meant was, in effect: The Germans feel that this is the best course of action because the Jews are undermining their society. But we Japanese are not Germans. We will protect ourselves from the Jews not by persecuting them but by putting them to good use for our own purposes.

Phases of Japanese Positions Toward the Jews

Japan's pro–Jewish policy developed during the years 1936–1938. It was to be manifested in the following developments which spanned the period from 1937 to 1945: The three conferences of "Far East Jewish Communities" held under Japanese sponsorship in 1937, 1938 and 1939; The plan for a "Jewish homeland" in Manchuria; The admission of Jewish refugees to Shanghai beginning in 1939; The granting of transit permits to German and Polish refugees for travel through Manchuria and Japan in 1940 and 1941; The use of Jewish go–betweens in 1941 in a final effort to avoid war with the United States; and finally, The attempts during 1943–1945 to use the Jews as peacemakers. (They were to intercede with their fellow Jews in the United States to the end that the American government should stop the war with Japan.)

Between 1931 and 1945 Japan's attitude toward the Jews seems to reflect four distinct phases. The first, from 1931 through 1935, was marked by indifference. The second, from 1936 until December 6, 1938 (the day it received official sanction from the government) saw the development of a distinctly pro–Jewish line. The third phase, from December 9, 1938 until

Pearl Harbor, may be described as an era of goodwill. The final phase, which spanned the war years, brought a sharp shift from the pro–Jewish position to one ranging between neutrality and outright anti–Semitism, but which never, even at its worst, as much as approached the extremism of Japan's Nazi allies.

The Japanese and the Jews in Manchuria

In Manchuria, the Japanese occupation brought an abrupt halt to the golden age the Jewish communities there had enjoyed since the end of World War I. The Jews of Manchuria, especially those of Harbin, were adversely affected by various political and economic changes that came with the Japanese takeover. The Jews of Harbin, most of whom were of Russian origin but had become "stateless" after the Soviet Union lost its extraterritorial rights in Manchuria in 1922, were also victims of vicious anti–Semitism from some of the large White Russian population. Anti–Jewish propaganda was spread by the Russian–language newspaper *Nash Put* (Our Way) which the White Russians published in Harbin. Many veterans of the Tsarist army served both the Japanese and the Soviets — as policemen for the former and as spies for the latter; they spied also for the bandit gangs that still roved Manchuria. Kidnappings and terrorist tactics, especially against wealthy individuals, including Jews, were frequent enough to cause a significant exodus of Jews from Harbin, notably to the Chinese cities of Tientsin and Shanghai.[20]

But while the Jews of Harbin were experiencing their most difficult period, plans were afoot that would change their situation for the better. Colonel Ishiwara and Itagaki were searching for ways to achieve their dreams of an industrialized Manchuria that would be the key to Japan's national defense. The problem was to secure the capital needed for this purpose. The *zaibatsu,* or big business conglomerates, were anathema to the radical army officers; hence the use of *zaibatsu* capital was out of the question. Consequently, Ishiwara and Itagaki sought the help of Gisuke Ayukawa, who was a relative upstart in the Japanese business world but who shared their views concerning the development of Manchuria.

Ayukawa was a strong advocate of the development of Manchuria on American capital with the aid of skilled, well–trained settlers — Japanese and Jews. In 1934, a plan by a staff member of the Ministry of Foreign Affairs was publicized for the first time, presumably at Ayukawa's request. The plan allowed Japan was to accept 50,000 Jewish refugees from Nazi Germany for settlement in Manchuria (where the

Japanese had set up the puppet state of Manchukuo). According to a Jewish executive who worked under and enjoyed a long and close relationship with him, Ayukawa had long sought Jews, whom he considered technically skilled and intellectually gifted, as pioneers for his Manchurian plan.

There is little doubt that Ayukawa's conception of universal Jewish power was influenced by his numerous discussions with his longtime colleague and friend, Baron Takahashi, the finance minister who was one of those assassinated in the 1936 army plot and who, we remember, portrayed Jacob Schiff in his autobiography as the internationally powerful Jewish money man.

The plan for the settlement of German Jews in Manchuria was supported by Ishiwara, Itagaki, and albeit somewhat less enthusiastically, by Yosuke Matsuoka, then president of the South Manchurian Railroad; a quasigovernmental agency that virtually ruled the country. (In fact, as early as 1933, a plan to settle German–Jewish refugees as a national entity in Manchuria had been proposed, probably by Ayukawa, to the world Zionist leader Chaim Weizmann. But Weizmann refused even to consider it "on the grounds that Manchukuo, a creation of the Japanese military occupation of Manchuria, was not recognized by the world community.")[21]

Among Ayukawa's friends were two other influential members of the Manchurian faction who strongly supported his plan to solicit American capital and especially powerful figures for the central government; Hoshino in the Cabinet Planning Board and Kishi in the Ministry of Finance. Like Ayukawa, they, too, may have formed their image of the Jews as international financiers on the basis of what they had learned or read from Takahashi.

Yet another friend of the "Manchurian faction" who shared the notion of the Jews as a world power was Hachiro Arita, an ultranationalist who in the late 1930s became foreign minister in the cabinet of Prince Fumimaro Konoye, which formulated Japan's official policy toward the Jews. Arita's image of the Jews reportedly had been shaped at least in part by two close colleagues. One was Toshio Shiratori, a virulent anti–Semite who became ambassador to Fascist Italy. The other was Mamoru Shigemitsu, later ambassador to China, who also believed in "the Jewish influence over world opinion."[22] In April, 1942, Arita was to publish an article entitled, "The Japanese and the Jews" in *Yudaya kenkyu,* the organ of the Japanese anti–Semites, accusing the Jews of plotting to control the world.

Armed with such knowledge of Jewish skills and the Jewish threat, the advocates of Manchurian development intended to make full use of Jews for their purposes. The only problem was that, until 1936, when a five–

year plan for the industrialization of Manchuria was first adopted, all the talk about importing American capital produced no practical results. Only during the crucial year of 1936 did a number of factors converge to necessitate a practical implementation of the earlier, purely theoretical policy toward the Jews.[23] The year marked the beginning of a distinct Japanese tilt in favor of the Jews, which reached its height during the three years preceding Pearl Harbor.

In 1936 Japan signed the Anti–Comintern Pact with Nazi Germany to counteract the threat of Soviet Communism and expansionism in East Asia. In the wake of this agreement the Japanese made sporadic attempts to please their racist partner by dismissing a number of Jewish academicians, such as the economist Kurt Singer.[24] However, these scattered cases had little real significance in overall Japanese policy.

As early as 1935 voices in the Japanese Foreign Ministry expressed concern that protests against the mistreatment of Jews in Manchuria might have an adverse effect on public opinion in the Western democracies.[25] These protests had been led in Harbin by Dr. Abraham Kaufman and in Shanghai by N.E.B. Ezra, editor of the newspaper *Israel's Messenger*. Undoubtedly it was the Manchurian faction, eager to cultivate the goodwill of the democracies and of the Jews for its plans in Manchuria, that was responsible for the establishment of the Far Eastern Jewish Council, headed by Dr. Kaufman. This organization secured Japanese recognition for the autonomous status of the White Russian anti–Semites. The liaison officer between the Council and the Japanese authorities in Dairen was none other than Colonel Yasue, who had become chief of the Japanese military mission in that city and advisor on Jewish affairs. In other words, the Jews of Harbin could henceforth appeal, through the Council and Yasue, to the Japanese authorities for redress of any injustice.[26]

The second move by the Japanese to allay the fears of Manchuria's Jewish community was the closing of the anti–Semitic sheet *Nash Put,* an act in which, as already mentioned, Colonel Yasue was instrumental. The third step was the calling of the first Conference of Far East Jewish Communities, which took place in December, 1937.[27] Earlier in 1937, hostilities between Japan and China had erupted in Shanghai and Japan found herself mired in a conflict from which she was unable to extricate herself. In November, 1938, impressed by Hitler's success in the Munich Agreement, Premier Prince Konoye signed a cultural agreement with Germany. Japan's war with China, and her gestures of friendship toward Nazi Germany, led the Western democracies to equate the policies and attitudes of Japan with those of Adolf Hitler. One direct result was a United

States moral embargo on shipments of aircraft and aviation fuel to Japan.[28] But even as the Japanese moved closer to Nazi Germany for protection against these international pressures, and against the Soviet Union, they increasingly cultivated the Jews as possible intermediaries between themselves and the Western democracies, notably Britain and the United States.

The next three Conferences of Far East Jewish Communities (1937, 1938 and 1939), represented an important instrument in Japan's policy toward the Jews. The Conference of December, 1937, for example, was attended by over 1,000 Jews, including delegates from five East Asian communities. What benefits did the Jews hope to obtain through these conferences? At the same time, what did the Japanese expect to gain?

The Jews hoped, first of all, to achieve a larger measure of protection from the White Russians in Manchuria, better and more direct relations with the Japanese authorities, and, as a by–product, the recognition of Zionism as a legitimate Jewish goal. Also, the tiny Jewish minority, scattered over the vast region of Manchuria and China hoped to gain a greater sense of unity through stronger national and religious ties. Above all, however, the Jews wanted to know, and to let it be known, that other people cared enough to try to help them in their precarious situation. That is why they so eagerly accepted the Japanese suggestions in 1936 and 1937 to establish the Far Eastern Jewish Council and the Conference of Far East Jewish Communities. Perhaps this is also the reason why the Jews in East Asia frequently responded with the same enthusiasm to other Japanese overtures even though they were aware that they were being used by Japan for her own purposes.[29]

What the Japanese expected to gain from the Jews of Manchuria, China (particularly Shanghai) and the United States can be gleaned in part from the reports and lectures by Captain Inuzuka and Colonel Yasue. A report made by Inuzuka on October 12, 1938, notes that after the outbreak of war between Japan and China, the wealthy Sephardic Jews in Shanghai had been concerned about the policy of the Japanese authorities, who were now in virtually absolute control of Shanghai. Inuzuka therefore suggested, "Now is the best chance for us to conduct a Jewish operation" (sic); i.e., a campaign for Jewish support. He asserted that the $700,000 credit which wealthy Sephardic Jews in Shanghai had advanced for a Japanese project was an example of Jewish attempts to "sound out Japan." Inuzuka urged a dual approach" in making use of the Jewish people" that would combine friendly overtures with firm authority, avoiding extremes in either direction. Regarding Jewish wealth, he continued, "it will be advisable to utilize their economic power in China to our inter-

ests.'' Such a plan, however, required the formulation of a basic, consistent Japanese policy toward the Jews.

Inuzuka went on to outline steps toward a viable Jewish policy. First,
he advised that a civilian agency such as the Japan Economic Federation
(*Nihon Keizai Renmeikai*) rather than a military authority should deal
with the Jews. In the following year the Japan Economic Federation was
to establish the External Relations Committee (*Taigai Iinkai*) to attract
American investments. Inuzuka further urged the formation of a committee that would study the Jewish problem and would ''keep in touch with
the government.'' He also called for greater coordination and exchange
of information between the various intelligence gathering agencies in
Shanghai.

However, the Japanese had other aims that were much more far-
reaching. Therefore much depended on how successfully they would be
able to manipulate the Conference of Far East Jewish Communities. We
have seen that Japan, in order to counteract Soviet and Communist expansion, entered into the anti–Cominter Pact with Germany. At the
same time she sought to promote closer relations with the United States in
order to develop Manchuria. She also wished to maintain and perhaps
even to improve trade relations with both the United States and Britain,
because she still depended on these two countries for raw materials.

A lecture delivered by Yasue in the fall of 1938 reveals what role would
be assigned to the Jews of Manchuria in pursuit of these objectives. As
Yasue put it and as recorded by the Japanese Foreign Office in a somewhat quaint English translation:

> The Jewish people in the Far East will solemnly denounce Communism and
> proclaim their gratitude for Japan's efforts in fighting against the USSR, the
> enemy of mankind.
> The Jewish people, while both Japan and Manchoukuo (Manchuria) render
> protection to them, will contribute to the interests of the two countries.
> Idealistically we will first solidify the Jewish people in Manchuria, then
> proceed to the indoctrination of those in North, Middle and South China and
> finally of those all over the world.[30]

In other words, the Jews of Manchuria would be expected to influence
the Jews of all East Asia, who in turn would impress the Jews in all the rest
of the world, especially in the United States, with the righteousness of
Japan's cause. It was hoped that powerful American Jews would then
sway U.S. public opinion in favor of Japan so that U.S.–Japanese relations might improve and Americans would no longer feel morally bound
to withhold aircraft and aviation fuel shipments to Japan, which had no oil

reserves of its own. At the same time American Jews would be encouraged to emulate Jacob Schiff and arrange for financial assistance to Japan. If all this could be achieved, Ayukawa's dream of inducing large numbers of technically skilled Jews to settle in Manchuria could be fulfilled. Most of all, a strong, united Jewish community, forming a separate national entity in the multiracial state of Manchuria, might act as a counterfoil to the Soviet Jewish "autonomous republic" of Birobidjan.[31]

What were some of the practical steps taken to implement the grandiose ideas of Ayukawa and of the Manchurian faction? And how did this lead to the emergence of a pro–Jewish policy from a Five Ministers' Conference held in Tokyo on December 6, 1938 — less than two weeks before the second Conference of Far East Jewish Communities and three weeks prior to the public announcement of Ayukawa's five–year plan for Manchuria which had been adopted two years before?

First of all, the first Conference of Far East Jewish Communities, under Japanese tutelage, passed the following resolution, given here in its somewhat awkward official English rendition:

> We Jews, attending this racial conference, hereby proclaim that we enjoy racial equality and racial justice under the national laws, and will cooperate with Japan and Manchuria in building a new order in Asia. We appeal to our coreligionists.[32]

Copies of similar resolutions and declarations made at the first and subsequent conferences were sent to all major Jewish organizations and published in Harbin's Russian–language Jewish newspaper, *Yevreskaya Zhizn* (Jewish Life). This propaganda was meant to convince American Jewry of Japan's goodwill toward the Jews. In addition, a first–hand personal report about the generous treatment the Japanese were giving to Manchurian Jewry was to be conveyed by a Jewish emissary from Manchuria to key Jewish leaders in the United States, including Cyrus Adler, president of the American Jewish Committee and Rabbi Stephen S. Wise, president of the American Jewish Congress. Since Wise was considered a confidant of President Roosevelt, the Japanese assumed that he had strong influence on the president. Indeed, many Jews shared this belief. At least one recent historian agrees that Wise, "more than any other figure represented American Jewry and as such was patronized by Roosevelt, Hull, and other top–ranking (American) government officials."[33]

A Manchurian Jew named Lew Zikman, on a business trip to the United States, was asked by Dr. Abraham Kaufman of Harbin, the chairman of the Far Eastern Jewish Council, to represent the Jews of East Asia at the convention of the American Jewish Congress scheduled for May, 1938. Zikman submitted to the convention a report given to him by Kaufman and entitled, "The Situation of the Jews in Japan and Manchu-Kuo," including statements made by Dr. Kaufman and parts of an address delivered by General Kiichiro Higuchi of the Ishiwara–Yasue–Inuzuka Manchurian faction at the 1937 Conference.[34]

We know from a letter written by Rabbi Wise to Zikman, dated November 22, 1938, that Wise adamantly opposed the request of the East Asian Jews for American Jewish support to Japan:

> I write to you again in order to say, I am in complete disagreement with your position. I think it is wholly vicious for Jews to give support to Japan, as truly Fascist a nation as Germany or Italy.
>   . . . Japan is like Germany (and) Italy, a nation that is bound to take an anti–Semitic attitude, and indeed has already done so (author's italics).

The next day Zikman, in desperation, sent Wise the following reply:

> In the name of the15,000 Jews in the Far East, I implore you to think of us; not to throw us upon the waves of disaster and not take upon yourself the responsibilities of any consequences where there might be at least the minimum hopes for betterment of our situation.[35]

This unanswered appeal is really the basis for the cooperation of the Jews with the Japanese in their attempt to survive under extremely difficult conditions. For obvious reasons Wise's letter was never communicated to the Japanese. Japan's next step in the quest for better relations with Manchurian Jewry was to invite Dr. Kaufman to visit Japan for a month in May, 1939. In hopes that this would impress American Jewry,[36] Kaufman was given a gala reception in Tokyo as he made the rounds from one government office to another, learning first hand from the highest officials how the Japanese intended to handle the Jewish problem. One of his meetings was with a group of economic leaders including Finance Minister Seihin Ikeda. The discussions on that occasion undoubtedly touched upon the investment of American Jewish capital in Manchuria. Ikeda reassured Kaufman that Japan had no reason to persecute Jews and that she did not condone racism or any other form of discrimination.

Six weeks earlier, the Japan Economic Federation extended to a supposedly influential American journalist, William O. Inglis, an invitation to visit Japan, in hopes that his reporting would "dispel misunderstandings in the U.S. about Japan and bring (about) Japanese–American amity." Given the social and diplomatic conditions in Japan at the time this meant that the scheme to import capital from the United States, especially from or through American Jews, had to be wrought with extreme care. Probably for this reason there is only one extant public document concerning the aims of the External Relations Committee established by the Economic Federation. This document states:

> The External Relations Committee, established within the (Japan Economic) federation in April, 1939, has as its objective the dissemination of information abroad and the carrying out of research in order to promote understanding and cooperation with various foreign countries concerning the longterm industrial and economic construction of Japan, Manchuria and China.[37]

In June, 1940 the Economic Federation again invited prominent Americans for the purpose of generating American goodwill — and capital — for Japan. General John O'Ryan, an attorney, responded to the invitation and spent weeks in Japan. However, nothing seems to be known about the results of the visits by either Inglis or O'Ryan. Since much more concern and planning was devoted to the Jewish aspect of attracting American capital, it would not be at all surprising to find out someday that the visits on Inglis and O'Ryan themselves were only by–products of the overall scheme to utilize the Jews on behalf of Japan.[38]

The foregoing accounts show that by the end of 1938, there had evolved in Japan a decidedly pro–Jewish policy advocated, or at least accepted, by the country's highest authorities. Born of — or perhaps despite — hardening British and American opposition to Japan's declaration of a New Order in Asia and to her cultural pact with Germany, this policy was maintained and strengthened with a tenacity probably due to the influence of the Manchurian faction under the military prowess of Ishiwara and the businessman Ayukawa.

It was these men who pushed hardest for using the Jews of the Far East as a means of easing American–Japanese tensions and attracting American–Jewish capital for the development of Manchuria. This plan had the support not only of politically influential persons as Kanji Ishiwara and his friend Seishiro Itagaki (the latter had become minister of the army) and their associates in the East Asian League, Norihiro Yasue and Koreshige Inuzuka, but also of powerful economic and financial leaders. The pro–Jewish policy proposed by these individuals received formal recognition at the Five Minister's Conference on December 6, 1938, which was attended by Prime Minister Prince Konoye, Itagaki as minister of the army, Arita as foreign minister, Ikeda as minister of finance, and the minister of the navy. The conference adopted the following declaration:

> Our diplomatic ties with Germany and Italy require that we avoid embracing the Jewish people, in light of their rejection by our allies. But we should not

reject them as (Germany and Italy) do because of our declared policy of racial equality, and their rejection would therefore be contrary to our spirit. This is *particularly true in light of our need for foreign capital and our desire not to alienate America* (Author's italics).

This declaration was followed by statements to the effect that "at present" Japan would treat Jews "presently living in Japan, Manchuria and China" on a par with "other foreigners;" that the same treatment would be accorded also to Jews who would enter these territories in the future, and that Japan would not "extend a special invitation to Jews to come to our territories, *but capitalists and engineers will be mentioned* (author's italics).[39]

The above decisions adopted by the Five Minister's Conference set the tone for Japan's relations toward the Jews for the next three years and constituted one of the factors that set in motion the stream of Jewish refugees from Germany and Austria to East Asia. On January 1, 1939, only weeks after the adoption of this policy toward the Jews, the former five-year plan for the development of Manchuria was incorporated into a new "Four-Year Plan for the Expansion of the Industrial Capacity of Japan."

The official adoption of the Manchurian faction's pro-Jewish policy explains why thousands of Jewish refugees were able to enter Shanghai during the first half of 1939 without any public protests from the Japanese. Only in August, when Shanghai's refugee population had grown to 14,000, and in response to pleas from Shanghai's Japanese community that Hongkew was becoming overcrowded and that the Jews were creating increased economic competition for the local population, did Japan take steps to control the refugee influx. But, as we remember, the Japanese authorities did so only after receiving reassurances that Jews in other parts of the world would not protest, and even then, they did not close the doors entirely. The restrictions which worked against the refugees who had no financial means, were not opposed by Shanghai's established Jewish population because the small community of the older settled Jews, too, did not want a flood of many thousands of destitute newcomers, especially since they received no assurances from the American Jews of ongoing support. Moreover, they feared the spector of increased anti-Semitism that would accompany the mass of newcomers.[40] However, neither the unexpected flood of refugees that entered Shanghai, nor the eventual restrictions on their entry, caused a change in Japan's policy toward the Jews. In fact, the presence of the refugees intensified Japanese efforts to use the Jews in order to obtain American Jewish capital.[41]

A subsequent example of the special treatment accorded by the Japanese to Jewish refugees involves 2,000 Polish Jews (including 300 students and teachers of the famous Talmudical academy of Mir), who for several months in 1940–41, found asylum not in Manchuria or Shanghai but in Japan proper. In 1939 these refugees, along with thousands of others, had fled from Poland to Lithuania, which had then been annexed by the Soviet Union. They were helped by Senpo Sugihara, the Japanese consul *pro tem* in Kovno (Kaunas) Lithuania, the Dutch Ambassador Dekker, and the Dutch Consul Zwartendijk in Kovno.

Sugihara gave the Polish Jews transit visas which permitted them to reach the Japanese seaport of Kobe by way of Siberia. He was able to issue documents on the basis of fake immigration visas to Curacao which the refugees had obtained from Zwartendijk, originally authorized by Dekker. After hundreds of refugees started to pour into Japan, the Japanese authorities in Tokyo twice instructed Sugihara to grant no more transit visas but still allowed all refugees with the Curacao visas to enter Kobe. Dozens more were eventually admitted to Japan also although stopped by Japanese officials at the Siberian port of Vladivostok for using forged passports and other illegal papers to enter Japan.

The refugees received a cordial welcome not only from Kobe's tiny Jewish community but also from the local Japanese populace. Of even greater significance, however, was the fact that the Japanese not only permitted them to enter Kobe with papers of obviously dubious legality, but also allowed the vast majority to extend their transit visas, which officially expired after seven or fifteen days, for periods ranging from three to eight months. The refugees were able to utilize the additional time to badger Western consulates in Tokyo and Yokohama for real immigration visas to such countries as the United States. Much of the credit for the extension of the transit visas must go to Professor Setzuso Kotsuji, a Japanese Bible scholar who had served as advisor on Jewish affairs to Foreign Minister Yosuke Matsuoka when the latter had been president of the South Manchurian Railroad.

It seems that the chairman of Kobe's Jewish community, having heard Kotsuji deliver an address in Hebrew in 1939, appealed to the scholar to intercede with his former superior, Matsuoka, on behalf of the refugees. It is noteworthy that Kotsuji, as the only Hebrew–speaking Japanese at the time worked for Matsuoka in Manchuria as his expert on the Jews. It was Matsuoka who as part of the Manchurian faction, with a particular interest in Jews, had been responsible for surprising and impressing the Jews of the Far East Conference by having Kotsuji give a speech in Hebrew. It is not too difficult then to envision Matsuoka concocting some kind of

deal involving the "Jewish power." In his reminiscences Professor Kotsuji (who eventually was to embrace Judaism) hints a little further at what
may have been the foreign minister's reasoning. We do not know the
exact context, but we have the record of Professor Kotsuji himself:

> His (Matsuoka's) idea was truly something, like wisdom revealed in Hell. Five
> thousand (sic) refugees were saved because of his scheme. I kept that only to
> myself. No one knew about this. After this he entrusted me with a plan to be
> carried out sometime in the future. Nobody will believe me today, even if I told
> about this secret agreement between him and me. His great scheme in dealing
> with the Jewish power was born out of the idea of protecting Japan. . . . I am
> not going to reveal the contents of this scheme, for I am afraid that it will be
> laughed at by people of malice. Matsuoka was not dissembling. He was eager
> to win the Jewish people over to the Japanese viewpoint. My task was to
> advise him, *to tell him what the Jews wanted, and how best to obtain their
> good opinion* (author's italics).[42]

The Germans made various attempts to influence Japanese anti–Semites
and high level Japanese policy toward the Jews. In late 1940, undoubtedly
in the wake of the Tripartite Pact, the German embassy succeeded in
getting the Japanese authorities to cancel, almost at the last minute, the
planned Fourth Conference of Far East Jewish Communities. This was
Germany's protest against the strong anti–Nazi line adopted by the three
preceding Conferences. Judging from the close timing, it seems that the
forced semi–retirement of Colonel Yasue, too, was also the result of
pressure from the Germans, who regarded him as a "friend of the Jews."
Meanwhile the Germans made diligent use of diplomatic channels to
spread the Nazi gospel among the Japanese.[43]

Only in light of all these developments can we now fully comprehend
the earlier mentioned pro-Jewish radio broadcast in November 1940.
Since all radio broadcasts in Japan were under strict government control
this broadcast caused uneasiness at the German embassy in Tokyo and
brought inquiries from Berlin about the influence of that "friend of the
Jews" in official Japanese circles. The Germans did not know that Inuzuka was identical with Kiyo Utsonomiya, author of many widely read
anti–Semitic writings which they themselves had praised extravagantly.

The fact is that the Japanese, notwithstanding the Tripartite Pact and
pressures from Germany, had no desire to reverse the pro–Jewish policy
proclaimed at the Five Ministers' Conference in 1938. Japan had a compelling reason for this, and for her behavior toward the Jewish refugees.
Following Japan's entry into Indo–China in July, 1941, the United States,
in conjunction with the British and the Dutch, had frozen all Japanese

assets and enforced an oil embargo against Japan. This cutoff from primary sources ultimately led Japan into war with the United States and Great Britain. But even while the military made plans for the confrontation, the diplomats attempted to preserve peace. And here again, the Japanese attempted to use the Jews, or their associations with Jews, in a last ditch effort to prevent war.

Two American priests, Bishop E. Walsh and Father James M. Draught, came to Japan on a private peace mission. They gained the ear of Premier Konoye, who, through them, tried to "sound out the U.S. government on the subject of negotiations and to report to Tokyo." Walsh and Draught carried with them credentials that still opened many doors in Japan: a letter of recommendation from Lewis Strauss of Kuhn, Loeb and Co., the firm which once had been headed by Jacob Schiff. The letter was addressed to Strauss' friend Tadao Ikawa, director of Japan's Central Agricultural and Forestry Bank and, incidentally, the author of an anti–Semitic work entitled *The Origin of Radicalism*.

Ikawa proved a valuable contact for the two Americans Walsh and Draught because he was on friendly terms with Minister of Finance Seihin Ikeda, and with Naoki Hoshino and Nobusuke Kishi, who, along with Gisuke Ayukawa, had been so closely involved in the scheme to import American Jewish capital for the development of Manchuria. Ikawa also worked closely, on this peace mission with Colonel Hideo Iwakuro of the ministry of war. This is the same Iwakuro, who, according to John Toland, had claimed part of the credit for having persuaded his superiors in Manchuria to permit Jewish refugees transit through Manchuria and Japan during 1940–41 "on the grounds no true Japanese could deny: a debt owed the Jews; the Jewish firm of Kuhan, Loeb and Company had helped finance the Russo–Japanese War." However, this peace mission met with opposition from Foreign Minister Matsuoka because the negotiations that resulted from them went on largely outside the surveillance of his ministry.

On February 11, 1941, Admiral Kichisaburo Nomura, a known friend of America, was sent to the U.S. by the Konoye government on behalf of Foreign Minister Matsuoka in an attempt to find a way out of the growing impasse with Washington. Ironically, only one month after he had approved the transit visa extensions for the Polish refugees in Kobe and after Nomura's peace mission, Matsuoka went to Berlin seeking to cement relations between Japan and Germany.

Two weeks before Pearl Harbor the new prime minister, General Hideki Tojo, who was part of the close–knit Manchuria faction was responsible for, or at least acquiescent in, one more last minute appeal to international Jewish power: Inuzuka had the Jews of Shanghai send a cable, dated November 23, 1941, to the major Jewish organizations in the U.S. as well as to Henry Morgenthau, Jr., Roosevelt's secretary of the treasury, pleading for negotiations to avert war:

> This day when the fate of the Pacific is in balance we voicing opinion of a large community deem it necessary to emphasize that *irrespective of the fact that Japan is allied to the Axis* its people are against national hatred and oppression stop War in Pacific would bring untold hardships to many millions and in the interest of humanity we hope a peaceful mutual understanding will be reached stop *convey this sincere unsolicited opinion* all influential organizations (author's italics)[44]

> > Shanghai Ashkenazi Communal Association
> > Topaz, President

Perhaps this cable, sent to a rather puzzled Morgenthau, points as well as anything else to the key to understanding why the Japanese brand of anti–Semitism was responsible for the rescue of 18,000 potential Jewish victims of the Holocaust.

Notes

1. This citation is a composite from the works of Colonel Norihiro Yasue, written during the 1930s.

2. For these quotations from the writings of Captain Koreslinge Inuzuka, see Rudolph Loewenthal, Japanese and Chinese Materials Pertaining to the Jewish Catastrophe, pp. 24–49, (Loewenthal *JCM*) an unpublished 293 page manuscript prepared for YIVO in 1955 with an index added in 1970. This manuscript and hundreds of other related documents and news clippings are part of this author's Loewenthal Papers, reproduced courtesy of Dr. Loewenthal.

3. For the detailed story of this unusual refugee community and the role of the Allies as well as the Jewish organizations, see David Kranzler, *Japanese, Nazis and Jews: The Jewish Refugee Community of Shanghai 1938–1945*. (Kranzler, *Shanghai*) (New York: Yeshiva U. Press, 1976), esp. chaps. 6–8.

For Yasue's role, see undated cable sent to Tokyo by the Japanese consul–general in Harbin (FO–S–9460–3–536). This series of documents from the Japanese Foreign Office, including those designated as FO (Foreign Office) and other official reports re: Jews, are part of what is known as the Kogan Papers (KP). For details, see Kranzler, *Shanghai*, pp. 600–604. Cf. also FO (Secret) No. 2221, Dec. 5, 1935, p. 4. The closing of *Nash Put* was announced in the report of the 1937 Far Eastern Conference by the chairman, Dr. Abraham Kaufman, in October 1938, p. 1.

4. See Abraham Kaufman, *Testimony Concerning Jewish Life in Manchuria* (Kaufman, Manchuria), a 90 page memoir in Hebrew translated from the Yiddish, May 1967 (Yad Vashem Archives No. 03/3168) p. 19; Hideaki Kase, "Jews in Japan" *Chuo. Koron*, V. 86, No. 6 (May 1971); Rudolph Loewenthal, *Japanese and Chinese Materials Pertaining to the Jewish Catastrophe 1939–1945* (Loewenthal *JCM*) pp. 265, 268. This is a 293 page unpublished manuscript containing summaries in the English language of important Japanese anti-

Semitic material. This manuscript and numerous other documents and news clippings from the English language press in China re the Jews of the Hitler era, are part of the Loewenthal Papers (*LP*) made available in photocopies to this author by Dr. Loewenthal. Dr. Loewenthal is an authority on the ancient Jewish community of Kaifeng and lived in Peking during 1935–1947.

5. The entry of Yasue's name in the Golden Book on July 14, 1941, over the signature of Menachem Ussishkim, chairman of the executive committee of the Jewish National Fund, is noted by Morinaka Yokoo, "The History and Recent Activities of the Japan–Israel Association" an undated extract of an article (ca. 1958).

6. See Cyrus Adler, *Jacob H. Schiff: His Life and Letters* (Adler, *Schiff*) (2 vols.) (New York: Doubleday, 1928), esp. chap. VII.

7. Ibid., For the story of Schiff's loans to Japan see Tokahashi's secretary's memorandum quoted in full by Adler, *Schiff*, v. 1, pp. 213–30. This memorandum is also quoted in fully by Kase, "Jews in Japan," pp. 17–20.

8. *Jewish Consulate*, pp. 104–5. This unpublished manuscript by Mr. S., a German–Jewish businessman, and longtime resident of Japan who maintained close connections with important Japanese officers and industrialists. In his correspondence with this author, Mr. S. requested anonymity. Parts of this manuscript and his detailed correspondence are in this author's files.

9. From Inuzuka's report to the Naval General Staff, January 18, 1939, cited by Kase, "Jews in Japan."

10. For the early contacts of the Japanese anti–Semites with their White Russian mentors in Siberia, see Masayuki Kobayashi, "Kametaro Mitsukawa's War Against Anti–Semitism: Sidelights on the Early Years of Anti–Semitic Propaganda in Japan," (Kobayashi, "Mitsukawa") *Kaigai Jijo* Vol. 22 (Feb. 1974), p. 2. See also Hyman Kublin, "Star of David and the Rusing Sun," *Jewish Frontier*, Vol. 25, (April 1958), pp. 15–22; Herman Dicker, *Wanderers and Settlers in the Far East: A Century of Jewish Life in China and Japan* (New York: Twayne, 1962), pp. 75–76; Hiroo Yasue, *Brief Biography of Colonel Yasue* (a brief, unpublished sketch of Yasue by his son) (KP); Nobutaka Shioten, *Election Bulletin*, April 30, 1942. This Bulletin contains an autobiographical sketch. (KP)

11. For the dissemination of the *Protocols* by White Russians throughout the world see Norman Cohn, *Warrant for Genocide* (New York: Harper and Row, 1967), chaps. 5–7. Cohn noted that Admiral Alexander Kolchek, the commander–in–chief of the White Russian forces in Siberia, was so obsessed by the *Protocols* that he published an edition right there in Siberia.

12. Ben–Ami Shillony, *Revolt in Japan: The Young Officers and the February 26, 1936 Incident* (Princeton, N.J.: Princeton University Press, 1973), esp. p. 15. For one of the principal sources of inspiration for the idealists, and their discontent with conditions in Japan, see George M. Wilson, *Radical Nationalist in Japan: Kita Ikki, 1883–1937* (Cambridge, Mass.: Harvard University Press, 1969), esp. chap. 5; Mark R. Peattie, *Ishiwara Kanji and Japan's Confrontation with the West* (Peattie, *Ishiwara*) (Princeton, N.J.: Princeton University Press, 1975); Yoshikashi Takehiko, *Conspiracy at Mukden: The Rise of the Japanese Military* (New Haven: Yale U. Press, 1963), esp. pp. 107–18.

13. For the most detailed discussions of Manchuria as a panacea for Japan's problems, see Peattie, *Ishiwara*. Ishiwara most clearly defined the concept of Manchuria as a haven for multi–ethnic groups. See Chapter 5, especially pp. 145–50, 165–66. For Japanese plans for the conquest of Manchuria, and their implementation, see Chapter 4, especially pp. 96–101.

14. Peattie, *Ishiwara*, p. 44.

15. Ibid., p. 150.

16. FO–S–9460–3–746, October 12, 1938, pp. 1–3. See also Loewenthal *JCM*, p. 116,

for England as a "Jewish dependency." See Ibid., pp. 75, 77, 88, 89, 95, 98, 101, 120. Namoru Shigemitsu also subscribed to the theory that Japan should take advantage of "Jewish influence over world opinion." See Namoru Shigemitsu, *Japan and Her Destiny* (Shigemitsu, *Japan*) (London: Hutchinson, 1958), p. 95.

17. See both articles by Kobayashi, "Mitsukawa." See also some of the titles of the anti-Semitic works in Loewenthal, *JCM,* such as *Jewish World Conquest Movement, The Cabal (Against the World) By the Jewish People* (by Shioten), *Jewish Aggression in the World.* In the latter, for example, the author attributes various European revolutions to the Jews, who allegedly used such techniques as means of attaining economic control over these countries (p. 202)

18. Yasue, in an article entitled, "The Struggle Between Two Jewish Trends of Thought" (1936), contends that Zionism seems to be the goal of the Jews but that this is merely a ploy to conquer the world. Yasue had "studied" Zionism at first hand in Palestine. Loewenthal, *JCM,* p. 269.

19. Loewenthal, *JCM,* pp. 171, 102, 78.

20. The excerpts from "Utsunomiya" are cited in Loewenthal, *JCM,* pp. 242–43; Kase, "Jews," p. 12. For the Japanese views of loans to China, see Katsumi Usui, "The Role of the Foreign Ministry," in Dorothy Berg and Shumpei Okamoto (eds.), *Pearl Harbor As History: Japanese–American Relations, 1931–1941 (Pearl Harbor)* (New York: Columbia U. Press, 1973), p. 135.

20A. For conditions in Manchuria during the 1930's see Kranzler, *Shanghai,* chap. 2.

21. "WZO Rejected Manchuria as 1930's Jewish Refuge," *Jerusalem Post,* March 8, 1982, p. 1.

22. Yukio Cho, "An Inquiry Into the Problem of Importing American Capital Into Manchuria: A Note on Japanese–American Relations, 1931–1941," *Pearl Harbor,* pp. 377–410. For Kishi's and Hoshino's relationship with Ayukawa and other sin the "Manchurian faction," see Robert J. C. Butow, *Tojo and the Coming of the War* (Butow, *Tojo*) (Princeton U. Press, 1961), particularly pp. 72–75. Cf. also Kranzler, *Shanghai,* p. 262, n. 108.

23. Cho, "Manchuria," p. 391.

24. See Kurt Singer, *Mirror, Sword and Jewel: A Study of Japanese Characteristics* (New York: George Braziller, 1973). For his dismissal, see p. 11. Others, such as the conductor Joseph Rosenstock, were retained despite Nazi pressure.

25. FO–S–9460–3–541, October 14, 1935. See also FO September 19, 1936, Chotaro Sato, Consular Officer in Harbin, to Shigeru Yoshida, Japanese ambassador to Britain.

26. The Council was probably set up in 1937 during the First Conference of Far East Jewish Communities.

27. For the closing of *Nash Put,* see Lew Zikman–Herman Dicker correspondence, October, 1938, p. 2 in this author's possession. See also FO Tanaka to Hirota, February 23, 1938.

28. See Akira Irye, "Japan's Policies Toward the U.S.," *Pearl Harbor,* pp. 443–54.

29. Dicker, *Wanderers,* pp. 44–47. This status of the Jews as an autonomous entity of sorts fitted well with Ishiwara's concept of Manchuria as a multiracial, autonomous state. Zikman–Dicker correspondence, May 20, 1959, pp. 2-3.

30. FO 13, October 13, 1938, p. 2.

31. 10, July 7, 1939, pp. 3–11. For the idea of a "counterfoil" to Birobidjan, see KP 6, June 5, 1939, p. 12 (addition, June 7, 1939); Kase, "Jews," p. 13; S–Tokayer correspondence, March 1, July 9, and September 19, 1974, *Jewish Consulate,* p. 100. See also Shigemitsu, *Japan,* pp. 94–95.

32. FO–S–9460–3–1640–154, January 11, 1940, p. 12 (should be p. 7; pagination not clear on manuscript). See also Dr. Abraham Kaufman's report and version of this resolu-

tion, given to Zikman, titled, "The Situation of the Jews in Japan and Manchu–Ti–Kuo (sic) pp. 3–5; Zikman–Dicker correspondence; Dicker, *Wanderers*, p. 46.

33. See Saul S. Friedman, *No Haven for the Oppressed: United States Policy Toward the Refugees, 1938–1945* (Detroit: Wayne University Press, 1973), pp. 151–52.

34. For the Japanese view of Stephen S. Wise, see FO–S–9460–3–1369 A.B. See also Karl Kindermann to Mr. Niwa June 7, 1940, and Wise's reply to a letter from Kindermann, June 10, 1940. Mr. Zikman's assignment is found in the Zikman–Dicker correspondence, September 30 (especially pp. 2-3, 5), October 11, 1959. This correspondence, together with other papers from the Dicker Files are in this author's possession. For Kaufman's report, see Zikman–Dicker correspondence, 1939. See also Dicker, *Wanderers*, p. 56-57; *KP* (Bei–(sic)–3–Confidential 291), Ambassador Ueda to Foreign Minister Arita, May 16, 1939.

35. Letters in archives of World Jewish Congress. See also Zikman–Dicker correspondence.

36. See speech by A. Kaufman, *KP* Bei–3–Confidential–291. Ambassador Ueda to Foreign Minister Arita, May 16, 1939.

37. Cho, "Manchuria," p. 378.

38. Ibid., p. 379.

39. For the text of the declaration, see Inuzuka, "Secret," p. 3. References to this policy are found in the FO S–9460–3–2516, Code 2149, 2152, January 17, 1942.

40. For details, see Kranzler, *Shanghai*, chap. 8.

41. For various plans by Inuzuka to attract Jewish capital, see Kranzler, *Shanghai*, chap. 7.

42. See the translation of a section of a biography of Matsuoka entitled *Matsuoka Yoseki, The Man and His Life*, (Tokyo: Committee for Publishing Biography of Matsuoka Yoseki, Kodansha, 1975). The section or article by Kotsuji was written especially for this book. The author is grateful to Chaplain Maruin Tokayer for securing this translated portion. Cf. also Abraham Kotsuji, *From Tokyo to Jerusalem* (Kotsuji, Tokyo) (New York: Bernard Geis Associates, 1964), p. 149. (In keeping with Jewish tradition, Kotsuji, upon his conversion, adopted the name Abraham.)

43. For the general pressure, see Kranzler, *Shanghai*, pp. 485–488. See also *Peking Chronicle*, December 3, 1939 (*LP*)

44. Copy of this and other cables from the World Jewish Congress Archives in this author's files.

5 THE HOLOCAUST IN NORWAY

Samuel Abrahamsen

The Problems

None of the Scandinavian Jewish communities suffered such staggering losses during World War II as did the Jews of Norway. Forty-nine percent of her Jewish population was murdered, a percentage higher than that of France (26 percent), Bulgaria (22 percent), or Italy (20 percent).[1] Finland, which was a co–belligerent with Nazi Germany from 1941 to 1944, protected her Jewish population throughout the war. As an Axis partner, Finland was the only German "ally that was never pressured into deporting its Jews."[2] Denmark, which was invaded on the same day as Norway, April 9, 1940, offered only token resistance and was considered by Germany as a "model protectorate" until August 27, 1943. Up to this date, Denmark had enjoyed a degree of autonomy unheard of in a country

The preparation of this publication has been supported, in part, by grants from National Endowment for the Humanities, American Council of Learned Societies, Royal Norwegian Ministry of Foreign Affairs, Memorial Foundation of Jewish Culture, and PSC/CUNY Faculty Research Awards.

109

under Nazi domination. Her Jewish population, which dates back to 1622, was rescued in October 1943 *en masse* to Sweden, which remained neutral and was the only European country that doubled its Jewish population by opening its borders to thousands of Holocaust survivors and refugees from over twenty–seven different nationalities.

That leaves us with the tragic saga of Norway's Jews. Why was their fate so different from those in other Scandinavian countries, especially in Denmark? Several theories have been advanced to explain the discrepancies between Denmark and Norway. A prominent Norwegian social scientist, Dr. Johan Galtung, took Norway as an example of an extremely nonpluralistic society, explaining that Norway "is found together with countries strongly dominated by one denomination . . . The Evangelical Lutheran Church is thus even more strongly dominant in Norway than the Roman Catholic in Brazil, or the Buddhist in Thailand."[3] Dr. Galtung added that the catastrophe which hit the Norwegian Jews had some remote connection with the national rejection of Jews and dissenters in general.[4]

In the face of a small Jewish population and the absence of any "disruptive Jewish cultural minority," one might expect Norway to be free of anti–Semitism, but anti–Semitism had become an issue long before the Jews were admitted in 1851. Could the difference between the two countries be due to the longer and deeper degree of emancipation and acculturation that marked the history of Denmark's Jews, compared to the counter–emancipation of Norway where Article Two of the Constitution of 1814 prohibited the entry of Jews until 1851? A noted author asked: "Was our Constitution perfect? Keeping Holocaust freshly in mind, Article 2 becomes exceedingly painful."[5]

Was this lack of cultural and social integration of Jews into the nonpluralistic Norwegian society a contributing factor to victimization? Norwegians "have a profound sense of community feeling" notes Harry Eckstein in his well received study.[6] Does this signify that Norwegian community feeling did not include Jews, as implied by Haakon Holmboe?[7] This conclusion is strengthened by Professor Johan Vogt's assertion that the fate of the Jews during World War II was, for nonJews, one of the war's many problems and for quite a few, one that was mostly on the periphery. Most nonJews, including his countrymen, were "spectators and indifferent to the persecution of the Jews in Norway."[8]

Another example of Norwegian xenophobia and dislike of Jews is found in Ragnar Ulstein's fundamental work on rescue from Norway to Sweden. He relates an episode from a training camp for Norwegian police in Dalarna, Sweden in 1944, where a film was to be shown. The movie projectionist was "short and dark and reminded the soldiers of a Jew . . . When he entered the hall, one shouted, and many joined in, 'Get out that Jewish devil!'" Another refugee, who knew the projectionist well, shouted in despair, "You err, he is no Jew, he is one of us!" The author adds that "anti–Semitism was not dead among Norwegians."[9]

Did racial theories play any role in registration, arrest, and deportation of Jews? In his diary, Odd Nansen wrote: "We are guilty of a disgraceful action. We are accepting the German division of mankind into two classes, Jews and scoundrels in one, other people in the other."[10] This shows, of course, that Nazi propaganda had not been ineffective. It should be noted, however, that the extent of indigenous anti–Semitism did not always have a bearing on the number of Jewish victims during the Holocaust. For example, Holland is commonly regarded as having a low degree of anti–Semitism. The country did, however, have a high degree of victimization. Old Romania (i.e., Romania without its provinces lost during World War II), notorious for intense anti–Semitism, had a relatively low degree of victimization.

Is an explanation to be found in the fact that the Danish Jews were forewarned about their impending deportation in October 1943 by Georg Ferdinand Duckwitz, the German naval attaché, who worked in the office of Dr. Karl Rudolf Werner Best, the German plenipotentiary in Denmark? Is it also true that the German anti–Nazi movement had given forewarning to the Norwegian resistance movement through such individuals as Theodor Stelzer, Carl Friedrich Goerdler, and Helmut James von Moltke. In *Mellom Frontene* (Between the Fronts), Professor Arvid Brodersen stated that von Moltke, during his second visit to Oslo in September 1942, "warned us that an anti-Jewish action was expected, but he knew neither the precise time nor the definite timing."[11]

Another explanation for the success of rescue in Denmark has been generally attributed to the small Jewish population of the country: about 7,000. However, Norway's Jewry was even less: about 1,600. The closeness of Denmark to Sweden has also been cited, but Norway has a border of 1,100 miles in common with Sweden while Denmark is separated by the Øresund, Skagerakk, and Kattegat straits. These explanations, however plausible they may sound, do not stand up to rigorous examination.

Other explanations may be more accurate. A factor of great importance was the attitude of the local population. While some expressed active sympathy and support, many displayed apathy, indifference, and direct hostility leading to betrayal of Jews in hiding or direct participation in the destruction machinery. Other factors also played a role: cooperation by local Nazi members, assistance by local police, temptation to obtain Jewish property or to receive rewards, threats of severe punishment for assisting Jewish rescue. All these factors must be considered in a dispassionate analysis of the Holocaust in Norway.

Compared to the Nazi machinery for destruction, no significant countervailing forces for rescue existed, except in a few countries such as Denmark. True enough, warnings of impending round ups and arrests had been received by Jews, including those in Norway. By the time this happened (October 1942), effective means had been developed in Norway to alert the general population about impending arrests of other groups such as trade union members, teachers, students, and clergymen. It was through the use of *parole* (directive) that the civilian resistance movement managed to develop a *holdningskamp*, i.e., a steadfast moral struggle against Nazification and strong solidarity in the population with the various persecuted groups.

The *parole* gradually assumed the status of an order. Whenever a group was threatened with encroachment of civil or legal rights, a sizeable machinery went into effect to thwart arrest, secure release, and prevent deportation. Civil protests reached a climax in May 1941 when forty–three professional organizations, representing more than 750,000 Norwegians, delivered a formal protest to *Reichskommissar* Joseph Terboven protesting the attempted nazification of these organizations.[12] Tore Gjelsvik, an authority on civil resistance, called the *parole* "an effective and distinctive instrument of warfare in the Norwegian resistance against nazification."[13]

No nationwide directive, however, was ever issued to alert the population not to assist or cooperate with quislings or Nazi authorities in any aspect of Jewish persecution: registering of Jews; confiscation and selling of Jewish properties; identification, round up, arrest, and deportation of Norwegian Jews. This was probably the only group destined for destruction that did not receive support and potential protection through a *parole*.

Nonetheless, hundreds of would–be rescuers of Norway's Jews did not wait for any directive from any organizations to assist their Jewish countrymen. A spontaneous outburst of help from willing hands provided aid to many of the endangered Jews. The rescuers followed their own consciences and went forth to do magnificent deeds against heavy odds, risking their lives. It was as if the rescuers had adopted the Talmudic saying that "the one who saves one life is regarded as having rescued all humanity."

Rise of the Quisling Party

Vidkun Quisling's name has become synonymous with treason and a symbol of European Nazi collaboration. During World War II most European states had native traitors who sought positions of power. These self–styled national leaders did not see themselves as traitors but as patriots "who would save their countrymen from the corruption and inefficiency of democratic government."[14]

Vidkun Abraham Lauritz Jonssøn Quisling (1887–1945) openly met the conquering Nazis as their closest collaborator. Born on July 18, 1887 in the valley of Fyresdal (southern province of Telemark), he graduated with distinction from the military academy of Norway and served as an officer on the General Staff (1911–1918). His special interest in Russia and his fluency in the Russian language brought about his appointment as military attaché to the Soviet Union and a diplomatic post in Helsinki (1919–1921). He became assistant to Fridjof Nansen, internationally renowned for aiding famine–stricken Ukraine in 1922. After completing several humanitarian tasks on behalf of the League of Nations, Quisling returned to Norway after Nansen's death in 1930: "I had to return home and contribute what I could to save Norway."[15]

Though opposed to the democratic way of life and to the Norwegian democratic government, Quisling was appointed Minister of Defense in 1931 in the government of Kolstad and Hunseid of the Farmer's Party. In 1933, Quisling founded his own party, the *Nasjonal Samling* (National Union).[16] *Nasjonal Samling,* with its vague program, never gained popular support. At the last free parliamentary election in 1936, the party received only 26,576 votes (1.8 percent of the electorate), substantially less than the first election in 1933. It was never able to elect a single delegate to the *Storting* (Parliament). During the occupation, its membership reached a peak of 43,000 in 1943,[17] but including the youth organizations, the number was close to 60,000. The membership came from all strata of Norwegian society. It included Knut Hamsun, the well-known writer, who enhanced the legitimacy of Norway's Nazi Party.[18]

From 1935 on, Quisling stressed anti-Semitism in his political campaigns, stating that it was the "goal of secret international circles, international Jewry, international democracy, and international Bolshevism to drag the British Empire and the Nordic countries into a fratricidal war on the continent, which would lead to their mutual destruction."[19] He placed the major share of the blame on the "eternal Jew, who is once again on his wanderings." Quisling accused the Jews of having representatives in every country dedicated to promoting the interest of their race rather than of the country that had given them sanctuary.[20]

The movement towards a racist ideology led, in 1935–36, to a split in the Quisling party over two different policies: whether to adhere to basic concepts of Christianity or to follow the German Nazi's racial outlook on life. After the split, Quisling's attitude became increasingly racist. Anti-Semitism, the Jewish problem, and pure racial theories became central issues for the development of *Nasjonal Samling*. Suffering defeats in parliamentary and municipal elections (1936, 1937), Jews became the scapegoat for these disasters. Hatred for the Jews became a dominant theme in the Quisling press, especially in Vestlandets Avis (The Western Coast Newspaper), Hedemark Fylkesavis (Hedemark People's News), *NS–Ungdommen* (The Youth of NS), and in the main publication, *Fritt Folk* (Free People). Quisling's outlook was reflected in his establishing, in 1937, the clearly anti–Semitic *Det Stornordiske Fredssamband* (The Greater Nordic Peace Union). Benjamin Vogt stated that Quisling "was a Jew–baiter in a country where there were hardly any Jews and no Jewish problem."[21]

More than any other Norwegian, Dr. Jon Alfred Mjøen (1860–1939) contributed to the dissemination of racism by establishing a "racial hygienic institute" in Oslo and publishing, from 1919 to 1932, a periodical, *Den Nordiske Race* (The Nordic Race). In 1938 he reissued an extended edition of his *Racial Hygiene* which became the main source for racial theories within the Quisling party.[22] Quisling was convinced about the inequality of races. The Jews had a low rating because of their inherent impurity. Quisling's belief in the superiority of the Nordic races made it easy for him to accept Nazi race theories.[23] By the time persecution of Norway's Jews started in 1941, Quisling had fully accepted vulgar anti–Semitism, quoting in his writings and speeches the falsifications against Jews contained in *The Protocols of the Elders of Zion*.[24]

The program of *Nasjonal Samling* incorporated several of Dr. Mjøen's theories, especially those stipulating that the Nordic race was to be protected and that habitual criminals, the insane, and hereditary imbeciles should be sterilized. Furthermore, Norwegian foreign policy should seek worldwide connections with race and culture related peoples. Dr. Mjøen had "proven" how important it was to prevent bloodmixing with inferior races. In 1934, the *Storting* passed a law to permit sterilization which, for some members of Quisling's party, indicated a "clear acceptance of Mjøen's negative part of the race–hygienic program."[25] Racism and biology, including elements of both anti-Semitism and race biology and claiming superiority of the Nordic race, were commonly propagated throughout Scandinavia.[26]

Under the impact of the rise of Nazism in Germany, Quisling's anti–Semitic and anti–democratic attitudes were strengthened.[27] Eager to prove himself a true follower of Hitler's racial theories and to explain to the Germans the "Jewish danger" in Norway, he travelled to Frankfurt–am–Main in March 1941 to address the inauguration of "The Institute for the Exploration of the Jewish Question." Here he stated that the main problem in Norway was not the small number of Jews, but the force of their destructive ideas. Jews had secured key positions and found eager followers, and thus had had a fatal influence on the inner development of Norway. The Jews had "maliciously attacked Norway leading to a national catastrophe for the country."[28]

However, Norway's small Jewish population was a problem for Quisling. To increase the number of Jews, Quisling invented the term *kunstige jøder* (artificial Jews), allowing the population to be inflated at will. Quisling estimated the number of Jews to be 10,000, a figure contradicted in a somber report by Terboven on November 6, 1942: "There are about 1,200 racial Jews who had led a quiet and secluded life. They have in Norway never succeeded in reaching a position in the economy. There are among them even capable farmers and craftsmen who are well–regarded (*die in gutem Ansehen stehen*) and who up to now have been considered as absolutely loyal citizens."[29]

Quisling and his fellow travellers consistently assisted the German invaders in their anti–Semitic policies, participating "actively in the persecution of the Jews of Norway."[30] Their aim was to build up a "New Norway," similar to Hitler's Nazi Germany. The Quisling regime had its own Brown Shirts — the *Hird* — the party's para–military force organized on the model of the Nazi S.A. and led, until January 1937, by J. B. Hjort, the powerful *Fylkesfører* (county leader) of Akerhus.[31]

Some Aspects of the German Invasion and Occupation

Although Quisling had sought contact in the 1930s with Nazi leaders, especially Alfred Rosenberg, *Reichsleiter* and head of the NSDAP Foreign Policy Bureau, German interest in Quisling and his movement did not become apparent until the summer of 1939.[32] Rosenberg and Quisling met in Berlin in June and again in December 1939, when a meeting with Admiral Raeder and Adolf Hitler was also arranged. They discussed a proposal for a peaceful German occupation to forestall a British invasion of Norway. On December 18, before returning to Norway, Quisling had a last audience with the Führer. Quisling believed he had been promised Germany's cooperation in a peaceful takeover by invitation from a pro–Nazi Norwegian government with himself as prime minister.[33]

During April 1940 there was a race for the occupation of Norway by Great Britain and Germany. Norway declared neutrality on September 1, 1939, referring to the previous declaration of May 27, 1938, issued together with Denmark, Finland, Iceland, and Sweden. Small states, however, cannot defend their neutrality by armed forces "unless the two opponents are equally interested in preserving it."[34]

Germany could not afford to lose the advantages of Norwegian neutrality. She decided to strike hard and fast ahead of the Allies to secure naval and airbases as well as the supply of iron ore from the Swedish mines in the Kirüna–Gallivare mountains through the port of Narvik. Hitler had stated that Germany could, under no circumstances, afford to lose the Swedish ore, "If we do, we will have to wage war with wooden sticks."[35] On February 21, 1940, Hitler put General Niklaus von Falkenhorst in charge of preparing the invasion of Norway, under the code name *Weserübung*.[36] On April 8, the British laid mines in Norway's territorial waters under the code name "Wilfred," named after St. Wilfred because, in the usual British style of understatement, the operation was "so small and innocent."[37]

Relying on speed, surprise, and camouflage, German air and naval forces successfully occupied five major Norwegian cities extending from the southern coast to the Arctic Circle — Kristiansand, Stavanger, Bergen, Trondheim, and Narvik — during the early morning hours of April 9. They suffered no serious losses. The main battle, to secure Oslo, was delayed when the German heavy cruiser *Blücher* was sunk with highranking officers and Gestapo staff on board.[38]

Warnings of possible German invasion of Norway had reached Whitehall from various sources,[39] but the British and Norwegian forces could not prevent the Germany military from successfully invading and occupying the country. The Norwegian government left the capital without giving orders to destroy vital means of communication. At 7:30 P.M. on April 9, 1940, Vidkun Quisling suddenly appeared on the radio announcing himself as prime minister in charge of a new government with the obvious support of Germany.[40] Although Quisling thought he would be Hitler's deputy in Norway, he was not kept abreast of Germany's invasion plans.[41]

The German Commander–in–Chief, General von Falkenhorst, issued a proclamation on April 14, 1940, stating in part:[42]

> It is my task to protect Norway against an attack by the Western powers. The Norwegian Government has declined several offers of cooperation. The Norwegian people must now themselves determine the fate of their fatherland. If my proclamation meets with the obedience which was very sensibly accorded by the Danish people when faced with similar circumstances, Norway will be spared the horrors of war. If opposition is offered and the hand of friendship is rejected, I shall be forced to employ the severest and most relentless means to crush such opposition.

Instead of cooperation from the majority of the Norwegian population, widespread and strong opposition characterized the reaction to the "new order" of a Quisling racist state based on German military power. Quisling was forced to resign as prime minister on April 15,[43] and the *Administrasjonsrådet* (Administrative Council) established on the same date. The Council was appointed by the Supreme Court with seven members of unimpeachable integrity, among them, Didrik Arup Seip, President of the University of Oslo, who was later arrested and sent to Germany.

The appointment of Josef Terboven as *Reichskommisar* came through a *Führer–Erlass* of April 24, 1940.[44] Upon entering his office that same day, he found a political power distribution not to his liking. His first declaration, issued on April 26, 1940, outlined his functions and powers.[45] He had two fundamental aims: first, to establish a government subordinate to his wishes and, second, to utilize his power to win World War II by all means. The occupation organization that he established — known as *Reichskommissariat für die besetzten Gabiete Norwegens* (Reich Commissariat for the Occupied Areas of Norway) — was to function throughout the war. Their offices worked closely with the willing collaborators, the quislings. The Administrative Council, which had the support of the rest of the population, was abolished on September 25, 1940. In his order of the same date, Terboven stated that the Royal House of Norway and its government have "no further political importance and will not return to Norway."[46] A Quisling government was appointed by the *Reichskommisar* on September 25, 1940.

With this proclamation, Terboven introduced the new official policy of Germany: the nazification of the Norwegian people with the help of Quisling's party. The issues had been clarified during *Riksrådforhandlingene* (Negotiations for an Occupation Settlement) from June to September 1940. The German policy went far beyond a military occupation of Norway, which Hitler had characterized as *das Schicksalgebiet in diesem Kriege* (the fateful territory in this war).[47] Among the Norwegian people, the proclamation of September 25 gave rise to the organized resistance movement, a response which turned defeatism into hope and eventual victory over the occupation regime. It has been ironically stated that "Terboven was the real founder of the Norwegian resistance movement, and that Quisling, through *Nasjonal Samling,* created national unification."[48]

A power struggle ensued between Terboven and Quisling. According to Hans–Dietrich Loock, one of the purposes of the occupiers was to establish a new Norwegian Nazi party, built on *Nasjonal Samling* but without Vidkun Quisling as "Führer."[49] However, in a memo of October 25, 1940, Quisling demanded an independent Norwegian government and the abolition of Terboven's civilian administration. Quisling's demand was ignored. Terboven regarded Quisling as an "uncomfortable competitor"[50] and wanted to rule without him. Quisling, however, had important support from Berlin through Alfred Rosenberg. Desirous of preventing Quisling from acquiring further power and becoming Norway's Chief of State,[51] Hitler effectively blocked his quest by appointing him "Minister President" through the Act of State of February 1, 1942. The interplay between the two protagonists is crucial for an understanding of the Norwegian Holocaust. Ultimate power, however, remained in the hands of the *Reichkommissariat* and Terboven.[52]

Ever since Hitler declared Norway an enemy state as of April 18, 1940,[53] her economy had been exploited by Germany with the cooperation of Norwegian workers who flocked to complete the enormous construction and armament work benefitting the German war machine. The figure of three thousand who were sentenced for profiteering after the war, "hardly conveys the lamentable willingness of many Norwegians to take the inflated wages offered for work which served the German interests."[54] Since Hitler was convinced about a forthcoming Allied invasion of Norway, *Festung Norway* (Fortress Norway) was constantly being reinforced.

Having suffered defeats in the attempted nazification of Norway's organized associations, legal and sports organizations, labor unions, teacher and student groups, churches, and the civil servants' union, Quisling and the Nazi leaders turned their undivided attention towards a defenseless group — the Jewish communities in Norway.

Stages in the Persecution of Norway's Jews

The triumvirate of General von Falkenhorst, *Reichskommisar* Josef Terboven, and *Obergruppenführer* (Lieutenant General) Rediess of the SS and Police, together with the eager cooperation of Quisling and the Norwegian police, set the stage for the destruction of Norway's Jews, characterized as "the saddest chapter of the history of occupation."[55]

The official book containing correspondence between the Norwegian Government in Exile and the resistance movement does not document what was done to assist Jews to escape or to go into hiding. Was there any such policy? What was the relationship between the resistance movement, the Jewish communities, and the rescue of Jews? Were any directives issued by the Government in Exile, the resistance movement, or the Jewish community leaders to rescue people condemned to death solely because they were Jews?

The official publication, *Regjeringen og Hjemmefronter under Krigen* (The Government and the Home Front During the War), throws no light on these issues and mentions Jewish persecutions in only two documents. One is a letter of December 2, 1942, from the Home Front to the Government in Exile in London stating: "The all overshadowing event has, of course, been the Jewish pogroms. People have little by little become careful about talking loudly in the streets, but in these days this rule has been broken. All of this has been so revolting that people have not been able to resist expressing their feelings."[56]

The other document, dated Oslo, June 28, 1944, is also from the Home Front to the Government in Exile: "We may remind you about the excellent work done by the transport organizations when it was important, upon the shortest possible warning, to transport the Jews and later the students."[57]

The leaders of the allied governments had detailed information about the Holocaust by the summer of 1942. Eyewitnesses from the death camps had arrived in London, where the Polish Government in Exile provided a steady flow of information about the massacre. The London *Daily Telegraph* reported in June 1942 that 700,000 Jews had been gassed. By December 1942, "every European government had heard the news, if not necessarily most of its citizens."[58]

What did the Norwegian Government in Exile do with this information? Why were relatively few notices about Jewish persecutions published in the underground press? In September 1942 a report appeared in *Norsk Ungdom* (Norwegian Youth), stating that "at this time, 700,000 Jews have been killed through wholesale murder."[59] This was followed by six brief notices from October 26 to November 26 in *Norske Nyheter* (Norwegian News, London), *Free Fagbevelgelse* (Free Trade Unions), *For Konge og Federland* (For King and Fatherland), and *Friheten* (Freedom).[60] On December 3, 1942, *Håndslag. Fakta og Orientering for Nordmenn* (Handshake. Facts and Orientations for Norwegians), a widely read paper published in Sweden but distributed in Norway and edited by Eyvind Johnson, stated: "The Jews in Oslo were, at first, taken to Bredtvedt, and from there a few days later to the new prison camp in Sem, which shall only be a temporary place of residence. Later on, all shall be sent for compulsory labor either to Northern Norway or to Poland."[61]

London Radio, another of the approximately 250 illegal newspapers during the German occupation,[62] gave the following account on December 4, 1942 under the heading "The Fate of the Jews in Occupied Countries":[63]

> The constantly increasing strong measures against the Jews in Norway is a part of the systematic policy of extermination which the Third Reich has over a long period of time perpetuated against Europe's Jewish population. The English section of the World Jewish Congress reported on August 6 (1942), that out of seven million Jews living in the occupied countries, one million have already lost their lives.

This report detailed the fate of the Jewish population in Poland:

> In the concentration camp Ozvizim (Auschwitz) in Southern Poland, where Poles and Jews are incarcerated together, 50 (sic) persons die every day. There is really no reason to disbelieve that the total number of Jewish victims now adds up to 700,000.

However, a more correct estimation of the number of Jews murdered by the end of 1942 was four million, according to Dr. Korherr's report to Heinrich Himmler of March 23, 1943: "The Final Solution of the European Jewish Question."[64] Despite information such as this, the destruction of the Jews did not become a principal concern of the Norwegian Government in Exile.

In Norway, anti–Semitic activities increased following the German invasion. The occupying power moved quickly to establish police power. The *Reichssicherheitshauptamt* (The Reich Main Security Office) was represented in Oslo by *Oberregierungsrat* and *SS–Oberführer* (Colonel) Franz Walter Stahlecker, who had been ordered on April 10, 1940 to be Himmler's personal representative in charge of German police in Norway. From January 28, 1942 to February 23, 1945, the Gestapo in Norway was headed by *SS–Sturmbahnführer* (Lieutenant) Hellmuth Reinhard.[65] Other high Gestapo officials in Norway were *SS–Oberführer* Heinrich Fehlis, *Obersturmbannführer* (Lieutenant Colonel) Gerhard Friedrich Ernest Flesh, and *Hauptsturmführer* (Captain) Wilhelm A. K. Wagner.

Anti–Semitic propaganda escalated after the invasion. From 1940–1942 the Jews were exposed to the familiar process of discrimination, arrests, torture, and deportation. Radios belonging to Jews were confiscated in May 1940. The Administrative Council minutes of May 16, 1940, noted that Oslo police had confiscated the radios "upon order from the German authorities." Hans Dellbrügge, the German negotiator, explained that the Jewish problem had to be handled on an international basis and that the "legal basis" for the confiscation "was to be found in one of Hitler's ordinances."[66] The Chief of the Oslo Police, Kristian Welhaven, stated that the police had obeyed the German order because they thought they had no right to oppose such a decree and, furthermore, that protests would be of no avail. This reaction is typical of the defeatist attitude that characterized Norwegian reaction to the first few months of occupation. The Administrative Council chose to deny Norwegian Jews the same legal protection as other Norwegians. There was no moral or legal foundation for confiscating Jewish radios or for condoning discriminatory actions directed solely against Norway's Jews. The Council had an opportunity to clearly protest anti–Semitic actions; however, it failed to do so.

By confiscating radios, two aims could be achieved: preventing listening to foreign broadcasts and identifying Jewish families. More systematic efforts to identify Jews were made in the fall of 1940 when demands for membership lists from the two organized Jewish communities in Trondheim and Oslo were made and complied with. Simultaneously with this harrassment, the systematic attempts at nazification started. The Nazis, calling for a crusade against the 'Jewish international danger," expected that the Norwegian population would react positively to the German policy. In the fall of 1940, the quislings painted anti–Jewish slogans on store windows belonging to Jews.[67]

The campaign against individual Jews led to withdrawal of licenses issued to nine foreign medical doctors. Furthermore, an announcement was made by Edward Sylou–Creutz that all Jewish music should be banned, and that performers should be members of *Nasjonal Samling*. In the fall of 1940, Per Reidarson, a well known musician, submitted a proposal for a *Norges Kunster–og Journalistlaug* (Union of Norwegian Artists and Journalists) suggesting that only carefully selected persons, anti–Semites, and members of NS would be eligible for membership. This resulted in harrassment of a leading musician, Ernst Glaser, who was scheduled to appear as soloist in Sinding's violin concerto at a concert in Bergen on January 16, 1941 using Ole Bull's Guarner del Gesu violin from 1742. While Mr. Glaser was entering the hall, a vicious anti–Semitic demonstration took place organized by the local NS party who insisted that a Jewish artist should not be permitted to perform. Glaser was not allowed to play. Instead demonstrations took place inside the hall and leaflets were distributed proclaiming that no Jews be permitted to play an Ole Bull's violin, which was considered a national treasure.[68] The demonstrators shouted "Down with Jews!", fist fights ensued, police were called; things finally quieted when the orchestra played the national anthem. The demonstrators were not prosecuted. Further harassment took place in July 1941 with the dismissal of Jews in public service. Jewish lawyers in private practice and other professionals were deprived of their licenses.[69]

Towards the "Final Solution" in Norway

With the German invasion of the Soviet Union in June 1941, arrests of Jews were made in Northern Norway. In Harstad, Narvik, and Tromsø, Norwegian and stateless Jews were arrested on June 22, 1941 and sent to the concentration camp at Vollan prison in Trondheim or to Grini internment camp near Oslo which had been used as a prison camp since April 14, 1940. By the end of the war, over 15,000 prisoners from all over Norway and eighteen foreign countries had been interned at Grini. Haakon Holmboe described the brutal treatment of Jews at Grini. On June 22, the day of the German invasion of the USSR, the Jews at Grini were singled out for savage beatings and for placement into special "rapid work groups." They had their hair torn off, skin and all. Afterwards, the Jews had to clean up the "bloody mess." Holmboe noted that the German contempt for foreigners gradually infected some of the Norwegian prisoners who, little by little, accepted the German view of East Europeans as belonging to an inferior race. The yellow Jewish star had been introduced at Grini.[70]

During the fall of 1941 and 1942, the campaign against the Norwegian Jews intensified in the press and on the radio. On October 10, 1941, the Norwegian State Police was requested in a letter from the *Befehlshaber der Sicherheitspolizei* (Chief of Security Police) to prepare a law for stamping all identity cards belonging to Jews with a J for *Jøde* (Jew). The law stated that the "stamping is *gratis* . . . and that as far as possible it should be done in red ink."[71] On January 10, 1942, Jonas Lie, the Minister of Police, issued an order to have a large J stamped into identification cards of Jews. This intensification of Jewish persecution had started with the arrival in Oslo on February 13, 1941, of Eichmann's representative, *Hauptsturmführer* Wilhelm Artur Konstantin Wagner as head of the Office for Jewish Affairs (IVB4). His immediate supervisor was Helmuth Reinhard.[72]

At this time regulations were issued clarifying "who is a Jew," based on the First Ordinance to the Reich Citizenship Law, published in Berlin in 1935, which defined who is a Jew, German, and so–called *Mischlinge* (mixed blood). The quisling government, through its minister of Church and Education, Ragnar Schancke, had during the summer of 1941 proposed changes in the marriage laws whereby mixed marriages would be prohibited. However, Bishop Eivind Berggrav, leader of the Church, expressed forcefully that the Church stood united against any attempt to introduce aryan marriage laws, whether against the Jewish or Lappish population. The proposal was postponed and when put into effect, was directed only against Jews.

Soon after his installation as Minister President, Quisling and his ministers reintroduced (February 1, 1942) Article two of the Norwegian Constitution of 1814. In March, 1942, the *Norsk Lovtidend* (Norwegian Legal Gazette) published the following change in the Constitution: "Jews are furthermore prohibited from admission to the Kingdom," i.e., the exact wording of Article 2 as originally adopted in 1814 by the Constituent Assembly at Eidsvold. This law received immediate coverage in the controlled press under the heading "Article Two of the Constitution Again in Its Original Form."[73] Minister Sverre Riisnaes praised Quisling for having resurrected the country's Constitution by prohibiting Jews from entering Norway, and added:[74]

> *Nasjonal Samling* builds the new state with the Constitution as foundation. At the time of our ancestors at Eidsvold we had still preserved our Nordic view of life. Our people acknowledged that one of the first duties of a people to gain its right to live is to take care of the people's race. This sound race–conscious thought is closely connected with the ideological view of NS. That is why there is so much stronger reason for Vidkun Quisling to re–establish this constitutional prohibition since Judaism today is a much more dangerous enemy for our race than it was at the time when the Constitution was adopted.

This law did not have any practical effect, but it was an expression of racist ideology and another example of the intensification of Jewish persecution.

On March 7, 1942, the first executions of Norwegian Jews took place when four Jews were shot in Trondheim on trumped up charges of spreading hostile propaganda for a foreign power. They were Abel Bernstein, David Isaksen, Wulf Isaksen, and David Wolfson.[75] A fifth person, Efraim Schilowsky, arrested at the same time in January 1942, was released because he was a Swedish citizen.

In the city of Trondheim, where about 150 Jews remained in April 1941, the synagogue was confiscated by the Germans without warning. It was completely vandalized. The main sanctuary was used as a barrack, the women's gallery as a barbershop, the Mogen Davids in the stained glass windows were replaced with swastikas, and all Hebrew inscriptions removed. Two of the four Torah scrolls were brought to safety to the home of Aron Mendelsohn, founder and leader of the Jewish congregation. His home was used as a synagogue until his arrest in October 1942. A room of the Methodist Church was also used for some time as a synagogue during 1942.

In sharp contrast, the synagogue in Oslo at Bergstein 13 remained almost intact. The superintendent took good care of all the possessions, including the Torah scrolls, throughout the occupation. The synagogue at Calmeyer Street 15, belonging to *Den Israelitiske Menighet* (The Israelitic Congregation), however, was vandalized, but not to the extent of the one in Trondheim.[76]

After the confiscation of the synagogue in Trondheim, Arne Fjellbu, Dean of the Cathedral, warned the local Nazis and quislings in private conversations that if this action indicated a general persecution of Jews, "I can assure you that the church will sound the alarm from one end of the country to the other. Here the Norwegian church stands one hundred percent united. Such a thing we will not tolerate."[77]

The church's protest was not the only example of sympathy and practical help extended to Norway's Jews. Notable were the personnel within customs control who had strict orders to confiscate all packages to Jews, especially food packages from Denmark or Sweden. The personnel, however, would contact the recipients immediately without informing the Nazi authorities. Jews could expect no help from the local quislings, but patriots extended whatever assistance they could under difficult conditions. Some of the Jews arrested in 1942 had actually fled to Sweden in 1940, only to return to Norway believing in the promise of amnesty for those who had fled during the invasion, or in Terboven's speech on September 25th of that year promising protection of all religious denominations which the Jews had interpreted in their favor. However, during the summer of 1942, ten Jews including Rabbi Julius Samuel, vacationing at Naersnes near Oslo, were arrested. Rabbi Samuel was deported and subsequently killed in Auschwitz in December 1942.[78]

Preparations for the Deportation of Norway's Jews

During the fall of 1942, the tempo of Jewish persecutions increased under the leadership of the Gestapo chief, Ernest Flesch, one of the most dangerous Nazis in Norway. On October 6, the Nazi authorities declared a state of emergency in the Trøndelag province following serious sabotage committed against German installations at Majavatn and Glomfjord.[79] Terboven took a terrible revenge. Thirty–four hostages were shot, among them Hirsch Kommisar, a leading member of the Jewish community in Trondheim who had been arrested in January 1942. That a Jew had been shot together with thirty–three other patriots reinforced the impression that no particular attack on Jews as Jews was forthcoming.

The next day, October 7, 1942, all male Jews over the age of 14 were arrested and sent to the Falstad prison camp near Levanger where the execution of the hostages had taken place. The Jews were brutally treated while at Falstad and three were executed.[80] An Auschwitz survivor, As–riel B. Hirsch, testified at the Quisling trial that he was taken by Norwegian police to Falstad where the Jews were executed because "they were weak; they became ill during their stay at Falstad because of mistreatment. One night, at 11 P.M., they were shot."[81] The person in charge of Falstad concentration camp was *SS–Obersturmführer* Denk who was under the command of *Obersturmbannführer* Flesch in Trondheim.[82]

In southern Norway, especially in Oslo which had a Jewish population of about 800, there had been only a few indications of the Nazi intent. Harry Koritzinsky, the longtime Secretary of the Oslo Jewish Community, stated that until the fall of 1942 the Jews in Oslo had undergone a relatively calm period. "Terboven's declaration of September 25, 1940 had, by and large, a quieting effect on the Norwegian Jews."[83] There were, of course, requisitions of apartments and houses for the benefit of the Germans, but that happened to all Norwegians and the Jews felt fairly safe that there would be no specific actions taken against them as Jews. They had gone through the same problems of occupation as everyone else and had adjusted themselves to the daily attacks in the controlled anti–Semitic press. The Norwegian Jews wanted to share the same difficulties as the rest of the nation; little did they know that they were singled out for destruction.

The state of siege and arrests of Jews in Trondheim and other parts of Norway in the beginning of October 1942 had affected the tranquillity of the Jewish community in Oslo. Escape to Sweden was one way out. Despite a decree on October 12, 1942 ordering the death penalty for assisting Jews, about 850 Jews managed to escape to Sweden in 1942 and 1943, often with the assistance of the Norwegian resistance movement. "Altogether, about 700 persons of Jewish descent arrived from Norway during 1942. About 500 of these have Norwegian citizenship. Among the refugees who arrived during 1943, about 150 are made up of Norwegians and of stateless Jews living in Norway. The majority of these arrived in Sweden at the beginning of 1943."[84]

An order had been given on September 24, 1942 by Wilhelm A. Wagner to the Norwegian STAPO (State Police) to arrest all Jews with a J on their identity cards, as well as their families, in order to deport them from Norway.[85] During the Quisling Court Proceedings in 1945, however, it was established that the Germans decided to permit solution of the Jewish problem in Norway according to the wishes of the Quisling government.[86]

The pretext for the start of the persecutions in Oslo was an event that happened on October 22, 1942, when nine young Jews tried to escape to Sweden by train under the leadership of Karsten Løvestad, a resistance member who served as a border pilot. On the train between Skjeberg and Berg, a border policeman, Arne Hvam, asked for identification. The Jews had a J stamped on their cards. The leader evidently panicked and shot the policeman. The trip had been arranged so hurriedly that the conductor had not been told about the rescue mission. Normally, it was his assignment to warn all refugees about possible inspection of identity papers. Now, with the policeman shot, the Nazis immediately searched the whole district and arrested the nine Jews. The next day, the families of the arrested men were rounded up.[87]

At 9:30 PM on Friday, October 23, the Norwegian State Police received orders to start preparing for general arrests of Jews. During the weekend, the STAPO worked at full speed compiling as complete lists as possible of all male Jews, assisted by *Nasjonal Samlings Statistikkontor* (National Union's Statistical Office). On Monday, October 26, a law confiscating Jewish property was promulgated with immediate effect[88] and arrests of all male Jews were carried out by the Norwegian police.[89] These arrests were based on a Quisling law of October 24, 1942, and on Terboven's decree of September 25, 1940 ordering arrests of persons hostile to the state.[90]

These actions against the Jews were initiated and carried out by Norwegians. The registration of Jews in Norway was undertaken by the Office of NS Statistics and "exclusively by this office without pressure by the Germans. The aim, as far as it is possible to ascertain, is to collect material for statistical preparation of the Jewish problem in Norway," according to Criminal Inspector J. Wiehrmyhr's report of October 27, 1942.[91]

While preparing the rules governing "who is a Jew" and thus defining who would be subject to registration, arrest, and deportation, Quisling's government cooperated closely with German authorities. Although the order was claimed to have come from the German Security Police, the

Quisling authorities exercised great initiative and zeal. The problem of "who is a Jew" was clarified on January 10, 1942 and published in *Fritt Folk* (Free People) on November 19, 1942 when the "Law of Registration for Jews" was promulgated.[92] The order to arrest all male Jews between the ages of 15 and 65 was issued by the Chief of the State Police, K. A. Marthinsen on Saturday, October 24th.

The procedure for the arrest can be followed in detail in a report of October 4, 1946, by Thorbjørn Frøberg and Knut Ebeling, where it is stated that altogether 260 male Jews were arrested between October 26 and 27, 1942.[93] The three police inspectors, Sverre Dürbeck, Jörgen Wiermyhr, and Thorvald Undhjem, brought along the *spørreskjema* (inquiry forms) which the Jews had filled out in the spring of 1942 and filed with local police throughout the country. In charge of preparing the lists of names and addresses was Police Officer Homb and eight other civil servants. Police Inspectors Knut Røed, Ragnvald Kranz and others arrived on Sunday, October 25th. The mimeographed lists of Jews to be arrested were distributed to arresting squads consisting of all available personnel from the State Police, forty members of the Oslo police, the Germanic *SS–Norge,* and others totalling 124 persons. The action was led by Deputy Chief of Oslo State Police, Knut Røed.

On Monday, October 26, everyone involved met at 5:30 AM at Kirkevien 23. The 124 policemen were divided into 62 task forces. Each received an envelope with ten names. Inspector Røed gave instructions as to the arrests, which cars were to be requisitioned, and how to proceed in hunting for individual Jews. The zeal of the Norwegian police is illustrated by the repeated attempts to arrest Jews who were not at home at the first call; in those cases, second and third calls were made. The arrest was a Norwegian action in which Norwegians arrested other Norwegians, leading to the destruction of nearly half of Norway's Jewish population.[94] Dr. Robert Savosnick, survivor of Auschwitz, testified that he had been arrested at Orkdal Hospital and sent to Oslo "guarded by two Norwegian patriotic policemen."[95] All the preliminary work was done by Norwegians.[96]

The arrested Jews were transported first to Bredtvedt, a detention camp outside of Oslo, and then to Berg concentration camp near Tønsberg. Ernest Aberle, a refugee from Czechoslovakia, arrested in his home at Lillehammer (about 150 miles north of Oslo), gave a detailed description of those events. He recounts that the Berg camp was under Norwegian administration, with Major Eivind Wallestad and Lieutenant Leif Lindseth in command. The camp was totally unfit for human habitation. There was no water and no toilet facilities at all.[97]

A group of about 350 Jews arrived on October 28 and were greeted by Lindseth's statement that they would receive the harsh treatment they deserved; any attempt to escape would result in being shot. Suffering from hunger, lack of medicine, clothing and bedding, they received some help from the Norwegian Red Cross and a local doctor, Anton Jervell, who sought to bring in additional supplies but was prevented from doing so by Wallstad's statement that help was not needed. The prisoners' stay came to an abrupt end at 4 AM on November 26 when about 280 Jews were transported by special train from the Berg concentration camp to Oslo with police officer Ragnvald Kranz in charge. He had received orders during the night not to deport Jews married to aryan women. Lindseth stated that "those who claim to be married to an aryan but are not will be shot."

H. O. Christophersen noted many years later:[98]

What for us was most grotesque — disregarding the Jews' own tragic fate — was that it was the *Norwegian* and not the German police that implemented the action. It is difficult to understand that the national elements within our so-called state police did not refuse to participate out of hand. They could not be in doubt that they transferred our Jewish countrymen to an inhuman fate.

Arne Skouen, a Norwegian columnist, was also surprised to learn about the involvement of the Norwegians:[99]

I saw Norwegians that terrible afternoon, Monday, October 26, from the gate in Ebells Street . . . I thought it was *Germans* I saw in action . . . I seem to remember that it was mentioned as a pure German action by the late Egil Meidell Hopp, who gave me the assignment to cover the district around Calmeyer Street for the courier mail to Stockholm. Most of the Jews lived there and they were among the poorest and most uninformed, so that the warnings had not caught their attention. Most of them were at home. It happened here that soldiers in *German* uniforms pushed the Jews towards the cars, while wives and children ran crying, being brutally stopped and shoved away. Now, for the first time, I am being informed that it was Norwegian SS Officers I saw in action. . . .

Deportations of Norway's Jews to Auschwitz

The main deportation of Norway's Jews took place on November 26, 1942, from Oslo via Stettin to Auschwitz. The night of November 25–26 has been recorded as the most fateful for Norway's Jews. A large and well organized force of about three hundred Norwegian police was prepared for action: sixty from the State Police, sixty from the Oslo police, sixty from the *Hird,* thirty from *Germanske SS–Norge* (Germanic SS–Norway), and about one hundred from *Statspolitiets Beredsskapsavdeling* (The Rapid Deployment Force of the State Police).[100]

Detailed instructions for deportation of all Jews still at liberty, especially women, children under 14, men over 65, the sick, the mentally ill, and the retarded, had been issued by K. A. Marthinsen, Chief of Norwegian Police.[101] "Exceptions are made for women and men married to persons not having J in their passports, and persons with British, American, Central or South American citizenships, the neutral countries and those countries allied to Germany."[102] About 55 persons of mixed marriages were interned in Norway until early May 1945, at which time they were safely moved to Sweden.[103] Marthinsen's report stated that he had received orders on November 24, 1942 at 8:00 PM from the German Security Police *Hauptsturmführer* Wilhelm A. Wagner.[104]

In his written report of November 27, 1942, Marthinsen made several complaints. The Oslo police had hesitated to provide the only suitable lodging for Jews arriving from out of town — the gymnasium of the Oslo police barracks. This problem was settled only after many hours of negotiation. Another complaint was that he had received a message from Germany Security Police at 8 PM on November 25, notifying him of a change in evacuation plans: families where a spouse was an aryan would not be evacuated at all. This caused many problems since initial lists and preparations had been based on the original instructions. Furthermore, he complained that he had been given too little time to prepare such an extensive action; he should have had as many days as he had hours.[105]

The action was carried out in the following manner. On November 24, Marthinsen called together all police officers to clarify special assignments. Inspector Sverre Dürbeck was assigned to arrange for the arrest and transportation of Jews from Østland (Eastern Norway), Sørlandet (Southern Norway), and if possible from Trondheim and Bergen. At his disposal he had the civil servants at police headquarters, the local chiefs of police, and the out of city precincts of the State Police. Inspector Knut Røed was in charge of the arrest of Jewish families in the Oslo and Aker precincts and of having the arrested families brought to Pier I where a ship would be available. Røed was also in charge of embarking the prisoners. *Politifullmektig* (Police Lieutenant) Ragnvald Krantz was assigned to arrest Jews in hospitals, the mentally ill and retarded at other institutions, as well as male Jews over the age of 65 within the Oslo and Aker precincts. Krantz also organized the transportation of about 300 Jews from Berg concentration camp to Oslo. *Politifullmektig* Lindvig was in charge of ordering about one hundred taxis and buses for local transportation in

Oslo on November 26, and also for obtaining the necessary provisions for the duration of the voyage.

During the late evening of November 25, air raid sirens went off repeatedly between 9 PM and midnight to keep people off the street. At 5 AM, November 26, the well planned and executed roundup of Jews took place. The Norwegian police went from house to house according to lists carefully compiled from the *spørreskjema* (questionnaire) which the Jews themselves had filled out during the spring and summer of 1942. Some turned out to be inaccurate because of changes in addresses, but the zeal of the police, already manifested the previous month, was repeated. By utilizing the *Folkregisteret* (The National Register), most of the changed addresses were traced. The men worked constantly throughout the day; altogether, 562 Jews were arrested.[106]

Those who had avoided arrest during previous roundups were now brought to Pier I for embarkation on board the S/S *Donau aus Bremen*. Special trains and buses from the various detention camps arrived at the pier where those previously arrested "were united with their families."[107] Willy Brandt gave this description of the pier prior to the deportation:[108]

> While children cried and mothers pleaded for mercy, they were thrown into cars and driven down to the German troop ship, *Donau*, which was laid up at the pier of the Norwegian American Line. At the pier the most heartbreaking scenes took place. The Quisling police behaved in a most brutal way even when it concerned women and babies. The sick on stretchers were thrown on board. Even mentally deranged from Ullevold Hospital were fetched for deportation.

Arne Skouen reported watching at a distance Norwegian Jews being taken to the *Donau*, "which awaited them in Bjørvika, to the gas chambers . . . I am standing outside the lock–up street and I hear children crying, and I still see the parents quieting them with whatever was left of hope and courage . . ."[109]

A survivor of Auschwitz from Oslo, Kai S. J. Feinberg, was arrested in October 1942 and brought on board the S/S *Donau* on November 26, 1942. He reported the deportation as follows:[110]

> On board I met my mother and father, sister and adopted brother. It came as a shock to me. I believed, of course, that they would not have permitted themselves to be arrested, because my father certainly knew what it was all about. But he told me: 'As long as you were arrested we could not think about escaping to Sweden.' And he also felt responsibility for the refugees from Central Europe. He did not speak much on board the *Donau* but made me understand that he knew what was going to happen. I remember one evening

when we youngsters went on deck and started singing, it was quite cozy. We imagined that we were being sent to work camps where the family could be together and survive the war. . . . There was a certain optimism on board, especially when we arrived at Øresund where Sweden was fully lit up on one side, and Denmark blacked out on the other. Should we jump overboard? No one did it. Then we arrived at Stettin. The German SS took care of us. We were called *Dreckjude* and *Schmutziger Jude*. They confiscated all the food we had with us and we received very little to eat. We were transported in cattle cars to Auschwitz, the men and women separately. We received nothing to eat or drink during the transportation. The trip from Stettin to Auschwitz lasted about two days. The cars were opened and, for the first time, we met other prisoners, Polish Jews with hair shaven off. They wore the striped prison uniforms. We paraded five and five for an SS officer, probably Josef Mengele. This was the 'selection.' Women, children and senior citizens were transported by cars. We did not know where to. Today we know all them went directly to the gas chambers. My mother, sister, adopted brother, grandmother, aunt and uncles, altogether thirty relatives, died this way. Only two of my uncles, a cousin and I went to camp Birkenau where we were tattoed on the arm. My number was 79108. The lowest number I have seen in Auschwitz was 26000, the highest 230000. It was only the men capable of working who came to this camp and received a number. In our transport it was 186 out of 532. All the others were gassed immediately. My father was beaten and brought to the hospital. Thanks to Professor Epstein who arrived with our transport from Norway, I managed to be at the hospital where my father died on January 7, 1943. I was left alone. I could not stand it any longer.

According to the official report contained in the *Kalendarium der Ereignisse im Konzenstrationslager Auschwitz–Birkenau,* 186 men were taken into custody as prisoners and received numbers 79064 to 79249.[111] The others were destroyed in the gas chambers. Thus, out of the 532 deported from Oslo — not from Bergen as listed in the official document — 346 were immediately sent to their death. The documents from Stettin showed that the Norwegian Jews had left the city by train at 5:12 PM on November 30. They arrived at Auschwitz at 9 PM the following day. The official notice had this laconic wording: "Auschwitz, December 1, 1942. *Confirmation of receipt:* Receipt of –532– Jews from Norway is hereby confirmed."[112]

One of the survivors of this transport, Hermann Sachnowitz, from Larvik, received No. 79235 and gave this description of daily life in Auschwitz:[113]

The working day lasted for ten hours. We were beaten repeatedly because we did not work fast enough . . . There were always guards nearby who kept watch on us . . . When an SS–man wanted to get rid of a prisoner, he might ask him to do something with angry shouts: "Los! Los!" Inexperienced prisoners would obey the order and run. "Shot attempting to escape!" Living targets were most attractive to the SS–soldiers.

Professor Leo Eitinger, a leading Norwegian psychiatrist and a survivor of Auschwitz, testified at the Quisling trial that it was only the Norwegian Jews who, without exception, were deported to the death camps and "that there can be no doubt that Quisling must take the main responsibility."[114] At the trial, the prosecutor noted that "Quisling was an active participant against the Jews, and . . . this is the reason why the Jewish question took on a much more dreadful development in Norway than, for example, in Denmark."[115] Quisling's attitude is revealed in a speech he made in Trondheim on December 6, 1942, where he commented on the deportations: "A Jew is not a Norwegian, not a European. He is an Oriental. Jews have no place in Europe. They are internationally destructive elements. The Jews create the Jewish problem and cause active anti–Semitism . . . For us there can be no compromise."[116]

Quisling, however, did not act in a vacuum. He received support from many influential Norwegians, among them Halldis Neegard Østbye, a former editor of *Fritt Folk*. In a letter to him dated October 7, 1942, she claimed that there was an urgent need for an Aryan Law against race mixing in Norway. The Jewish persecution, she said, should be undertaken "quietly and through stages," for example, by bringing the Jews to concentration camps without official orders. The final arrangement "must, of course, be radical and not sentimental as it concerns the security of our own people and of Europe against a new Jewish attack. They have to be killed quickly and painlessly."[117]

The Germans apparently were not fully prepared for the Norwegian deportations. At the Wannsee conference of January 20, 1942, called together at RSHA headquarters by Heinrich Heydrich for implementation of the "final solution." Martin Luther, Under Secretary of State of the German Foreign Office, warned that the Germans would meet obstacles in deportations of the small Jewish populations of Scandinavia. Luther argued for a postponement.[118] The Norwegian drive against the Jews reportedly came as a surprise to Berlin, for the quisling authorities had great difficulties obtaining the ships necessary for deportation. Only one month after the October arrests did the German navy provide the S/S *Donau* for deportation purposes. Until November 1942, Adolf Eichmann and his staff had not been concerned with the deportation of Norway's Jews, for he realized that without a ship, deportation could not have taken place.[119] Transportation by train over neutral Sweden was considered an impossibility.

Within Norway, public opinion had been aroused by the brutal treatment, arrests, and deportation of Jews. This sense of agony was best articulated by the heads of the Norwegian Lutheran Church.[120] The leaders of the church, who had themselves been removed from Office, were fighting a crucial battle against nazification. The seven dismissed bishops strongly protested the Jewish persecutions. In a letter of November 10, 1942 to Minister President Quisling, the bishops stated:[121]

The Minister President's law, announced October 17, 1942, regarding the confiscation of property belonging to Jews has been received by our people with great sorrow, which was deepened by the decree that all Jewish men over 15 years of age were to be arrested. When we now appeal to the Minister President it is not to defend whatever wrongs the Jews may have committed. If they have committed crimes, they shall be tried, judged and punished according to Norwegian Law, just as all other citizens. But those who have committed no crime shall enjoy the protection of our country's justice. For 91 years Jews have had a legal right to reside and earn a livelihood in our country. Now they are being deprived of their property without warning and the men are being arrested and thus prevented from providing for their propertyless wives and children. This conflicts not only with the Christian commandments to "love thy neighbor," but with the most elementary legal rights. These Jews have not been charged with any transgressions by judicial procedure. Nevertheless, they are being punished as severely as the worst criminals are punished. They are being punished because of their racial background, wholly and solely because they are Jews. When we now appeal to the authorities in this matter we do so because of the deepest dictates of conscience. By remaining silent about this legalized injustice against the Jews we would make ourselves coguilty in this injustice. If we are to be true to God's Word and to the Church's Confession, we must speak out.

If the worldly authority becomes a terror to good works, that is, to the one who does not transgress against the country's law, then it is the Church's God–given duty as the conscience of the State to object. The Church, namely, has God's call and full authority to proclaim God's law and God's gospel. Therefore, it cannot remain silent when God's commandments are being trampled underfoot. And now it is one of Christianity's basic values which is violated; the commandments of God which are fundamental to all society, namely law and justice. Here one cannot dismiss the Church with a charge that it is mixing into politics. The apostles spoke courageously to the authorities of their day and said: 'We ought to obey God rather than men.' (Acts 5:29). Luther says: 'The Church does not interfere in worldly matters when it warns the authority to be obedient to the highest authority, which is God.' With the power of this our calling, we therefore admonish the earthly authorities and say in the name of Jesus Christ: halt the persecution of the Jews and stop the race hate which, through the press, is being spread in our land! By the right of this our calling, we therefore warn our people to desist from injustice, violence and hatred. He who lives in hatred and encourages evil invokes God's judgment upon himself. The Minister President has on several occasions emphasized that *Nasjonal Samling,* according to its program, will safeguard the basic values of Christianity. Today one of these values is in danger. If it is to be protected, it must be protected soon. We have mentioned it before, but reemphasize it now in closing: this appeal of ours has nothing to do with politics. Before worldly authorities we maintain that obedience in temporal matters which God's Word demands.

This strong protest was supported by leading theologians, nineteen church organizations, and six nonstate church religious societies. A total of over sixty signatures from all sections of Norway's Protestant communities endorsed the protest. On two Sundays, November 15 and 22, prayers were said for the Jews from the pulpits and in some cases the text of the letter was read. The pulpits of the Protestant churches had become one of the most effective means of anti–Nazi communication with congregations during the occupation.

The Catholic church did not participate in this official protest. Bishop Mangers, who was in charge of the Catholic church during the occupation, sent a letter to the Department of Church and Education on the same day that the Protestant church sent its protest. The Bishop, however, had written to secure the release of five baptized Jewish families, namely those of Dr. Ernest Adler, Samyel B. Jaffe, Hans Huszar, the family Neubauer, and Adolf Neumann. The Bishop thought it would be inappropriate to send another letter before receiving a reply to the first one.[122] A letter of November 10, 1942 from Bishop Mangers to Ole Hallesby, a leader of the Protestant protest and chairman of *Den Midlertidlige Kirkeledelse* (Temporary Church leadership) stated that "another letter on my part will undoubtedly lead to no consideration for the first one, and thus harm Christians of Jewish descent."[123]

While the protests and prayers of the Norwegian Lutheran Church did not stop the deportation of the Jews, they made a deep impression on the Norwegians at home and abroad. Additional protests were received from the Swedish bishops, the British Broadcasting Corporation, and from many countries throughout the free world. The fight of the Lutheran Church to resist nazification had become identical with the fight for national freedom. The church struggled, not on the periphery, but in the center of the field of battle. The majority of the population realized, as Ferdinand Schjelderup expressed it, that resistance would pay off "cost what it may — to the bitter end!"[124]

The Germans tried to minimize the effectiveness of the protest. For example, in the daily reports of December 1942, it was mentioned that the

Norwegian churches had pleaded for the Norwegian Jews, but "the radical solution of the Jewish question will be forgotten by the egoistic Norwegians."[125]

A second large deportation took place on February 24, 1943. This time it was on board the S/S *Gothenland,* with the 158 Jews, most of them belonging to the Trondheim congregation. These Jews had arrived in Oslo nine hours too late to be brought on board S/S *Donau* on November 26, 1942. They had all been brought to the concentration camp of Bredtvedt, where they were incarcerated and brutally treated for three months, under the supervision of the *Hirdmenn.* Quisling made "no attempt to prevent this second deportation."[126]

The prisoners on board the S/S *Gothenland* were sent, via Stettin, to Berlin, where they were added to a transport of German Jews for Auschwitz. About 120 from this group of 158, mainly from the districts of Nordland, Trøndelag, Møre, and Romsdal, were sent to the gas chambers immediately upon arrival. Those fit to work were sent to camp Buna–Monowitz, after having been tatooed on the left underarm. One prisoner, Julius Paltiel, received number 105362.[127] Of those who were gassed, the youngest was a baby boy, 14 months old, Harry Shotland from Harstad (born August 20, 1941); the oldest was Mendel Becker, 80 years old (born October 15, 1862). The murder of these innocent Jews took place on March 3, 1943 which, according to the Jewish calendar, was Yom Rishon (the first day) of the month of Adar, a leap year. This is a day of Holocaust commemoration for Jews deported and killed from Northern Norway.[128]

Altogether, 6,193 Norwegians were deported during World War II, among them, 762 were Jews. Out of the 5,431 nonJews, 649 died; i.e., 12 percent. Out of the 762 Jews deported, 739 perished; i.e., 97 percent.[129] In addition to the 739 Norwegian Jews killed in the various German concentration camps, 22 more Norwegian Jews perished as a result of other war related actions.[130]

In 1940 there were 1,364 Jews living in Norway's eighteen *fylker* (counties).[131] Because of severe immigration restrictions, only about 200 central European refugees were living in Norway in 1940.[132] The total loss of the Norwegian Jewish population during World War II was 761 persons. The small Jewish community of Norway sustained a loss of "nearly half its members."[133]

To commemorate the murdered Norwegian Jews, the small Jewish community of Trondheim erected in 1947 a monument inscribed with 130 names. In Oslo, the following year, members of the Royal family, government officials, and members of the diplomatic corps unveiled a monument with 620 names. At the ceremony, thanks were expressed to the Norwegian people for having rescued hundreds of Jews to Sweden. For this, the Yad Vashem gave official recognition to members of the Norwegian resistance movement in 1977, naming them as one "of the Righteous among the Nations."[134]

Notes

1. Lucy S. Davidowicz, A Holocaust Reader, New York: Behrman House, 1976, p. 381. The estimated number of Jews killed in these four countries: "France, 90,000 out of 350,000; Bulgaria, 14,000 out of 64,000; Italy, 8,000 out of 40,000; Norway, 900 out of 1,800." The latter figures are too high. 739 Jews perished out of 762 deported during the Holocaust which has been defined as "the destruction and martyrdom of European Jews under German occupation during the Second World War," Ibid., p. XIII.

2. Raul Hilberg, The Destruction of the European Jews, Chicago: Quadrangle Press, 1961, p. 291. In respect to the Finnish Jews, Hilberg was probably in error. Recent research by Elina Suominen, Kuolemanlaiva S/S Höhenhorn. Juutalaispakolaisten kohtalo Syomessa (The Ship of Death SS Höhenhorn. The fate of Jewish refugees in Finland), Helsinki: Werner Söderström Osakeyhtio, 1979, stated that nine Jews, all former citizens of Lithuania, Germany or Australia, were arrested on October 6, 1942 by the Finnish Security Police headed by Arno Anthoni. The Jews were deported on board S/S Hohenhorn to the Gestapo in occupied Estonia. They were transported from "Tallin to the Birkenau concentration camp, and Georg Kollman was the only one to survive. He is now living in Israel." As quoted in a review by Tapani Harvianinen in Nordisk Judaistic (Scandinavian Jewish Studies), Stockholm, Vol. 3, No. 2, March 1981, pp. 57–58.

3. Johan Galtung, "Norway in the World Community," in Natalie Rogoff Ramsøy, ed., Norwegian Society, New York: Humanities Press, 1974, pp. 395,398.

4. Gerd Gordon, The Norwegian Resistance During the German Occupation, 1940–1945; Repression, Terror and Resistance: The West Country of Norway, Ann Arbor: University Microfilms International, 1981, p. 485.

5. Elizabeth Aasen, "Vår nasjonale kulturarv" (Our national cultural heritage), Samtiden, Oslo, Vol. 90, No. 1, 1981, p. 76.

6. Harry Eckstein, Division and Cohesion in a Democracy. A Study of Norway, Princeton: Princeton University Press, 1966, p. 79.

7. Haakon Holmboe, "De som ble tatt" (Those who were caught), in Sverre Steen (ed.), Norges Krig (Norway's War), Oslo: Gydendal Norsk Forlag, 1950, Vol. III, p. 480.

8. Johan Vogt, Det store brennoffer. Jødenes skjebne under den annen verdenskrig (The Holocaust. The Fate of Jews During World War II), Oslo: Universitetsforlaget, 1966, pp. 14–15, 24.

9. Ragnar Ulstein, Svensketrafikken. I. Flyktningar til Sverige, 1940–1943 (Swedish Traffic. I. Refugees to Sweden, 1940–1943), Oslo: Det Norske Samlaget, 1974, p. 250.

10. Odd Nansen, From Day to Day, New York: Putnam, 1947, p. 171.

11. Arvid Brodersen, Mellom Frontene (Between the Fronts), Oslo: Cappelen, 1979, p. 68. A more detailed account is given by Professor Brodersen in an article, "Norsk kontakt med mennene bak Hitler–attentatat" (Norwegian Contact with the Men Behind the Attack on Hitler's Life), Farmand, Oslo, March 8, 1975, pp. 38–43.

12. Johns. Andenaes. O. Riste, and M. Skodvin, Norway and the Second World War, Oslo: Johan Grundt Tanum Forlag, 1966, p. 68.

13. Tore Gjelsvik, *Norwegian Resistance, 1940–1945,* London: C. Hurst and Company, 1979, p. 31.

14. George N. Kren and Leon Rappaport, "Resistance to the Holocaust: The Idea and the Act," in Yehudah Bauer and Nathan Rotenstreich (eds.), *The Holocaust as Historical Experience,* New York: Holms and Meier, 1981, p. 212.

15. *Straffesak mot Vidkun Abraham Lauritz Jonssøn Quisling,* Utgitt på offentlig bekostning av Eidsivating lagstols landssvikavdeling, (Court Proceedings Against Vidkun Abraham Lauritz Jonssøn Quisling), Oslo: 1946, p. 752. Hereafter referred to as *Quisling.*

16. Paul M. Haynes, *Quisling. The Career and Political Ideas of Vidkun Quisling, 1887–1945,* London: David and Charles, 1971, p. 103.

17. Tore Gjelsvik, *op. cit.,* p. 14.

18. Hans Frederik Dahl, Bernt Hagtvet, and Guri Hjeltnes, *Den norske nasjonalsosialismen. Nasjonal Samling, 1933–1945, i tekst og bilder* (Norwegian National Socialism. The National Union Party, 1933–1945, in Text and Pictures), Oslo: Pax Forlag, 1982, pp. 100, 151ff.

19. Haynes, op. cit., pp. 123–124.

20. Vidkun Quisling, *Kampen mellem arier og jødemakt. Tale i Frankfurt, 28. Mars 1941 om jødeproblemet* (The Fight Between Aryan and Jewish Power. Speech in Frankfurt about the Jewish Problem, March 28, 1941), Oslo: Nasjonal Samlings Rikstrykkeri, 1941, pp. 5ff.

21. Benjamin Vogt, "Quisling. The Man and the Criminal," *The American–Scandinavian Review,* XXXVI, No. 1, March 1948, p. 41.

22. Dag O. Bruknapp, "Idéene splitter partiet. Rasespørsmålets betydning i NS's utvikling" (The Ideas Split the Party. The Significance of Racial Questions in the Development of the National Union Party), in Rolf Danielsen and Stein Ugelvik Larsen (eds.), *Fra idé til dom. Noen trekk fra utviklingen av Nasjonal Samling* (From Idea to Sentencing. Some Aspects of the Development of the National Union Party), Oslo: Universitetsforlaget, 1978, pp. 26–27ff.

23. Haynes, op. cit., pp. 312–313.

24. See, for example, *Fritt Folk,* No. 72, 1941.

25. Bruknapp, *op. cit.,* p. 42.

26. Tomas Hammar, *Sverige at Svenskarna* (Swedes for Sweden), Stockholm: Calso Boktryckeri, 1964, pp. 367 and *passim.*

27. Sverre Hartmann, *Fører uten folk. Forsvarsminter Quisling — has bakgrunn og vei inn i norski politikk* (Leader Without People. Minister of Defense Quisling — His Background and Path to Norwegian Politics), Oslo: Tiden Norsk Forlag, 1970, p. 167.

28. Interview of Vidkun Quisling by Professor Hans Günther, author of *Die Rassenkunde Europas* (Race Knowledge of Europe), during the inauguration of the "Institute for the Exploration of the Jewish Question," Norwegian Broadcasting Tape No. 54319/2, March 1941.

29. *Strafsache gegen Hellmuth Reinhard* (Court Proceedings Against Hellmuth Reinhard) held in Baden–Baden, February 1, 1967, Yad Vashem Archives, Jerusalem, Doc. No. TR–10/608, p. 17.

30. Johs. Andenaes, *Det vanskelige oppgjøret. Rettsoppgjøret etter okkupasjonen. De offentlige tjenestemenn* (The Difficult Accounting. The Legal Accounting After the Occupation. The Civil Servants), Oslo: Tanum, 1979, pp. 47–48.

31. Oddvar Høidal, "Hjort, Quisling, and *Nasjonal Samling's* Disintegration," Scandinavian Studies, 1975, Vol. 47, No. 4, p. 467.

32. Magne Skodvin, *Kampen om Okkupasjonnstyret i Norge* (The Fight About the Occupation Regime in Norway), Oslo: Det Norske Samlaget, 1956, pp. 22ff.

33. Andenaes, Riste, and Skodvin, *op. cit.,* pp. 37–38.

34. Jacques Mordal, *La Campagne de Norvège. Preface du Général Weygand*, Paris: Self, 1949, p. 10.

35. Nils Ørvik, *The Decline of Neutrality, 1914–1941*, Oslo: Johan Grundt Tanum, 1953, p. 237.

36. International Military Tribunal, Vol. 28, Doc. 1809–PS, p. 406.

37. Magne Skodvin, "Norge i stormaktsstrategien: Fra Finlandsfreden til 'Wilfred' " (Norway in the Great Power Strategy. From the Peace in Finland to 'Wilfred'), in *Norge og den 2 verdenskrig: 1940, fra nøytral til okkupert* (Norway in the Second World War. 1940, From Neutral to Occupied), Oslo: Universitetsforlaget, 1969, p. 90.

38. Othar Lislegaard and Torbjørn Børte, *Skuddene som reddet Norge? Senkningen av "Blücher" 9. April 1940* (The Shots that Saved Norway? The Sinking of the "Blücher," April 9, 1940), Oslo: Aschenhoug, 1975,

39. Public Records Office, London, FO 371/24815/N3776/2/63 and N3990/2/63, reports from British Naval Attaché in Oslo and British Minister in Copenhagen, respectively.

40. Hans Frederik Dahl, *Dette er London. NRK i krig, 1940–1945* (This is London. Norwegian Broadcasting System During the War, 1940–1945), Oslo: Cappelen, 1978, pp. 61–62.

41. Brodersen, *op. cit.*, p. 27.

42. Curtis, *op cit.*, pp. 73–74.

43. *Quisling, op. cit.*, p. 42.

44. Monica Curtis (ed.), *Norway and the War, September 1939–December 1940*, London: Oxford University Press, 1941, pp. 78–79.

45. For text, see Curtis, *op. cit.*, p. 80.

46. For text, see *Ibid.*, pp. 140–141.

47. Chr. R. Christensen, *Vårt Folks Historie* (Our People's History), Vol. IX, Oslo: Aschehoug, 1961, p. 239.

48. Sverre Kjellstadli, *Hjemmestyrkene. Hovedtrekk av den militaere motstand under okkupasjonen* (The Home Front. Features of the Military Resistance Under Occupation), Vol. I, Oslo: Aschehoug, 1959, p. 20.

49. Hans-Dietrich Loock, *Quisling, Rosenberg und Terboven, Zur Vorgeschichte und Geschichte der nationalsozialistichen Revolution in Norwegen*, Stuttgart: Deutsche Verlags-Anstalt, 1970, pp. 546, 558–562.

50. Sverre Steen, "Riksrådforhandlingene" (Negotiations for an Occupation Settlement), in *Norge og den 2. verdenskrig, op. cit.*, p. 137.

51. Magne Skodvin, "Det store fremstøt" (The Great Advance), in Sverre Steen (ed.), *Norges Krig, op. cit.*, Vol. II.

52. Helge Paulsen, "Litt om forholdet mellom NS og Reichkommissariat i Norge 1940–1945" (Something About the Relationship Between NS and RK in Norway), in Danielsen and Larsen (eds.), *Fra idé til dom, op. cit.*, p. 205.

53. Finn Palmstrøm and Rolf Nordmann Torgersen, *Preliminary Reports on Germany's Crimes Against Norway*, Oslo: Grondahl & Son, 1945, p. 64.

54. Olav Riste and Berit Nøkleby, *Norway, 1940–45: The Resistance Movement*, Oslo: Johan Grundt Tanum Forlag, 1970, p. 58.

55. H. O. Christophersen, *Av nød til seir* (From Distress to Victory), Oslo: Grøndahl & Søn Forlag A/S, 1977, p. 184.

56. *Regjeringen og Hjemmefronten under krigen. Aktstykker utgitt av Stortinget* (The Government and the Home Front During the War. Documents Published by the Parliament), Oslo: Aschehoug and Co., 1948, p. 139.

57. *Ibid.*, No. 242, pp. 422–23.

58. Walter Laqueur, *The Terrible Secret Suppression of the Truth About Hitler's "Final Solution"*, Boston: Little Brown and Co., 1980, p. 6.

59. Terje Halvorsen, "Holocaust og de illegale avisene" (Holocaust and the Illegal Newspaper), *Dagbladet* (Daily News), July 18, 1977, quotes also from the illegal paper *Hjemmefronten* (The Home Front) which in January 1944 stated that "no one knows how many Jews have been murdered by the Hitler regime. The guess varies from 2.5 to 4 millions."

60. Kaare Haukaas, *Faktaregister for Okkupasjonen* (Factual Record of Events During the Occupation), Oslo, 1947, pp. 32–33. Mimeographed.

61. *Håndslag*, No. 14, December 3, 1942, p. 23.

62. Tor Dagre, *Nytt fra Norge* (News From Norway), November 23, 1981.

63. *London Radio*, December 4, 1942, p. 1.

64. Yitshak Arad, Yisrael Gutman and Abraham Margaliot, *Documents on the Holocaust, Selected Sources on the Destruction of the Jews of Germany and Austria, Poland and the Soviet Union*, Jerusalem: Yad Vashem, 1981, pp. 332–334.

65. Odd Bergfald, *Gestapo i Norge* (Gestapo in Norway), Oslo: Hjemmenes Forlag, 1978, p. 84.

66. *Protokoll for møter i det Administrasjonsråd som er oppnevnt av Høyesterett mandag den 15 April, 1940. År 1940 den 16, mai* (Minutes of Administrative Council, appointed by Supreme Court, Monday April 15, 1940. May 16, 1940), pp. 108, 115.

67. Magne Skodvin, "Det store fremstøt," *op. cit.,* p. 617. Examples: "Jødisk forretning!" (Jewish Store!), "Jøde!" (Jew!), "Lukket!" (Closed!), "Jødisk parasitt!" (Jewish Parasite!), "Palenstina kaller! Jøder tåles ikke i Norge!" (Palestine Calling! Jews Not Tolerated in Norway!).

68. Hans Jørgen Hurum, "Musikk under okkupasjonen" (Music During the Occupation), *Kultur Nytt* (Cultural News), Oslo, Vol. 7, No. 7, 1981, pp. 22–23.

69. For a sample of the letters sent to the Jewish lawyers, see the one addressed to Willy Rubinstein of Oslo on September 6, 1941, signed by Sverre Riisnaes and Reinhard Breien, Norwegian Dept. of Justice, Ref. No. 511/41.S. Norwegian Telegraphic Agency, Inc., Oslo.

70. Holmboe, "De som ble tatt," *op. cit.,* p. 450.

71. *Stempling av jøders legitimasjonsbevis* (Stamping of Identity Cards for Jews), January 10, 1942, from Chief of Security Police, Reference No. 5289/41A.

72. *Straffesak mot Wilhelm A. Wagner* (Court Proceedings Against W. A. Wagner), *Politiforklaring* (Declaration to the Police), July 25, 1945, pp. 23, 72. Hereafter referred to as *Wagner*.

73. *Norsk Lovtidend* (Norwegian Legal Gazette), March 12, 2nd Edition, Oslo: Grøndahl & Søn 1942, n.p.

74. *Afterposten*, March 14, 1942.

75. *Fritt Folk* (Free People, March 9, 1942.

76. Interview on July 4, 1981 with Mendel Bernstein, President, 1939–46, *Det Mosaiske Trosamfund* (The Mosaic Religious Society) of Oslo.

77. Arne Fjellbu, *Minner fra Krigsårene* (Memoires from the War Years), Oslo: Land of Kirke, 1945, p. 106.

78. Henrietta Samuel, *Eichmann Trial, District Court,* Jerusalem Criminal Case No. 40/61, November 5, 1961, p. N1.

79. Sverre Kjellstadli, *Hjemmestyrkene* (The Fighting Home Forces), Oslo: Aschehoug, 1959, pp. 166, 404.

80. The Jewish Cemetery in Trondheim has these memorials: "Shot in the Falstad Forest, November 13, 1942, during the German reign of terror: Herman Schidorsky, b. 1887;

Kalman Glick, b. 1877, Moritz Nevesetsky Abrahamsen, b. 1884. Buried here June 16, 1947." Abrahamsen was shot even though he was married to a nonJewish person. A separate memorial was erected for "Hirsch Kommisar, b. June 9, 1887, shot as a hostage by the Germans, October 7, 1942 in the Falstad Forest."

81. Asriel B. Hirsch, Testimony, *Quisling, op. cit.,* p. 159.

82. Bergfald, *op. cit.,* p. 255.

83. Harry Koritzinsky, *Jødene i Norge, 1940–1942. Redegjørelse avgitt i Stockholm, 30. november 1942* (The Jews in Norway, 1940–1942. Statement Given in Stockholm, November 30, 1942), p. 14. Mimeographed.

84. *Sveriges Forhällande till Danmark och Norge under krigsåren. Redogörelser avgivna till den svenska utrikesnämnden av ministern for utrikesärendena 1941–1945* (Sweden's Relation to Denmark and Norway During the War Years. Reports Given to the Swedish Committee of Foreign Affairs by the Minister of Foreign Affairs, 1941–1945), Stockholm: Nordstedts and Söner, 1945, p. 149.

85. *Wagner, op. cit.,* p. 71.

86. *Quisling, op. cit.,* p. 203.

87. Ullstein, *op. cit.,* p. 206. Among those arrested was Hermann Feldmann. His foster parents, Rakel and Jacob Feldman, fled in panic to the Løvestad farm, where they sought help in escaping to Sweden. The rescue party set out early on October 27 for the Swedish border; however, when the two pilots, Peder Pedersen and Haakon Løvestad reached *Skrikerud Pond,* they murdered the Feldmanns, stole their money and jewelry, and left their bodies in the pond. The bodies were not discovered until the following spring. Pedersen and Løvestad were not tried until 1947, when they were acquitted for murder and given only minor sentences for theft. They defended themselves by claiming that the Feldmann's would not have been able to reach Sweden because of their weakened condition and that the pilots had been afraid that if captured, the Feldmanns would reveal to the Gestapo the resistance routes to Sweden. The acquittal of Pedersen and Løvestad caused the greatest debate in the history of Norway's rettsoppgjør (legal accounting) after the war. See Ted Olson, "Death at Skrikerud Pond," *Harper's Magazine,* Vol. 206, No. 1236, May 1953, p. 70; *Yad Vashem Archives,* Doc. B/28–1, p. 10; Sigurd Senje, *Ekko fra Skriktjenn. En dokumentarroman basert pa "Feldmann–saken," 1942–47* (Echo from Skrik Pond. A Documentary Novel Based on the Feldmann Case, 1942–1947), Oslo: Pax Forlag, 1982; Even Stengelknoll, "Også vi tok livet av jøder" (We Also Killed Jews), *Dagbladet,* Oslo, August 4, 1947; Ingebjørg Sletten Fosstvedt, "Noen spørsmol til minelandsmenn om Feldmann–saken" (Some Questions for my Countrymen Regarding the Feldmann Case), *Dagbladet,* Oslo, September 4, 1947.

88. *Lov av 26 oktober 1942 om inndraging av formue som tilhører jøder . . . Denne lov trer i kraft straks* (The Law of October 26, 1942 regarding the confiscation of Jewish properties . . . This law is effective immediately), signed by Quisling, Hagelin, Sverre Riisnaes, and R. J. Fuglesang.

89. Oskar Mendelsohn, "Jøder i Norge" (Jews in Norway), in Hallvard Rieber–Mohn and Leo Eitinger (eds.), *Retten til å overleve. En bok om Israel, Norge og antisemittismen* (The Right to Survive. A Book About Israel, Norway and Anti–Semitism), Oslo: J. W. Cappelens Forlag, 1976, p. 80.

90. Time Greve, *Bergen i krig,* 1940–1942 (Bergen at War, 1940–42), Bergen: J. W. Eide Forlag, 1979, p. 256.

91. J. Wiermyhr, *Registering av jøder i Norge* (Registration of Jews in Norway), letter of October 27, 1942, Ref. No. 1205/42B, p. 1.

92. *Fritt Folk* (Free People), November 10, 1942.

93. *Rapport til Oslo Politikammer, Landssvikavdelingen: "Aksjonene* mot jødene" (Report to the Department of Collaborators, Oslo Precinct: Actions Against the Jews), submitted by Criminal Assistant Thorbjørn Frøberg and Knut Ebeling, Oslo, October 4, 1946, pp. 1–2.

94. Dag Tangen, "Norges krystallnatt 1942: 10 jøder i hver konvolutt" (Norway's Crystal Night. Ten Jews in Every Envelope), *Dagbladet,* Oslo, April 4, 1979, May 28, 1979.

95. *Rettslige Forklaringer fra hjemvendte norske jøder* (Legal Dispositions by Returning Norwegian Jews), Testimony, February 26, 1946, Oslo, Department of Justice and Police, May 20, 1947, p. 17.

96. Frøberg and Ebeling, *Rapport til Oslo Politikammer, op. cit.,* p. 4. They note that the questionnaires and lists of names and addresses used for the roundup and arrests were prepared and printed by Norwegians.

97. Ernest Aberle, *Vi må ikke glemme* (We Must Not Forget), Oslo: Cappelen, 1980, p. 44; see also, Carl Haave and Sverre J. Herstad, "Redselsnatten" (The Night of Horror) in *Quislings Hønsegard, Berg Interneringsleir* (Quisling's Chicken Coup. Berg Internment Camp), Oslo: Alb. Cammermeyer Forlag, 1948, pp. 29–30.

98. H. O. Christophersen, "Akjonen mot jødene. Okkupasjonens tyngste slag" (The Actions Against Jews. The Heaviest Blow During the Occupation), *Afterposten* (Evening Edition), October 23, 1967.

99. Arne Skouen, "Ytring" (Remarks), *Dagbladet,* Oslo, April 6, 1979.

100. *Risadvokatens Meddelsesblad* (Supreme Court Decision), L.nr. 187, S.nr. 669/1946; Case Against Wilhelm A. K. Wagner, p. 26.

101. Instructions from the State Police, Oslo and Aker Precincts, November 25, 1942.

102. Holmboe, "De som ble tatt," *op. cit.,* Vol. III, p. 480.

103. Leni Yahil, "Scandinavian Countries to the Rescue of Concentration Camp Prisoners," *Yad Vashem Studies,* Jerusalem, VI, 1967, p. 219.

104. Report from Norwegian State Police of November 27, 1942, by K. A. Marthinsen. Document R.I.06644, *Eidsivating Lagstol, Lanssvikavdelingen* (Eidsivating Court, Department of Collaborators), *Evakuering av jøder* (Evacuation of Jews), pp. 1–6.

105. Marthinsen, *op. cit.,* pp. 5–6.

106. Frøberg and Ebeling, *op. cit.,* pp. 203.

107. Bengt Jerneck, *Folket uten frykt, Norge 1942–43* (The People Without Fear, Norway, 1942–43), Oslo: Johan Grundt Tanum, 1945, p. 30.

108. Willy Brandt, "Jøderpogromene i Norge oktober–november 1942" (The Jewish Pogroms in Norway, October–November 1942), in *Fram Norsk Magasin* (Forward Norwegian Magazine), London, July 24, 1943.

109. A. Skouen, "Ytring" (Remarks), *Dagbladet,* Oslo, August 20, 1973.

110. "Kai Feinberg — norsk jøde i Auschwitz" (Kai Feinberg–Norwegian Jews in Auschwitz), *Dagbladet,* Oslo, February 24, 1979.

111. *Hefte von Auschwitz,* 1960, Vol. 3, p. 104: "December 1, 1942. RSHA Transport, Juden aus Bergen (sic) Norwegen"

112. T. Friedmann, *Dokumentsammlung über Die Deportierung der Juden aus Norwegen nach Auschwitz,* Stadt-Verwaltung Ramat Gan, Israel, 1963, p. 13.

113. Herman Sachnowitz, *Det angår også deg* (It Concerns Also You), Oslo: Cappelen, 1976, pp. 51–53.

114. *Quislingsaken. Samlet Rettsreferat* (The Case Against Quisling. Complete Legal Accounting), Oslo: A/S Bokkomisjon, 1945, p. 131.

115. *Quisling, op. cit.,* p. 23.

116. *Fritt Folk,* Oslo, December 7, 1942.

117. From *The Verdict of December 22, 1948 of Hilldis Neegard Østbye, Oslo Byrett* (The Court of the Municipality of Oslo), pp. 1, 2.

118. Hilberg, *op. cit.*, p. 355.

119. Friedmann, *op. cit.*, p. I.

120. Einar Molland, "Kirkens Kamp" (The Fight of the Church), in Steen (ed.), *op. cit.*, Vol. III, p. 36.

121. *Norsk Tidend* (Norwegian News), London, published by the Information Office, Royal Norwegian Government, November 26, 1942.

122. Personal communication by Pastor Johs. J. Duin of the Hamar Bishopric, dated February 22, 1982.

123. Letter of November 10, 1942 from Bishop Mangers to Professor Ole Hallesby. See also, Torleiv Austad, *Kirkens Grunn. Analyse av en kirkelig bekjennelse fra okkupashonstiden 1940–45* (The Foundation of the Church. Analysis of an Ecclesiastical Confession from the Occupation 1940–45), Oslo: Luther Forlag, 1974, pp. 19–20.

124. Ferdinand Schjeldrup, *På Bred Front* (On a Broad Front), Oslo: Grøndahl and Søns Forlag, 1947, p. 301.

125. *Anlage 120 zum Tätigkeitbericht December 1942 Abt Ic Niederschrift Über die Ic–Besprechung beim AOK Norwegen in der Zeit vom 8.–11.12 1942: 1. Tag 8.12 1942.*

126. *Quislingsaken, op. cit.*, pp. 170–171.

127. Julius Paltiel, "Seks ganger på dødens terskel" (Six Times on the Threshold of Death), in Hans Melien (ed.), *De kjempet for vår frihet* (They Fought for Our Freedom), Oslo: Aschehoug, 1979, p. 57.

128. Det Mosaiske Trossamfunn (The Mosaic Religious Society), *Våre falne norske jøder* (Our Fallen Norwegian Jews), Oslo, n.d., pp. 2,36, in *Vad Vashem Archives*, B/28–1.

129. Leo Eitinger, "On Being a Psychiatrist and a Survivor," in Alvin H. Rosenfeld and Irving Greenberg (eds.), *Confronting the Holocaust, The Impact of Elie Wiesel*, Bloomington: Indiana University Press, 1978, p. 189.

130. Oskar Mendelsohn, "Jødene i Norge" (The Jews in Norway), in Egil A. Wyller and Terje Gudbrandson (eds.), *Jødene og jødedommen. Fra det gamle testamente til Midt–Østen konflikten* (Jews and Judaism. From the Old Testament to the Conflict in the Middle East), Oslo–Bergen–Tromsø: Universitetsforlaget, 1977, p. 84.

131. Martin Gilbert, *Atlas of the Holocaust,* Map 46: "The Jews of Norway Living at the Time of the German Invasion," Jerusalem: Steinmatsky, 1982: Finnmark (7), Troms (22), Nordland (13), Nord-Trøndelag (1), Sør-Trøndelag (227), Møre (34), Opland (3), Hedemark (14), Buskerud (25), Telemark (5), Bergen (27), Rogaland (10), Vest–Agder (4), Aust–Agder (1), Vestfold (50), Oslo (749), Akerhus (134), and Østfold (38).

132. *Encyclopedia Judaica*, "Norway: Holocaust Period," Jerusalem–New York: MacMillan Publishing Co., 1971, Vol. 12, p. 1224.

133. Huge Valentin, "Rescue and Relief Activities on Behalf of Jewish Victims of Nazism in Scandinavia," *YIVO Annual of Jewish Social Science*, New York, 1953, Vol. III, p. 234.

134. *Jødisk Meninghetsblad for Det Mosaiske Trossamfund, Oslo og Trondheim* (Jewish Journal for the Mosaic Religious Community, Oslo and Trondheim), Vol. 2, No. 3, December 1977, pp. 13–32: "Yad Vashem–medalje til våre redningsmenn' (Yad Vashem Medal to Our Rescuers). The Vad Vashem medal is given to nonJews who endangered their own lives to save Jews from the Nazi persecutions.

IV REACTIONS TO THE HOLOCAUST

6 IN HISTORY'S "MEMORY HOLE": THE SOVIET TREATMENT OF THE HOLOCAUST

William Korey

History and Historiography in the Soviet Union

Historical writing in the Soviet Union, in the words of George Orwell, is a "process of continuous alteration" with the past "brought up to date" to conform to the current Communist Party line. Each modification in the Party line required the elimination of previous histories. Events and personages disappeared or were completely reinterpreted and distorted. Half truths and even total fabrications became commonplace, especially if the historical subject was the recent past. The Bolshevik Revolution, together with events leading up to it and flowing from it, were marked by endless official revisions.

A critical subject ineluctably re-examined and "brought up to date" was World War II. How was the historian to explain the Nazi–Soviet Non-Aggression Pact, or the initial victory of the Nazi armies, or the collaboration of some Soviet nationalities with the Hitlerian invaders, or the imperial subjugation or acquisition by the USSR of non-Soviet territories in Eastern Europe? The initial focus was Great Russian chauvinist patriotism which flowed from the notorious "anti–cosmopolitan" cam-

145

paign, itself linked to anti–Semitism. The glorious Motherland of Soviet Russia must be lauded even as the historian's function inevitably had to be oriented to resisting "all attempts to belittle the significance of our national history." Nor would the disclosures by Nikita Khrushchev about the "cult of personality" weaken the pointedly xenophobic emphasis. Events and the personages might be falsified but the thrust was to remain the same.

The corollary to Great Russian nationalism, as it had been during the Tsars, was destined to be anti–Semitism. Anti–cosmopolitanism and anti–Zionism required the removal of the Jew from Russian history, where he had played a prominent role culturally and intellectually. Indeed, his presence was to be erased from world history while the State of Israel, whether in the ancient or contemporary world, required denigration if not elimination. The pulverization of Jewish identity in history could not but exert a profound impact upon the treatment of the Holocaust.

The official Soviet attempt to erase the entire Jewish past is remarkably revealed in an episode related by Pulitzer Prize winner Arthur Miller, following a visit to the USSR. A prominent Soviet author had written a children's book entitled *The Story of the Bible*. The editors, though enthusiastic about the book, were unhappy with the author's treatment of certain concepts, such as God and Jewish people. As the editors put it, "God is a mythological construction, and in any strict sense mentioning God is really unnecessary." But what disturbed the editors even more than the reference to God were the repeated comments about the Jewish people. "Why is that necessary?" the editors asked. When the author began to answer that "the Bible, you see is . . . ," he was cut off with the following:

> Why not simply call them "the People"? After all, it comes to the same thing, and in fact it generalizes and enhances the significance of the whole story. Call them "the People".

Not only was the title changed to read *Myths of the People,* but the Jews suddenly, as if by magic, disappeared as an historical entity. They had been plunged down the memory hole of history.

This episode was no isolated incident. A close study of the history textbooks published since 1966 and used in the Russian Republic's elementary and secondary schools reveal that Jews are virtually invisible in Russian history or in world history. Not only are Jews rarely referred to, Jewish culture is never treated and the contribution of Jews to civilization is completely neglected. Both ancient and present day Israel, if mentioned at all, are discussed in a highly critical and condescending manner.

As disturbing as the neglect of Jews and Jewish culture as positive phenomena is the almost complete indifference to anti–Semitism as a negative factor in Russian and world history. Even the anti–Semitic racism of the Nazi epoch is understated.

It was insufficient to blot out the Jewish past from history textbooks. Pressing deeply upon the memory of every Jewish family was the trauma of the Nazi Holocaust, the greatest tragedy ever inflicted upon the Jewish people throughout its long history. Moreover, there was hardly a Jewish family in Soviet Russia that was spared the consequences of Hitler's genocidal plans. Expunging the Holocaust from the record of the past was hardly a simple matter, but unless it were done the profound anguish of the memory was certain to stir a throbbing national consciousness. Martyrdom, after all, is a powerful stimulus to a group's sense of its own identity.

How the Soviet authorities dealt with the Holocaust can be ascertained by examining five key indices: 1. Soviet textbooks; 2. Other scholarly and popular Soviet books; 3. the response to the historic Black Book of Nazi crimes; 4. Soviet press treatment of the Eichmann case; and 5. the official handling of Babi Yar.

History, as a separate subject in the USSR, begins in the fourth grade when the Soviet child is about eleven years of age. The standard fourth grade work for the Russian Republic covers in elementary fashion all of Russian history. Since the fifties, this textbook, in various editions, has not referred to Jews at all. Nor is anti–Semitism mentioned even when the authors have dealt with the Nazi invasion of the USSR and its occupation of critical Western Soviet areas. The current text, written by T. S. Golubeva and L. S. Gellershtein, contains an entire chapter of thirty pages devoted to World War II. Not a single reference to either Jews or anti–Semitism appears.

The contemporary history syllabus used in the upper and final two grades in secondary school — ninth and tenth grades — provides extensive discussion of the Nazi epoch. The syllabus is divided into two periods, 1917–39 and 1939 to the present. Much of the focus of the first period centers on the rise of Fascism in the interwar years. Strikingly, no reference is made to anti–Semitism as a core feature of Nazi ideology and practice. Indeed, a "Manual on the Methodology of Teaching Contemporary History" excludes totally the word and the concept of anti–Semitism, along with examples of Nazi persecution of Jews.

The standard textbooks covering these periods were prepared since the 1970s under the editorship of V. K. Furaev. The work embracing the interwar period devotes 18 out of 112 pages — a fairly sizeable amount — to

Germany. Mindboggling is the fact that anti–Semitism was completely excluded from the description of the Fascist dictatorship is defined as the "dictatorship of the most reactionary, the most chauvinistic and imperialist elements of finance capital," but whether this definition has any relationship to Jews or to Jewish persecution or extermination is left completely unanswered. Instead, almost by accident, the textbooks in a section dealing with terror and violence spoke of terrible Jewish pogroms. But such acts were by no means perceived as integrated into Nazi policy.

One of the more curious features of the volume is the fact that it gave emphasis to one of the Nazis' more notorious slogans: "Down with Jewish Finance Capital." Since this slogan was left unexplained and came just prior to the reference to Jewish pogroms, young readers might assume that the latter constitute justifiable retribution. Significantly, earlier editions of this work carried the Nazi slogan "Down with the Capitalist Plunderers." The provocatory slogan about Jewish capitalists had not been used.

The Furaev textbook on the second period of contemporary history contains 25 pages devoted to World War II. The Nazi invasion of various European countries together with their brutal occupation policies are closely examined. Yet not a single word is said about the massacre of Jews, even when Auschwitz is discussed. Nor is there reference to the Warsaw Ghetto Uprising.

During earlier periods, the distinctive Jewish trauma of the Nazi epoch did appear in several popular and scholarly works. In the course of the war books appeared written by V. V. Struve, G. Aleksandrov and S. Adamov, which had sympathetically alerted the reader to the Jewish plight and the Holocaust. Several volumes during the sixties performed the same function: V. Kral's *Crime Against Europe* (1963); G. L. Rozanov's *Germany under Fascism* (1964); and William Dodd's *Diary of an Ambassador* (1961). None of these volumes are obtainable in Soviet bookstores.

Instead of such types of analytic studies, the USSR in 1972 published a grossly distorted portrait of Nazism by M. S. Gus' entitled *The Madness of the Swastika*. It was clear that the Kremlin warmed to his thesis for the volume, 400 pages long, was published in an edition of 100,000 copies. That thesis carried crude anti–Semitic overtones. Thus, Gus' declared that many of the Nazi leaders were either one–half or completely Jewish or that Jewish bankers were among Nazi benefactors. According to Gus', the principal racial targets of the Nazis were Slavs and Negroes, not Jews. The obscene inversion of thought and morality was made palpably evident when he described a displaced person's camp which he personally visited and where he saw well–fed Jewish young survivors.

A major bibliographical study of Russian publications on Jews indicates that the blackout of the Holocaust in historical works was initiated at the end of 1948 when all Soviet Jewish institutions were closed. Prior to the curtain descending upon Jewish communal life, Soviet authorities did permit the publication in Russian of two books dealing with the Holocaust: one concerned Jewish resistance in the Minsk ghetto and the other discussed Jewish partisans.

The Jewish anti–Fascist Committee had planned to publish, in 1948, *The Black Book*, which was to include memorials and documents on the destruction of Soviet Jewry. It was never to see the light of day in the USSR and a blanket of silence would now envelop the Holocaust. The silence was broken only twice in the fifties and sixties with a Russian translation of *The Diary of Anne Frank* and a similar story by a girl who lived in the Vilna ghetto. A far more significant exception was the novel *Heavy Sand*, written by Anatoly Rybakov and published in 1978 in three large installments in the conservative journal, *Oktyabr* (October). It is an eloquent portrayal of the suffering and resistance of Jews in a Ukrainian town during the World War II culminating in their destruction. Only one printing was allowed, and, since then, the subject faded from public view.

The Soviet Authorities and The Black Book

The Black Book merits special attention. Indeed, the Kremlin's reaction to its planned publication in 1948 was the clearest indication of official Soviet determination to obliterate thoroughly all written traces of the specific Jewish suffering, of the horrendous trauma of this ancient people during the Holocaust. *The Black Book* was conceived by Ilya Ehrenburg and Vassily Grossman, another Jewish writer who, like Ehrenburg, served as a frontline correspondent for Soviet newspapers during the war. Their aim was monumental in character: to capture in documentary form through eyewitness accounts of letters, diaries and firsthand reports both the martyrdom of some two million Jews in dozens of towns and cities on Soviet territory and of the heroism of the Jewish partisan and resistance movement.

For Ehrenburg, it was to be a labor of love and devotion to which he gave an extraordinary amount of "time, strength and heart," as he related in his diary. The Nazi brutalities toward Jews moved him very deeply, indeed, roused, like nothing else ever did, every fiber in his being. He would later re–read the letters and diaries that went into the book and the deadly impact they exerted upon him. His recollection had an overpowering character: "I don't understand how we (Jews) lived through this and how we retained the strength to live." What was immensely disturbing was the realization that the Holocaust could be perpetrated in the twentieth century by inhabitants of a civilized country.

The book, Ehrenburg believed, would be more than merely a documentary account of a historic tragedy. It would offer the world, through the vastness of its canvas and the uniqueness of the horrors experienced by Jews, a guarantee that a repetition of the trauma would never recur. If the work was perceived as an exorcism of a horrendous evil, it was also seen as endowed with powerful enlightenment features.

Ehrenburg and Grossman, as early as 1943, began assembling the invaluable documentation utilizing the service of journalists working for military newspapers who were among the first to enter the liberated areas along with advance units. Additional material was provided by the legal branch of the military and individual officers and soldiers at the front. Of particular significance, the project won the cooperation of 27 very distinguished Soviet writers (mostly Jewish, a few nonJewish), in addition to the compilers. Each assumed responsibility for documenting a specific massacre, like Babi Yar or heroic act like the Warsaw Ghetto uprising, and assembling and editing the material appropriate to the section.

A total of sixty–five reports were incorporated in the massive volume which would run to 1200 typescript pages. Ehrenburg himself prepared 18 of them, testifying to his zealous commitment to the project. He would later recall how the diaries, letters, and eyewitness testimony would personalize the tragedy for him. "It seemed to me," he wrote, "that I was in the ghetto . . . and they were driving me towards the ravine or ditch." The plan was to have the massive volume translated into many languages. The compilers urgently wanted the world to know the dimensions of the tragedy as well as the heroism of a beleaguered and cornered people.

Grossman wrote the Foreword which, despite evident self–censorship and careful editing, is nonetheless remarkable for the honesty and integrity of the broad picture he paints. His central point, pressed determinedly, in numerous passages, is that the driving force of Hitlerism is anti–Semitic racism. Grossman traced the evolution of anti–Jewish bigotry in Germany and Austria over the previous century and showed how it impacted upon the population leading to the Nuremberg laws and ultimately to the acceptance of barbarities thought inconceivable in the modern world. In a comprehensive analysis of the theory and the practise of anti–Semitism, Grossman did not waver in depicting the techniques of annihilation extending to the gas chambers and crematoria.

Later of course the Grossman notion accepted by Western scholarship, that anti–Semitism was intrinsic to Hitlerism would be completely rejected and repudiated by Soviet authorities. Indeed, as the more recent history textbooks reveal, anti–Semitism was totally expunged from the record of Nazism, incredible as this may appear. Even at the time of the book's preparation, Grossman was having difficulties. His initial draft of the Foreword was scrapped. Clearly, a form of self–censorship, if not open censorship was apparent. Stalin was lauded by Grossman not only as the "genius liberator" but as a fighter against anti–Semitism. Even more striking was the absence from the entire work of any reference to Ukrainian and Lithuanian collaborators with Nazism, a subject which is known to have aroused the deepest anger of Ehrenburg and about which he wrote with considerable passion in his memoirs.

Neither the caution nor the censorship saved *The Black Book*. According to Ehrenburg, the manuscript was completed as early as the beginning of 1944. But by then, as Ehrenburg's memoirs record, "something had changed" with regard to discussing the Jewish issue. An assistant to Alexander Shcherbakov, a high Party official who was in charge of ideological indoctrination in the armed forces, told Ehrenburg that the latter's draft of a message to American Jews should not mention the exploits of Soviet Jews in the Red Army. When Ehrenburg protested to Shcherbakov, the Party leader sharply noted: "The soldiers want to hear about Suvorov while you quote Heine."

Still neither Ehrenburg nor Grossman were prepared to give up hope. The printing of their book was done in 1946. Yet not a single copy reached state libraries let alone bookstores. The entire edition was taken directly from the printing plant to warehouses. Toward the end of 1948 with Stalin engaged in a large-scale, orchestrated effort to liquidate every vestige of Jewishness in the USSR, including all its institutional forms, the books were destroyed along with the original type molds.

Many connected with the preparation of *The Black Book* were later linked to crimes against the state and sentenced to prison terms. Ehrenburg's memoirs indicate that dozens of sentences were imposed for imaginary crimes of which *The Black Book* was apparently one.

Fortuitous circumstances have enabled Yad Vashem in Israel to publish the original version of this outstanding contribution to Holocaust literature. An English translation was published in 1981 by the Holocaust Library in New York. Apparently, unbeknownst to anyone, a copy of the work arrived in Palestine in 1946. It was sent by the sponsor of the book, the Jewish Anti–Fascist Committee of Moscow, to the Palestine based League to strengthen Cultural Relationships with the Soviet Union. For reasons that remain unexplained, the manuscript was not discovered until May, 1965 when Shlomo Zirulnikov, a former League member, brought it to Yad Vashem. Soviet Jews, in time, may have access to an epoch making publication. It will fill in a huge and throbbing gap in their consciousness.

The Treatment of Eichmann's Capture and Trial

Particularly illuminating was the manner in which the Adolf Eichmann capture and trial was treated in the Soviet mass media. He was the veritable symbol of the Nazi murder machine and his capture by the Israelis, in the Spring of 1960, after fifteen years of hiding, brought forth an extraordinary amount of world attention. A detailed study of the Soviet press and radio coverage offers an unusual insight into the policy of Soviet leaders on the Holocaust. Prior to the opening of the trial on April 11, 1961, Soviet coverage of the case was marked first by relative paucity, then by an emphasis upon an alleged relationship between Eichmann's crimes and the then rulers of the Federal Republic of Germany, and finally by a general minimization of Eichmann's crimes against Jews as compared with his crimes against people generally.

Vechernaia Moskva (Evening Moscow), on June 7, 1960 published the first substantial Soviet account of the capture of the Nazi leader. A lengthy description of Eichmann as "one of the most bloodthirsty hangmen of Fascist Germany" was accompanied by an accusation that German Chancellor Konrad Adenauer was sympathetic to Nazism and permitted "yesterday's assistants of Hitler, Himmler and Kaltenbrunner" to occupy leading posts in West Germany. No mention was made of Jews. Instead the article spoke of "six million shot, burned in gas chambers." *Pravda* (Truth) on April 8, 1961 — three days before the opening of the trial — used the Eichmann case as a peg for a wideranging attack upon West Germany's leaders. In the course of this lengthy article, not once did the word Jew appear. Eichmann was identified as the "killer of millions" or as one "who exterminated millions of men, women and children in the furnaces of. . . .Hitlerite death camps." The opening of the Eichmann trial in Jerusalem on April 11 was marked in the Soviet press by silence. Neither *Pravda* nor *Izvestiia* (News) on that day carried any reference to the historic occasion.

In striking contrast to the Soviet mass media was the extent and character of the coverage of the Eichmann case in the mass media of Poland, Hungary and Czechoslovakia. As in the West, the press of these Communist countries provided frequent and extensive coverage of both the capture and the trial, with an extraordinary amount of background reporting added. Feature articles and editorials accompanied the newspaper stories. Significantly, the mass media of both Poland and Hungary gave emphasis to the theme of Jewish martyrdom. Even when criticism was directed against the West German government, stress was repeatedly placed on the Jewish Holocaust.

The Soviets and the Babi Yar Massacres

The Soviet attempt to obliterate the Holocaust in the memories of Jews, as well as nonJews, becomes especially pronounced in the method chosen to erase from the historical record Babi Yar, the site and symbol of Soviet Jewry's greatest single tragedy during the Nazi era. Almost from the beginning, Soviet authorities sought to blur this record. The official governmental report on the massacre, six months after Kiev's liberation, spoke of Nazi crimes against Soviet citizens generally rather than against Jews specifically.

Plans had been advanced for a monument to be built at Babi Yar. A well-known architect, A. V. Vlasov, had designed a memorial — "strict, simple, in the form of a prism," — and the artist, B. Ovchinnikov, had worked out appropriate sketches "dedicated to Babi Yar." But these plans were quietly shelved. And in March 1949, a Ukrainian–Jewish poet Savva Golovanivsky, who had written sympathetically about the victims at Babi Yar was denounced for "defamation of the Soviet nation." For over a decade, Babi Yar was blanketed in silence. While references to it simply did not appear in the public press, city officials in Kiev quietly advanced proposals to flood the site, then fill it and turn it into a park on which a stadium would be erected.

The proposals prompted sensitive intellectuals, encouraged by a broadening thaw, especially in literature, to react with revulsion. Viktor Nekrasov wrote in *Literaturnaia Gazeta* (Literary Journal) on October 10, 1959:

> Is this possible? Who could have thought of such a thing? To fill a . . .deep ravine and on the site of such a colossal tragedy to make merry and play football?

A much larger community, extending far beyond Soviet borders, was to be stirred by Yevgeny Yevtushenko in September 1961, almost twenty years to the day after the Babi Yar tragedy. In a poem recited to 1200 students in Moscow on September 16 and published three days later in *Literaturnaia Gazeta*, Yevtushenko bewailed the fact that "no monument stands over Babi Yar," a site which he deliberately presented as a link in a chain of major historical episodes of Jewish martyrdom. The official response was not long in coming. The poem was severly chastised by two prominent literary ideologists, Aleksei Markov and Dmitri Starikov, within eight days of its appearance. The latter specifically challenged the view that Babi Yar was "one of history's examples of anti–Semitism." The issue was taken up by no less an authority than the Party boss, Premier Nikita S. Khrushchev. At a conference of writers and artists held in the Kremlin on March 7–8, 1963, he declared:

> Events are depicted in the poem as if only the Jewish population fell victim to the Fascist crime, while (in fact) at the hands of the Hitlerite butchers there perished not a few Russians, Ukrainians, and other Soviet peoples of other nationalities.

Yevtushenko — Khrushchev contended — had displayed an "ignorance of historical facts."

The assault upon the Soviet poet was extended to Dmitri Shostakovich whose Thirteenth Symphony, in part, constituted a musical and chorale setting for Yevtushenko's Babi Yar. The symphony was first performed on December 18, 1962 and was accorded a tumultuous reception by the audience. But no review would appear in the major press organs. Only one day earlier, the top party ideologist, Leonid Ilyichev, had told an assemblage of party leaders and leading Soviet intellectuals that Shostakovich had chosen an undesirable theme for his symphony. A critic writing in a Minsk newspaper, on April 2, 1963, was to denounce the symphony for elevating "a petty incident to the rank almost of national tragedy."

A slight easing of political controls in literature in the summer of 1966 permitted the publication of the novel *Babi Yar* by Anatoly Kuznetsov in the pages of the liberal journal, *Yunost'* (Youth). The response was similar to that evoked by the Yevtushenko poem. As recalled by Kuznetsov:

> There was an unpublicized row over "Babi Yar". They suddenly decided that it ought not to have been published. At *Yunost'* they told me that it was practically an accident that it had ever appeared at all and that a month later its publication would have been out of the question. In any case they forbade the reprinting of it.

The final word on the novel was given in August 1967, by a Soviet military journal, *Sovetskii Voin* (Soviet Soldier). The work was declared to be unhistorical and offensive. Babi yar was by no means a Jewish tragedy: instead, those buried at the site are "Russians, Ukrainians, and other nations."

Those who dared suggest publicly that Babi Yar was symbolic of the

Holocaust faced jail sentences. In 1969, a young Jewish radio engineer of Kiev, Boris Kochubievsky was placed on trial, in part, for declaring at a Babi Yar memorial service: "Here lies part of the Jewish people." Together with other utterances of a similar nature, this assertion led to Kochubievsky's conviction of the crime of slander and to a sentence of three years in a labor camp.

A memorial was finally erected at Babi Yar in the summer of 1976. But it was scarcely the one hoped for by Soviet Jews and demanded by Yevtushenko and his associates among the Soviet intelligentsia. Fifty feet high and rising from the edge of the ravine, the huge bronze monument built at a cost of nearly $2 million contains nothing that even remotely suggests the Jewish agony. In the form of a frieze, the sculpture includes eleven distinctive figures, none of which is symbolic of Jewry. Instead, like dozens of other Soviet memorials which dot Eastern Europe from the Brandenburg Gate to the Urals, the frieze highlights the positive heroes. As characterized by a *Novosti (News)* blurb: "Proudly raising their heads, implacable and unconquered, the imprisoned soldier and the partisan are struck by the volley of bullets. Even in their last moments, they terrify the enemy with their hatred."

At the base of the memorial is an inscription which makes no reference to the Jewish trauma. It reads: "Here in 1941–43, the German Fascist invaders executed over 100,000 citizens of Kiev and prisoners of war." The veritable total effacement of Babi Yar as a symbol of the Holocaust was breached but once. Inexplicably, in October 1980, the Moscow Jewish Drama Ensemble was allowed to perform at a tiny theater an original play about Babi Yar, entitled *Ladies' Tailor* by Aleksandr Borshchagovsky. Powerful and moving, the play was permitted only a one week run. But that was an exception. A new Soviet Ukrainian 70-minute documentary film about Babi Yar mentions Jews but once. In the same film, Zionists are equated with Nazis.

Even the *Kaddish*, the traditional prayer for the dead, can no longer be said by Soviet Jews over their martyred relatives. On May 3, 1981 several hundred Moscow Jews had planned to hold a memorial service commemorating the Holocaust in a forest twenty-five miles east of Moscow, KGB officials told a Jewish activist: "We will not tolerate them any longer."

While this memorial service was called off, in the following week another group of over 100 Jewish persons braved the hostile official attitude and gathered at the Moscow forest site. Police units broke up and dispersed the group and arrested one of its leaders, Boris Chernobilsky, on charges of assaulting a member of the militia.

At Babi Yar, on the occasion of its 40th anniversary (September 29–30,

1981), the official reaction was the same. No assemblages, no memorial services. Moscow Jews planning to make the journey to Kiev were threatened with arrest. Five who were adamant in their determination to say the prayer over the dead were arrested by KGB and convicted. Only four persons broke through to the memorial. They were permitted to place a wreath at the site. Nothing more.

George Santayana once taught that he who chooses not to recall the past is doomed to relive it. Soviet Jews have chosen to recall the past. Babi Yar and the Holocaust as memory and martyrology cannot be erased. It remains a throbbing element of Jewish consciousness with its trauma seared into the very souls of Soviet Jews. Some day, they are convinced, they will be able to tell the story to their children and their children's children.

7 CONFRONTING GENOCIDE: THE DEPICTION OF THE PERSECUTION OF THE JEWS AND THE HOLOCAUST IN WEST GERMAN HISTORY TEXTBOOKS

Walter F. Renn

Introduction

Dieter Bossman's book, *What I have heard about Adolf Hitler*, caused an immediate sensation when it appeared in 1977, revealing once again the depths of confusion, ignorance and distorted images German young people had about events in the Third Reich. A few excerpts from the section "Persecution of the Jews" will indicate the anti–Semitic attitudes which continue to prevail among some students:[1]

> Kirsten, age 16; Adolf Hitler was himself a Jew and was mocked by everyone.
>
> Maria, age 17; It is assumed that his mother was a Jewess.
>
> Otto, age 16; He freed Germany of the Jews. In all the larger businesses there was a Jew. The Germans were oppressed.
>
> Ute, age 16; Concentration camps were later constructed where the Jews were gassed. The Jews were warned long beforehand, however, and told that they should emigrate.
>
> Hubertus, age 19; In order to get a pure race, they didn't have to resort to concentration camps right away. He could certainly have thought of something

157

that was not so 'gruesome.' Surely he could have given out Jewish expulsions from the German Reich.

Thomas, age 15; He ordered the following judgment: all Jews on the streets after 8 o'clock would simply be shot. (The worst was, that they didn't have watches!)

Joachim, age 18; The Jews had to be removed. Since no one wanted to admit them, not even Roosevelt himself, who was a Jew, they had to be killed.

Renate, age 15; I think about the Jews. He surely could have found another way to kill them.

Hanspeter, age 16; Adolf Hitler was right to do away with the Jews.

Frank, age 15; Aryan Race–German — Negroes, Jews–Animals.

Dietmar, age 15; He dismissed the Jews by way of the chimney. The Jews could perish in gas chambers. Some were allowed to take part in athletics. The Russians were permitted to play football, and the Jews were allowed to play leap–frog in minefields.

Heike, age 18; Even so, the people still inherited the problem with the Jews, who now meanwhile make their claims exclusively from a financial standpoint.

Thomas, age 17; Hitler also had the Jews killed, because he wanted to have only Germans in his Empire. If we didn't have so many foreigners today, there would be more jobs open.

There are, of course, many counterexamples by other young people in this revealing book, which show strong anguish and sympathy for Jewish victims of Germany and rejection of the Nazi regime. Significantly, though, only two students out of the 300 responses in this chapter held the German people responsible for the deeds of the Holocaust. The Bossmann book only confirms that German history texts have not yet succeeded in one of their self-proclaimed tasks, that of educating students to value tolerance and toward overcoming ethnic and religious prejudices.[2]

Such public events as Bossmann's book lead naturally to renewed concern with the teaching of history and the history textbooks of West Germany. The Federal Republic, of course, is highly sensitive about the content of its Holocaust educational program, which raises special pedagogical problems and challenges for the German education system. At the same time, many Germans have made clear their commitment to coming to grips with the National Socialist era, and have taken the initiative in correcting errors, prejudices and misrepresentations in their nation's textbooks.[3]

While it is no easy task to separate the influence of textbooks from other socialization processes, such as those of the family, peers, the church and the mass media, it is postulated here that textbooks, along with other factors, have a substantial and important role in shaping young persons' attitudes towards other peoples. As Margarete Dörr has written, "in view of the large numbers (of textbooks) printed and the intensity of their use, textbooks may be considered as belonging to the most influential of all books."[4] Indeed, a successful German textbook moulds the instruction in a given discipline and influences 100,000 or more young people each year.[5] This influence is further multiplied by the fact that the average successful textbook, with revised editions, remains in circulation from seven to ten years.[6] Hundreds of thousands of school children study history texts, often with keen interest, using them to form their earliest educational impressions of the historical past. For many persons, the school text may be their primary formal encounter with history. For these reasons, the historical picture taught in West German textbooks about critical issues in history should furnish significant insights into the understanding young people have of their past.

For this study, an examination was made of the sections on persecution of the Jews and the Holocaust as depicted in a major sampling of eleven West German history textbooks, workbooks and teacher's guides used in the late 1970s and the 1980s.[7] These are in use for 13 to 18 year olds in the intermediate level schools (*Hauptschule*), secondary schools (*Realschule*) and the university preparatory high schools (*Gymnasium*). This study surveys the text depiction of six topics: the Germans' relationship to the Nazi regime; the treatment of the background and motives of anti–Semitism; the depiction of German participation in the persecution of the Jews and the Holocaust; the assessment of German knowledge of the Holocaust; and the handling of the issue of German responsibility.

In brief, it was found that while the texts cannot be faulted on obvious matters of fact, they have been found remiss in the acknowledgment of German participation and responsibility for the persecution and mass killings during the Third Reich. Before turning to the evidence, it will be useful to comment generally on the strengths and weaknesses of these history texts.

General Improvements and Shortcomings

Some aspects of the history texts of the 1970s and 1980s are characteristically better than their predecessors of the 1950s and 1960s. There is a general trend to stress the more recent past over the earlier historical periods. In general, authors devote more space than earlier to the Third Reich, to the persecution of the Jews during the Nazi era and to the

Holocaust. Most texts now have political learning goals, such as education for democracy and education against totalitarianism, aims which sometimes influence the style of treatment of the Third Reich. Moreover, unlike earlier texts, those currently in use include a greater number of original documents of the Nazi period, despite warnings by some educators that first hand accounts of the Holocaust would be too shocking for young people.[8] It can certainly no longer be said that the authors do not depict the horrors of the mass shootings and gassings in sufficient detail. In general, texts have improved on the space allotted for a detailed treatment on the Holocaust, and all texts may be said to have a number of positive features.

But if the textbooks are generally better,[9] there is still much which may be done to improve them. Despite years of criticism by experts, most texts do not have sufficient historical background about Jews for students to know them in any other context than as victims. As late as 1976, the textbook analyst Heinz Kremers[10] found no textbook of history, social science or political education which dealt with the characteristics or history of the Jewish people. "The Jews surface here and there, always only in another connection." In many texts it is not at all clear that these are Jewish *Germans* being discussed and not simply alien Jews living in Germany. In order to more readily identify with Jewish victims of the Holocaust, German students must perceive them, like themselves, as fellow Germans, but of a different religion.

Another common omission in history texts is any discussion of the sociology of anti–Semitism. While there is usually some material on the evolution from religious to racial anti–Semitism, most authors neglect the background of religiously and nationalistically oriented anti–Semitism.

Only a few texts give attention to the economic, political and social functions of anti–Semitism. Without this analysis students cannot get a very clear insight into the uses made of anti–Semitism for political exploitation.

Only recently have history textbook authors begun to pay attention to the didactical strategies necessary for teaching this emotionally charged subject. But only small beginnings have been made in balancing the demands made on the emotions of students and the claims of objectivity and rationality when presenting the most horrifying events of this period.[11]

Finally, the history texts still make no attempt to evaluate the overall significance and historical meaning of the Holocaust. For the most part, the Holocaust is dealt with as a closed occurrence, unique and essentially unrepeatable, which partly explains the omission of the treatment of capitalism in connection with the events of the Holocaust. Unlike the East Germans, few Western texts include the association between capitalistic enterprises and the pauperization and exploitation of the cheap labor of the Jews in the camps.[12] Furthermore, the economic advantages gained by aryanization of Jewish property are scarcely mentioned.[13] Nor does any history textbook attempt to place the Holocaust in the historical perspective of a credibility crisis for Christianity, for the liberal assumptions of historical progress, or the challenge it poses to humanistic claims of mankind and civilization.

Enthusiasm for the Nazi Regime

None of the history texts, workbooks, or teacher's aid books allude to the fact that the Nazi government was the most popular regime in German national history. Friedrich Lucas in *Menschen in Ihrer Zeit* (Men in Their Time)[14] comes perhaps closest to discussing it. He asserts that the German people thought that the violence was a transitional phenomenon and that after the dissolution of the SA there would be no more violent action. He hints at national susceptibilities when he comments that "people were proud of Germany's reestablished power and greatness, which was exhibited to them as Germany's highest aim on every occasion. They did not ask the price." He stresses that "externally everything in Germany was steadily improving," and lists the early accomplishments of the regime, to explain how the Germans could be beguiled. He concludes that the majority of Germans were satisfied with their Leader. They did not concern themselves "much about what was happening to dissenters and to the (political) parties." In connection with the 1936 Olympics he points out that most foreign visitors were also deeply impressed. After a tour of Nazi showcase successes, Lucas analyzes the ruthlessness and corruption that were behind the façade, and ends by declaring that only later did most people understand what the Third Reich meant for Germany. The stress of the book was on Gestapo intimidation and the threat of concentration camps:

> *Fear and Mistrust* (emphasis in original) drove numberless people to be silent, to look the other way or even to cooperate in the evil which they had before their eyes. Innumerable others learned scarcely anything of the horrors which took place (*erfuhren kaum etwas von den Untaten, die geschehen*). They supported the regime in the belief that they were doing right, and not until later did they become aware how shamelessly they had been misused.

Such passages do more to explain away German enthusiasm for the Nazi regime than to acknowledge it. Lucas's aim is to counter the possible suggestion that Germans were enthusiastic about Hitler and the Nazis. In a later study assignment, Lucas seeks to arm students against the vestiges of the positive attitude towards the Hitler period still held by elements of the society. He asks the students to respond to the following contentions: "Hitler's social measures were very good." — "The entire people certainly cooperated." — "Hitler made Germany into a power again and created respect," and, finally, "Hitler governed well until the war, only he should have left the Jews alone."[15] In this study lesson, Lucas has made the popular contentions held in certain German circles the subject of his assignment.

But if Lucas is not quite able to acknowledge German enthusiasm for the Nazi government of the 1930s, he does a better job than most other textbook authors. Only Hans Deissler in *Grundzüge der Geschichte* (Principles of History) briefly broaches the subject with the statement: "As a rule the number of yes-votes (in plebiscites) was more than ninety percent. These voting results were probably falsified. For at all times during the Hitler dictatorship there was non-agreement and opposition."[16] Here is a statement which does more to conceal than to portray the attitude of the German masses upon which the dictatorship rested its power. No matter how German sentiments may have been manipulated and betrayed, there is scarcely any question that a large majority of Germans were idealistically allied to the regime and that it enjoyed genuine popular support. So long as this is denied or distorted, students will be unable to understand how the Nazis were able to achieve so many of their goals.

But why is there this strong avoidance of revealing the willing participation of Germans in the Nazi regime, a regime in which even its former Minister of Armaments and War Production, Albert Speer, stated that he did not feel in any way compelled to carry out persecutions or to even make anti–Semitic remarks?[17] In part, of course, it is because dealing with the embarrassing aspects of the regime's deeds, perpetuates condemnation of the perpetrators, that is, against the German people and nation. If one may postulate almost as a general rule of Holocaust text writing the assertion that "Nazis are not Germans,"[18] it is partly because textbook authors think that the stereotype of Germans abroad is that "All Germans were Nazis."

There are other reasons for this effort of dissociation. Educators may separate the Nazi regime from the Germans for pedagogical purposes. Since anti–Semitism is still strong in Germany, well intentioned educators may seek, on the one hand, to discredit the Nazi regime for its dictatorship and the murder of defenseless people, while, on the other hand, they may try to minimize the identification of the German *Volk* with the Nazis, in order to avoid acknowledging that anti–Semitic attitudes were widespread and popular. Such avoidance of close association between anti–Semitism and the German population allows teachers not to have to deal with the problem of teaching students that their parents and relatives held social values now considered cruel and shameful. It also reduces the conflict between home and school, in which the young find themselves involved in immense spiritual conflicts when they come to believe that their grandfathers, and earlier, their fathers, or older brothers, participated in murdering thousands of defenseless and innocent human beings.

Thus, it is far easier for pedagogues to declare the German people to have been innocent, misused and manipulated in their values than to concede that the previous generations held a number of inhuman and degrading values, among them racially based prejudice and virulent anti–Semitism.

Motives and Background for Anti–Semitism

Wolfgang Hug, in his workbook for history students, asks the compelling, if cosmic question, "*Auschwitz*: How is this outbreak of barbarism in the Europe of the 20th century to be explained?"[19] Though he does not begin to answer the question, it quite naturally evokes the question of German motives for anti–Semitism.

Most texts are disappointingly brief on the motives for anti–Semitism, and in some the subject is not treated at all.[20] The most superficial statements ascribe anti–Semitism as simply an aberration of Hitler's mind: "A sick delusion controlled Hitler's thinking."[21] Or, again, "Hitler lived in the delusion that the Jews belonged to an inferior race and that they sought to destroy the German people."[22]

R. H. Tenbrock in *Zeiten und Menschen* (Times and Men) makes a fair demonstration that "Hitler's struggle against Judaism was founded entirely upon prejudices against a minority, and was not justified by anything,"[23] but he makes no attempt to clarify the issue of why, then, the German people were so susceptible to such prejudices.

The textbooks, moreover, never call racial prejudice by its name. It is always racial illusions or mania — *Rassewahn* — which comes close to connoting insanity in German. The consequence of this is to render unnecessary any analysis of the sociology of prejudice to explain German susceptibilities to prejudice.

Some authors, in fact, leave the impression that the reason why racial theory is mad is that it squandered able bodied workers. Hug declares in *Geschichtliche Weltkunde* (Historical Social Science)[24] that:

> the murder of able–bodied men and the loss of considerable transportation space had to lead to increased disruption of the conduct of the war. But in this matter the only thing which counted was the insanity (*Wahnsinn*) of racial theory.[25]

In his accompanying workbook, Hug repeats this point: "The crimes of the 'Final Solution' hindered the effectiveness of the German economic and military war leadership."[26] If it is necessary to make this point, it would be better to state that even from the Nazi point of view, genocide was necessarily an insane policy because it was self–defeating. But the emphasis, of course, must be that any genocidal attempt against groups deemed racially inferior is morally repugnant, ethically bankrupt, nationally disgraceful, and cruelly inhumane from the perspective of a people which considers itself civilized. Further, the greatest German victory in history would not change this verdict in the slightest degree. Hug's pragmatic reasons for condemning racism are to be found in many other texts as well.

Hug attempts also to explain how the Nazis evolved racially founded anti–Semitism by quoting long passages from Nazi wartime textbooks and Hitlerian comments, and by describing 19th century ideas of Social Darwinism, the Survival of the Fittest, and "Capitalist and Imperialist" attitudes about the right of the stronger to rule.[27] But nowhere does Hug criticize these ideas or offer rebuttal, except to condemn them because they led to conquest and extermination. Since these ideas still hold sway in the West, it is essential that students hear counterarguments. Indeed, there are many teachers today who do not know how to argue effectively against Social Darwinist ideology.

Hans Heumann in *Unser Weg durch die Geschichte* (Our Path Through History) and Hans Muggenthaler in *Geschichte für Realschulen* (History for Secondary Schools) mention without discussion that there were religious, economic and political motives for anti–Semitism.[28] Muggenthaler additionally cites Christian envy and indebtedness to Jews, but all of these motives are in a retrospective section on medieval anti–Semitism. He then alludes to scapegoats and the practice of making Jews responsible for all the ills that befell Germany, including the Nazi policy whereby "Jews were made responsible for the diminished respect for Germany abroad." While this treatment is adequate, if brief, Muggenthaler's introductory statement to the section on Jewish persecution is surely questionable from a pedagogical standpoint:

> In this matter [of anti–Semitism] it was by no means a new phenomenon. Since the exile of the Jews from their native land and the minority status they took on in the foreign states, there were repeated anti–Semitic waves.[29]

While the accuracy of this teaching may not be objected to, its pedagogical purpose is dubious, for without considerable treatment of these manifestations of Christian prejudice, the young student may simply conclude that because Christians for centuries have been anti–Semitic, this prejudice is in some way vindicated. Muggenthaler also states, one page later,[30] that during the nineteenth century "the aversion to (*Abneigung gegen*) the members of the Mosaic faith was extended to all who were of Jewish ancestry." There are three problems with this sentence. The word aversion should read prejudice or intolerance; second, it is misleading, because many assimilated Jews experienced no disabilities because of Jewish ancestry; third, because of the author's indirect language, few students will understand that his meaning is that there was a shift from religious to racial prejudice in the nineteenth century that had ominous portent for the Jews.

It is particularly striking that the religious motives of anti–Semitism and the role of the churches and of Christianity are not raised in any textbook examined. Only Steinbügl hints at this significant factor in historical anti–Semitism by quoting Hitler's famous passage from *Mein Kampf*, that in struggling against the Jews he knew he was "acting in the spirit of the Almighty and fighting for the work of the Lord."[31] But, while Steinbügl certainly must have chosen the passage to allude to the Christian role in anti–Semitism, he nevertheless does not take up the theme.

Immisch, in *Zeiten und Menschen*, alludes to motives of economic exploitation for German anti–Semitism when he writes: "Jewish sworn testimony counted for less than that of nonJews; contracts with Jews could be much more easily evaded or broken,"[32] but again the statement is immersed in information dealing with another theme, and does not relate to economic motives in anti–Semitism.

Taken as a whole, the textbooks offer a variety of motives for anti–Semitism, though psychological and sociological explanations for prejudice are conspicuously lacking. Individually, the texts do little more than mention a few motives and give some treatment to racially motivated anti–Semitism, though even in this, one wonders if it is enough to repeat racist attitudes and then merely criticize them as insane.

German Participation in Persecutions

A related question is how authors handle German expressions of anti–Semitism and German participation in persecuting Jews. In general, it may be said that most texts are either silent or only briefly allude to German adherence to anti–Semitic attitudes and their violent and humiliating behavior towards Jewish Germans.

In their workbook for students, Ebeling and Birkenfeld[33] include a revealing quotation by which they seem to sense the remissness of their contemporaries. They quote A. Joseph's *Meines Vaters Haus* (My Father's House):

> Young people who learn history today could come to think that the persecutions of 1933 descended upon people who lived among us as aliens, (who were) provocative and disturbing in their differences from us. It could remain concealed from young people that Germans were hunted by Germans.

This is a forthright introduction to the relationship of Germans to Jews and anti–Semitism, but Ebeling and Birkenfeld leave the topic, citing instead the fate of Jewish citizens of Braunschweig. Seven Jewish citizens are selected from the fine *Braunschweiger Denkbuch* (Memorial Book of Braunschweig). Unfortunately for the choices (four emigrated and three were murdered in Auschwitz) the authors chose a ratio which does not correspond to the real picture of the fate of the Jews of Braunschweig.[34] In their text, *Die Reise in die Vergangenheit* (Journey Into the Past), Ebeling and Birkenfeld stress that "anti–Semitic slogans and propaganda were hammered into people, even into the smallest children,"[35] by way of explaining German behavior during the persecutions.

Lucas uses a *Stürmer* newspaper article to make a similar point, but the article chosen is so patently anti–Semitic that it is extremely doubtful whether one needs this sort of pedagogy simply to show that children were incited to hate Jews under the Nazis. The passage, purportedly a child's letter to the Stürmer, states:

> *Gauleiter* Streicher has told us so much about the Jews that we quite properly hate them. We wrote an essay in school on the theme: 'The Jews Are Our Misfortune.' Unfortunately many today still say: The Jews are also creatures of God. Therefore we must also respect them. But we say: Vermin are also animals, but nevertheless we exterminate them.[36]

This use of documentary overkill to make the simple point that children were incited to hate Jews, if it does not itself foster anti–Semitism, certainly prepares the young to expect that their elders could hardly have been anything but anti–Semitic. Its function seems to be to convince students that if Germans persecuted Jews, it must have been because they were so programmed that they no longer could distinguish humans from vermin.

Other texts come somewhat closer to mentioning German participation in anti–Semitic slanders. In *Geschichte für Realschulen*, Hans Muggenthaler states that "On the entrances to many restaurants and at the entrance to many villages were signs: 'Jews not wanted here,' "[37] though he does not mention that these signs were placed there voluntarily by the citizens, often in handlettered graffiti, the better to please the Nazis with evidence of their public spiritedness. Instead, Muggenthaler retreats into the frequently used passive voice of one (*man*). Writing about the systematic denial of human rights of Jews, he notes laconically, "Life was made intolerable for those remaining" after *Reichskristallnacht* (Reich Crystal Night).

Lucas uses some excellent documentary materials to illustrate the organized manhunts against the Jews in 1933 in which Nazi Brownshirts invaded restaurants and shops along the Kurfürstendamm, extorting, humiliating, chasing out and beating up Jews.[38] Such material could easily be used as a natural introduction to the question of bystander Germans' reactions. But it is not so used. There is no discussion based on these documents, whose purpose instead appears to be to personalize Jewish suffering at the hands of the Nazis.

German reaction to such measures as the Jewish boycott, the removal of Jews from public service, the Nuremburg Laws, and the removal of Jews from all public and cultural life is generally not mentioned. Some books maintain that these things had to be done without too much public fanfare so as not to disturb people. But Steinbügl and Schreiegg, for example, in *Geschichte: Von 1890 bis zur Gegenwart* (History: From 1890 to the Present), write succinctly, "Already, on April 1, 1933, the 'Aryan' people were summoned to boycott the Jews." That the Aryans are German citizens is not called to the students' attention. Similarly, on the next page, he states that to work in public service jobs one had to be of "Aryan descent," again without clarifying the term.[39]

In *Didaktischer Grundriss für den Geschichte* (Didactical Outline of History) Tenbrock assures his readers that "Aggressive anti–Semitism was not popular among the German people. This was why Hindenberg was able at first to oppose Hitler, and why anti–Jewish measures could not be allowed to penetrate too much into the consciousness of broad sections of the public."[40] One may be permitted to doubt some of the judgments in Tenbrock's statement. But what is important in this and many other passages is the effort to minimize the association of the German public with Nazi anti–Semitism.

One of the best textbooks used in the Federal Republic of Germany is Joachim Immisch's *Europa und die Welt. Das 20. Jahrhundert* (Europe and the World. The Twentieth Century), vol. 4, of the series *Zeiten und Menschen*. Yet even Immisch is reticent about German culpability for the persecutions. In one sentence he concedes that many Nazis enriched themselves on the property of the Jews,[41] and he has an incisive quotation, separated from the above sentence by four pages, from a 1934 newspaper article, "Expropriation in the New Reich," whose turgid but telling message could be used to introduce students to the economic uses of anti–Semitism:

> To the dangers which can justify expropriation of property by the government in an emergency, belong also some threats which only now are perhaps being recognized as such, namely the danger to blood and race. Thus, expropriation proceedings are underway against foreign racial elements and do not require legal empowerment in so far as they pertain to German ground and land. We must completely do away with the liberalistic ideas of the "just state". Our highest law is: What serves the German People; that is just.[42]

This quotation and the text commentary are admirable, but their purpose is not a discussion of German exploitation of the Jews, for there is no topic in the text which even remotely describes this. Similarly, Hans Deissler in *Grundzüge der Geschichte* (Principles of History) writes of party functionaries extorting Jews, and forcing them to "place their property in German hands at prices far below the value of the property."[43] In this case, again it was the Nazis who appear to force the passive Germans to enrich themselves at the expense of the Jews. Hug blames neither Nazis nor the German people, but retreats into vagueness when he states that, after *Reichskristallnacht*, the "forced aryanization of all Jewish enterprises, business, and factories enriched many who could now acquire the Jewish economic concerns for little money."[44] Hug does not examine who these many people could have been. Also, the term aryanization is a rather time bound Nazi euphemism which renders harmless the actual massive looting of the helpless victims' personal possessions.

Immisch actually comes so close to a discussion, one feels he is ready to address the subject. In the following passage he explains the Germans' entanglement in the persecutions:

> Indeed many Germans who believed they possessed some influence opposed these measures (against the Jews). Gradually, however, there arose a chasm between many non–Jews and their Jewish fellow men. Friendships were dis-

solved, neighbors were no longer greeted, Jewish children were taunted. This was, on the one hand, a consequence of surveillance into private lives through functionaries whose reports many wanted to avoid, and on the other hand, daily propaganda had its erosive effects. Anti–Semitic slogans were spread to the last little village; posters appeared and lettered banners; everywhere there were crude hate sheets in show windows. The Jews were made responsible for all the difficulties domestically and in foreign relations: They were the scapegoats.[45]

This exposition is more candid than that of any other text examined. Nevertheless, it stops considerably short of assessing German responsibility in these matters. And, as will be seen, the standard author's view is that the Germans were more the victims of the dictatorship than the victimizers.

In the textbook sections dealing with the persecution of the Jews, a few authors consider the question of German knowledge of the injustices, immorality and crimes of the Nazis. Heumann may be viewed as representative. He stresses that concentration camps were built "away from main roads so that the public noticed them as little as possible. Many Germans did not at all know what went on behind the high, encircling, electrically–charged, barbedwire fences . . . Whoever entered here . . . was not allowed to say anything under threat of heavy punishment."[46]

Heumann's emphasis, like many others, is more on the intimidation of the Germans than on whether they recognized the criminal nature of the regime. Writing of the events of *Reichskristallnacht*, Heumann declared that this "would have to have opened people's eyes to the true character of National Socialism."[47] But German reaction, except for fear and silence, is not discussed.

As a handy explanation for the ruthlessness, cruelty and injustices, the standard German text author invokes the names Adolf Hitler, Heinrich Himmler, the SS and the Gestapo. More often than not, Hitler is made the exclusive agent of the entire process of barbarism, as in Heumann's text:

> Hitler's sick anti–Semitism . . . which was expressed both in the Party program as well as in *Mein Kampf*, led to the murder of nearly six million Jews.

German Participation in the Holocaust

Let us now turn to the depiction of Germans in connection with the Holocaust itself. As in sections dealing with the persecution of the Jews, there is massive reluctance to portray Germans as active agents in these annihilations. There is considerable use of euphemism, many of which are unchanged from Nazi terminology, and frequent use of the passive voice to omit mentioning perpetrators. Steinbügl, for example, writing of the disposal of the dead, states that "in the beginning *one* threw the dead into mass graves; later *one* made the transition to the burning of the bodies."[48] By comparison, the words Germany, Germans, and the German people appear up to a dozen times per page in other sections of Third Reich coverage both before and after the section on the Holocaust. Two texts, Heumann and Schwander, make no mention whatever of Germans in depicting mass murders. Ebeling and Birkenfeld on the other hand introduce the subject Auschwitz, with this statement:

> There began the most ghastly event ever to take place in the name of the Germans.[49]

Unfortunately this turns out to be the only reference they make to a German connection with the Holocaust. Hug only lightly grazes the German connection:

> Until the Fall of 1944 trains carrying Jewish men, women and children rolled out of the German occupied areas to the extermination camps.[50]

Otherwise, he exhibits the tendency, found elsewhere as well, to link the perpetration of the massacres to other nationalities, as for example:

> *Einsatzgruppen* ravaged in Poland and in the occupied Soviet areas, supported in part by native anti–Semitic militia units.

The *Einsatzgruppen* are not plainly identified as Germans and they are linked to resident military units which thereby implicitly disperses responsibility. In the student workbook, Hug poses the intriguing question, "What contributed to the carrying out of mass murder organized by the state and participated in by many?"[51] While the text provides enough material for a reasonably detailed answer, the point here is that *the student is not made aware that this question pertains particularly to his nation.*

The authors also frequently use abstractions which leave the perpetrators anonymous and the killings taking place with almost mechanical autonomy: "The government of the extermination machine," writes Hug, "lay in the hands of the SS–police power."[52]

Deissler uses a similar mode of description: "Staffs of coldblooded desk murderers led the victims in freight trains and trucks from all the nations under German control into huge camps." Deissler describes the mass gassings in detail, mentioning the most notorious camps. He then enlarges upon the mechanistic model, names nationalities and imputes motives. But here is what the student reads:

> The million–fold murders took place according to general staff–like planning with bureaucratic precision using factory–like technology. Ukrainians, Poles, Lithuanians, and Jewish forced labor were compelled to carry out the crude activities under threat of death. The SS were placed in positions as administrative, supervisory, technical and medical personnel. Now and then there were devilish torturers. (But) the majority were simple, upright (*biedere*) family fathers, correct in their private life, citizens obsessed with duty, who convinced themselves that their dirty 'work' was in the service of the people and the fatherland.[53]

Deissler's details on German participation are illuminating because he reflects, in greater detail, a view which may be gleaned from many texts. The Germans are perceived as having been decent people gone wrong because of an obsession with patriotic duty. In truth, the motives were far more differentiated, and less noble than merely excessive nationalism and a compulsive sense of duty. German supervisors, administrators and guards may be classified according to at least five overlapping sets of characteristics: fanatical Nazis who hated Jews out of ideological fervor; purely destructive types who reveled in the chance to torture and murder; looters, who sought to enrich themselves on the booty of the victims; ambitious opportunists at all levels, who saw in their murderous work a means of gaining a better income and higher status than they could ever have hoped for in normal occupations; and, at all levels, conformists who merely took the line of least resistance, went wherever they were directed and did whatever they were told. Deissler's depiction merely highlights the simplistic results of unreflective generalizing about a subject.

Oddly, of the eleven texts and workbooks examined, only Hug and Immisch mention the important Wannsee Conference of January 20, 1942 at which the implementation of the Final Solution was discussed and resolved. This omission is even more striking because its inclusion would not disturb the general thesis of "bigwig desk–murderers" mechanistically planning genocide far removed from the slaughter, and inventing euphemistic terms to disguise their intents. A more serious shortcoming than the inadequate presentation of the plan for genocide is the abrupt closure of the subject, often by use of a document on some aspect of horror powerful enough to virtually cry out for commentary. Though the depiction of the killings is now more than sufficiently terrifying — harrowing enough to remain with any sixteen year old for years — in text after text, the authors quickly break off the subject with no effort at placing this most ghastly event in German history in any kind of perspective. No attempt is made to state any larger meaning of the Holocaust, to evaluate its significance, lessons or portent. Finally, there is no stress on the enormity of the murder of the European Jews, its historic magnitude or the awesomeness of the deed. While the authors by and large identify the number of victims correctly, they seem to suffer from a tragic failure of imagination, a partial repression, and general discomfiture in the presence of the event. It is hard to determine whether they are more in awe or embarrassment in the presence of a subject which poses so many difficulties for them to depict.

German Knowledge of the Holocaust

It remains to be described how the textbook authors treat the question of German knowledge of the most ghastly event ever to take place in the name of the German people. Remarkably, all textbooks treat the question of German knowledge, sometimes in some detail, which indicates that they are sensitive to the subject and recognize its psychological, and perhaps its historic, significance. Hug recounts that "though the SS sought to keep their terrible deeds a secret, it could scarcely be prevented that the greater part of the German people learned of the mass murders."[54] Unfortunately, Hug does not state when the Germans learned of the Holocaust, and does not further explicate this remarkable declaration. Almost all other textbooks are far more circumspect as, for example, Immisch, when he writes,

> Undisturbed from abroad and hidden from most Germans in the broad reaches of the east, Hitler was able to carry out his Final Solution of the Jewish Question.
> Since 1940 the German Jews had been 'deported' to the Eastern region where almost all were later to fall victim to the exterminating operations. By mid-1943, only a few thousand still lived in the Reich. The deportation did not remain hidden from the population. Some few Germans risked their lives and hid Jewish friends; they intuited the fate which, under the camouflage of a 'relocation action', awaited the Jews in the East.[55]

Steinbügl is briefer and more ambiguous about German awareness of the fate of the Jews:

> After the outbreak of the Second World War the Hitler regime finally showed its true colors [seine Maske fallen] and ordered the "Final Solution of the Jewish Question," in other words, the extermination of the Jews in Europe.[56]

It is not clear from this passage whether Steinbügl meant that the Germans knew, and he does not return to the question.

Ebeling and Birkenfeld make their judgment in much clearer terms and better explain their reasoning:

> All of this was carried out under the most extreme conditions of secrecy in remote areas. The guard companies were enjoined to the most strict silence, and only very seldom did a victim of these extermination machines escape in order to be able to report these things. When, indeed, sporadically something leaked through, it seemed so gruesome that no one wanted to believe it. Not until near the end of the war did the event in all of its inhumanity become known.[57]

Muggenthaler's description is particularly interesting:

> The murder of the Jews by the National Socialists was characterized by a completely unique factor: silence [*ein vollig neuartiges Moment: das Schweigen*]. While all dictators up to this time had their opponents publicly executed, now one [man] murdered thousands of people in all secrecy.[58]

Aside from the fact that many dictators did and do have their opponents executed in secret, Muggenthaler has neatly insinuated that the European Jews were somehow opponents of the Nazis, instead of being thus defined by the National Socialists for their own purposes.

Schwander treats the issue of German knowledge under the heading of Concentration Camps, and later in connection with the war. About the camps, he wrote:

> Many Germans did not know to what purposes they were being misused . . . Thousands, however, remained silent out of fear, although they deeply loathed the aims of National Socialism . . . The phrase, "protective custody" was nothing less than a mockery.[59]

But immediately, he then asserts,

> Most people did not learn until 1945 how inhumane things that went on there were. Many, of course, intuited that a human life in these camps did not possess much value to the "Nazis."

As to the public knowledge of the Holocaust, Schwander gives this section the title, *The Concealment of the Extermination Campaign (Geheimhaltung der Vernichtungsaktionen)*. Not surprisingly, and rather unconnectedly, he writes,

> The murders in the concentration camps were concealed from the German people. Hitler himself visited Treblinka extermination camp in August, 1942.[60]

Schwander's final verdict: Only a few knew the whole truth about the camps.[61] In view of the foregoing, it may be wondered what sort of assessment the authors will make of the question of German responsibility for the events of the Holocaust.

The Depiction of German Responsibility for the Holocaust

Turning to the authors' depiction of German responsibility for these tragic events, it may come as no surprise that only a few authors choose to take up the issue. Only four texts, in fact, broach the question even briefly. Heumann makes a fine concluding statement after describing the numbers of victims of the Holocaust. After pointing out that the final figures cannot be known with precision, he states that "The horror has already begun when we hear of a single person being murdered simply because he belongs to another religion, another nation or another race."[62] Heumann describes the event as "a dark, admonishing element of German history, and the reason why, even today, Germans frequently encounter the mistrust of foreign nations."[63]

Immisch writes sympathetically of the suffering of the Jews and he, too, informs the student that these sufferings "are said to have led to the deepest humbling of the reputation of the German people."[64] Though Hug does not discuss German responsibility, he does call upon students to discuss "the Wannsee Conference, the Höss statement on Auschwitz, the number of victims" (all of which are treated), and "the question of the distribution of guilt" [*Schuldanteil*] (which is not treated). Hug is also the only author who seems to sense an obligation to memorialize Jewish victims. In an assignment, he urges students, "to seek information about the fate of former Jewish citizens in your area."[65]

But in all texts far less space is devoted to the issue of distribution of responsibility than to depicting the horror of events and the intimidation of citizens by the regime. Since Germans were rarely mentioned in connection with these gigantic tragedies, any undue emphasis on German remorse would at this point seem in striking contrast to the standpoint taken in the rest of the text. This position, while not nearly so obvious as in early postwar texts, asserts essentially: "certainly Jews suffered, but so did Germans." So long as the Germans' intimate connection with the Nazi regime is suppressed, there will be no need to consider the fate of the Jews as a special burden for German sensibilities, and authors will continue to be inclined to give evenhanded sympathy to the suffering of the Germans and to the European Jews.

As much as texts have progressed since the 1950s and 1960s they have not been able to confront the fact of massive, willing German participation in injustice to other human beings during the Third Reich, both in peacetime and war. For this reason, authors persistently stress intimidation of the Germans and how little they knew. The German educator, Eberhard Quester, sought to warn his colleagues against these claims of German ignorance and innocence twenty years ago:

> It simply won't do to emphasize over and again that "only a very few" knew of these things: this may be pertinent to the events in the extermination camps — although here, too, the circle of those who did know comprised significantly more persons than merely the directly participating security forces — but the unjust and brutal expulsion of Jewish citizens from the life of the community *everyone* could see, and also *did* see. Unless the clear reprimand is accepted for at least *this* political and moral failure of tolerance — for this failure to recognize inhumanity — the greater part of the recent past will remain "unmastered," and contemporary history will take on the fatal character of an apologetic.[66]

As has been demonstrated, Quester's words have gone largely unheeded.

Conclusions

While the persecution of the Jews during the Nazi regime and the events of the Holocaust are treated at some length in recent German history textbooks, it has been shown that they omit or deny the fact that a majority of Germans loved and admired the National Socialist regime, that a considerable number of Germans, generally speaking, were anti–Semitic, that many participated in the persecution of the Jews, and that they, for the most part, had some knowledge during the war of the terrible fate that befell Jews rounded up and shipped to the East. There is also a subtle, but important, denial of German responsibility for events relating to the fate of the European Jews. In the presentation of the Nazi period, the cruel and tragic events are universally condemned, but there is a tendency to treat the subject as if anti–Semitism were a thing of the past, which therefore need not be addressed for any possible portents in the present or future. This may be observed in the omission or brief treatment of the history and cultural background of the Jews, in the tendency to minimize the German nationality of the Jews of their country, in the tendency to employ euphemisms, or the camouflaged language of the Nazis, and the use of the passive voice in the sections on the persecution and murder of the Jews.

It has been shown that German textbook authors exhibit remarkable agreement that the German people generally did not know the fate of the Jews during the Holocaust. The German textbook treatment is inadequate on this important point. A more balanced examination is needed to depict the deepening suspicion that many Germans shared, a terrible concern that something awful, dreadful, sinister, and almost too terrifying was happening to the Jews in the East.

Such declarations as *Das haben wir nicht gewüsst* — We didn't know that — have a direct connection with the Germans' unwillingness to take on the psychic burden of confronting what was perpetrated by their fellow citizens. Those who in 1945 were between the ages of twenty and forty years are now fifty-eight to seventy-eight years of age. The murderers among them are a small fraction of the overall West German population, but the compromised among them remains a significantly large and influential age group within the population. So long as they do not know how to come to grips with how much they were compromised by their attitudes and acts during the 1930s and 1940s, the past will remain unmastered and misunderstood by them. In consequence, they will be compelled to maintain massive defenses and selective memories, rather than to seek to understand the enormity of their deeds in the eyes of the world. Perhaps never before has a large historic event cast such a long shadow over a nation.

A large task haunts Germany, the inadequately considered settling-of-accounts with its Nazi past. It has not been reflected upon by the first generation, and they have passed on their apologia to the second generation who are similarly defensive about German responsibility for the events of the Holocaust. The general attitude taken in the textbooks reflects this general reluctance of the population to deal with the horrors of the Hitler regime. The inability of the Germans to look closely at their recent past, has been termed *The Great Evasion*.[67] Alexander and Margareta Mitscherlich have called it *The Inability to Mourn*. The Germans, of course, do not lack the capacity for grieving, and many millions of Germans have been deeply stricken, and penitent over the murder of the European Jews and other innocent people by the German government and citizens. But a majority of Germans have not, and perhaps cannot, reconcile their present selves with their past of forty years ago. For this reason, they repress the history of the Nazi era.

Most textbooks reflect this repression of the German participation in the Nazi past, which staves off a terrible confrontation with their former selves. The texts reflect a more usable past by accommodating to this national syndrome. It is one which allows older and younger Germans to remain in relative harmony and to share a usable history. They fear facing a representation of their attitudes, values and actions during or since the Nazi era in a manner which would rob them of their self-respect and dignity. Thus, the distortions of the era are maintained to avoid undergoing that painful process of all who are human: the process of mourning mistakes, grieving about injustices and crimes committed by oneself or in one's own name. It can only be hoped that the most recent efforts of a new generation of German textbook authors will begin to make headway against the massive logjam of the German collective repression of the sins of the fathers. Only in this way may the past be laid to rest and not visited upon succeeding generations.

Notes

1. The following examples were taken from Dieter Bossman (ed.), *"Was ich über Adolf Hitler gehört habe . . ." Folgen eines Tabus: Auszüge aus Schüler-Aufsätzen von heute,* Frankfurt/Main: Fischer Verlag, 1977, 164–179.

2. In his *Didaktischer Grundriss für den Geschichtsunterricht* (Schöningh: Schroedel Verlag, 1969, 41), R. H. Tenbrock states that the function of the materials is "to protect or preserve the young generation from any prejudice towards minorities by presenting its abominable consequences."

3. One major ongoing program, for example, is the bilateral projects for textbook revision between Germany and scores of other countries sponsored by the unique *Georg–Eckert–Institut for International Schoolbook Research* in Braunschweig. See Georg Eckert, "The Changing Picture of European History" in Walter Stahl (ed.) *Education for democracy in West Germany; achievements, shortcomings, prospects.* New York: Praeger, 1960, 119–120; and Rolf Joachim Sattler, "Schulbuchvergleich und Schulbuchanalyse in internationaler Zusammenarbeit" in E. H. Schallenberger (ed.), *Das Schulbuch — Aspekte und Verfahren zur Analyse,* Ratlingen: Aloys Henn Verlag, 1973.

4. Margarete Dörr, "Das Schulbuch im Geschichtsunterricht — Kriterien für seine Beurteilung" in Fäckel und Weymar (eds.), *Die Funktion der Geschichte in unserer Zeit,* Stuttgart, 1975, 294. Horst Schallenberger (Schallenberger, 1978, 36) sees textbooks in a dialectical relationship to the society at large: "School books exist in a connection with the total society and, in their creation and in the possibilities of their effects within the given historical situation, are to be seen as both response and factor . . . They are moulded by the spirit of the time and, in turn, mould it. As a political factor . . . the textbook exists in a dynamic relationship to the respective political system." E. Horst Sachallenberger, "Zur Darstellung der Schoah im deutschen Schulbuch der Gegenwart" in *Tribüne, Zeitschrift zum Verständnis des Judentums,* 17 Jg., Heft 67 (1978), 36.

5. Alfred Dauch, "Das Schulbuch aus der Sicht des Verlagers" in *Zur Sache Schulbuch,* Bd. 1 (1973), 44.

6. Arbeitsgemeinschaft Schulbuchproduktion, "Schulbuch — Produktion und Profit" in *Aus: päd extra* 3/4 (1973), 10; and Peter Timmann, "Teaching the Hitler Period at the West German Secondary School" presented at the Duquesne History Forum, October, 1978, manuscript copy from author.

7. For a listing of the textbook and related materials examined, see appendix. It should be noted that the following assessment does not reflect on the entire textbook, but refers only to those sections dealing with the persecution of the Jews and the Holocaust during the Third Reich.

8. Eberhard Quester, "Die Darstellung des Judentums in Geschichtsunterricht" in *Die Realschule*, November, 1963, 341.

9. West German textbooks are certainly more objective and candid than their East German counterparts with which they may be perhaps most fruitfully compared.

10. Heinz Kremers, "Die Darstellung der Juden in neuen Schulbüchern in der Bundesrepublik Deutschland" in Gerd Stein, E. Horst Schallenberger (eds.), *Schulbuchanalyse und Schulbuchkritik. Im Brennpunkt: Juden, Judentum und Staat Israel*, Verlag der Sozialwissenschaftlichen Kooperative, 1976, 149, fn. 2.

11. See Heinz Kremers, "Judentum und Holocaust im deutschen Schulunterricht" in *aus politik und zeitgeschichte* B 4/79 (27, January, 1979), 37-45; Chaim Schatzker, "The Teaching of the Holocaust: Dilemmas and Considerations" in Irene Schur, Franklin Littell (eds.), *Reflections on the Holocaust: Historical, Philosophical, and Educational Dimensions (The Annals of the American Academy of Political and Social Science)* Richard Lambert (ed.), vol. 450 (July, 1980), 218-226; and Arye Carmon, "Teaching the Holocaust as a Means of Fostering Values" in *Curriculum Inquiry* 9:3 (1979), 209-228.

12. Schallenberger, 46.

13. Albrecht Thiemann, "The Holocaust in German Schools: Personal Experiences and a Report" presented at the *Duquesne History Forum*, October 13, 1979, manuscript copy from author.

14. Friedrich J. Lucas et al., *Menschen in ihrer Zeit*, vol. 4, *In unserer Zeit*, Stuttgart: Ernst Klett Verlag, 1975 (6th edition), 86–89.

15. Ibid., 90.

16. Hans Herbert Deissler et al., *Von 1890 bis zur Gegenwart*, vol. 4 of Eugen Kaier (ed.), *Grundzüge der Geschichte*, Frankfurt/Main: Moritz Diesterweg, 1974 (5th edition).

17. Albert Speer, *Infiltration: How Heinrich Himmler Schemed to Build an Industrial Empire*. New York: Macmillan, 1981. 330. These are Speer's last lines.

18. Martin and Eva Kolinsky, "The Treatment of the Holocaust in West German Textbooks" in Livia Rothkirchen (ed.) *Yad Vashem Studies on the European Jewish Catastrophe and Resistance* vol. X, Jerusalem: Yad Vashem, 1974, 214.

19. Wolfgang Hug, et al., Lernimpulse 3, *Begleitheft zum Arbeitsbuch "Geschichtliche Weltkunde"* vol. 3, Frankfurt/Main: Moritz Diesterweg, 1976, 47.

20. For example, Josef Schwandner, et al., *Geschichte*, München: R. Oldenbourg Verlag, 1973.

21. Hans Ebeling and Wolfgang Birkenfeld, *Die Reise in die Vergangenheit: Ein geschichtliches Arbeitsbuch*, Westermann, 1976, 137.

22. Eduard Steinbügl and Anton Schreiegg, *Geschichte*, vol. IV, *Neueste Zeit*, München: Oldenbourg, 1973, 85. Steinbügl uses the passage to mention many creative and famous Jews as proof of their superior qualities.

23. R. H. Tenbrock, *Didaktischer Gründriss für den Geschichtsunterricht* vol. 4 *Zeiten und Menschen* (3rd edition) Schöningh: Schroedel, 1969, 123.

24. Wolfgang Hug, et al., *Geschichtliche Weltkunde*, vol. 3, *Von der Zeit des Imperialismus bis zur Gegenwart*, Frankfurt/Main, Moritz Diesterweg, 1976.

25. Ibid., 47.

26. Hug, *Begleitheft*, 47.

27. Hans Deissler in *Von 1890 bis zur Gegenwart* has a particularly well–handled section depicting how racists viewed Europeans in terms of superior and inferior stock and connect-

ing his description with the German penchant for order, to their "need to create, finally, a new biological, sensible order in European society." (p. 220).

28. Hans Heumann, *Unser Weg durch die Geschichte*, vol. 3 of *Die Welt gestern und heute*, Frankfurt/Main: Hirschgraben Verlag, 1976, 58; and Hans Muggenthaler, Wolfgang and Hannah Marks, vol. 4, *Geschichte für Realschulen*, vol. 4, *Neueste Zeit*, München: Kosel–Verlag, 113.

29. Muggenthaler, 113.

30. Ibid., 114.

31. Steinbügl, 85.

32. Joachim Immisch, *Zeiten und Menschen*, vol. 4 of *Europa und die Welt. Das 20. Jahrhundert.* (Schöningh: Schroedel, n.d.), p. 137.

33. Ebeling and Birkenfeld, 137.

34. See Richard Moderhack (ed.), *Brunsvicensia Judaica. Ein Gedenkbuch für die judischen Mitbürger der Stadt Braunschweig 1933-1945* Bd. 35, Braunschweiger Werkstücke. Veröffentlichungen aus Archiv, Bibliothek und Museum der Stadt. Braunschweig: Waisenhaus Buchdruckerei u. Verlag, 1966.

35. Ebeling and Birkenfeld, 137.

36. *Der Stürmer,* (Nr. 2., January, 1935) cited in Lucas, 88.

37. Muggenthaler, 115.

38. Lucas, 88.

39. Steinbügl, 85–86.

40. Tenbrock, 123.

41. Joachim Immisch, *Zeiten und Menschen*, vol. 4 *Europa und die Welt das 20. Jahrhundert*, Schroningh: Schroedel, 1966, 140.

42. Ibid., 136.

43. Deissler, 178.

44. Hug, 111.

45. Immisch, 136.

46. Heumann, 57.

47. Ibid., 59.

48. Steinbügl, 103–104. W.R. emphasis.

49. Ebeling and Birkenfeld, 138.

50. Hug, 160.

51. Ibid., *Begleitheft*, 47 "unter Beteiligung vieler."

52. Hug, 161.

53. Deissler, 221–222.

54. Hug, 161.

55. Immisch, 172.

56. Steinbügl, 86.

57. Ebeling and Birkenfeld, 139.

58. Muggenthaler, 134.

59. Schwander, 105.

60. Ibid., 129.

61. Ibid., 125.

62. Heumann, 58. Emphasis in the original.

63. Ibid., 59. Earlier authors closer to the events here depicted, while much briefer about the Holocaust, were sometimes more contrite: "Therefore, the German People earned the hatred and contempt of the whole civilized world." in *Lebendige Vergangenheit* (Klett Verlag, 1953, 119) cited in Kolinsky, 200.

64. Immisch, 136.

65. Hug, 161.
66. Quester, 341.
67. Walter Renn, "The Great Evasion: Teaching the Third Reich in Postwar Germany" in Wheeling College *Annual*, 1980, 1-27.

Appendix

LIST OF TEXTBOOKS, WORKBOOKS AND TEACHER–AID BOOKS CONSULTED:

Hans Herbert Deissler et al., *Von 1890 bis zur Gegenwart*, vol. 4 of Eugen Kaier (ed.), *Grundzüge der Geschichte*, Frankfurt/Main: Moritz Diesterweg, 1974 (5th edition)

Hans Ebeling and Wolfgang Birkenfeld, *Die Reise in die Vergangenheit: Ein geschichtlices Arbeitsbuch*, Westermann, 1976 (Teachers Aid book)

Hans Heumann, *Unser Weg durch die Geschichte,* vol. 3 of *Die Welt gestern und heute*, Frankfurt/Main: Hirschgraben Verlag, 1976

Wolfgang Hug, et al., *Geschichtliche Weltkunde*, vol. 3 *Von der Zeit des Imperialismus bis zur Gegenwart*, Frankfurt/Main, Moritz Diesterweg, 1976

Wolfgang Hug, et al., *Lernimpulse 3, Begleitheft zum Arbeitsbuch "Geschichtliche Weltkunde,"* vol. 3, Frankfurt/Main: Moritz Diesterweg, 1976

Joachim Immisch, *Zeiten und Menschen,* vol. 4, *Europa und die Welt Das 20, Jahrhundert,* Schröningh: Schroedel, 1966

Friedrich J. Lucas et al., *Menschen in ihrer Zeit,* vol. 4, *In unserer Zeit,* Stuttgart: Ernst Keltt Verlag, 1975 (6th edition)

Hans Muggenthaler, Wolfgang and Hannah Marks, vol. 4, *Geschichte für Realschulen*, vol. 4, *Neueste Zeit*, Munchen: Kosel-Verlag

Josef Schwandner, et al., *Geschichte*, Munchen: R. Oldenbourg Verlag, 1973

Eduard Steinbügl and Anton Schreiegg, *Geschichte*, vol. IV, *Neueste Zeit*, Munchen: Oldenbourg, 1973

R. H. Tenbrock, *Didaktischer Gründriss für den Geschichtsunterricht* vol. 4, *Zeiten und Menschen* (3rd edition) Schoningh: Schroedel, 1969

V CRIME AND PUNISHMENT

8 ERNST KALTENBRUNNER AND THE FINAL SOLUTION

Peter R. Black

Few of those who stood on the defendants' dock at the trial of the major war criminals before the International Military Tribunal at Nuremberg in 1945–1946 inspired more revulsion than Ernst Kaltenbrunner, erstwhile chief of the Reich Security Main Office (*Reichssicherheitshauptamt* — RSHA). Born in 1903, in Ried im Innkreis, Austria, this tall, hulking, scarfaced lawyer joined the National Socialist German Workers' Party (NSDAP) in 1930 and the elite *Schutzstaffel*, or SS, in 1931. In 1937, he was appointed chief of the underground Austrian SS; after the *Anschluss* of Austria into the German Reich a year later, he arrived in Vienna to take command of all SS and police forces in Vienna, Upper Austria and Lower Austria. On January 30, 1943, *Reichsführer*–SS Heinrich Himmler summoned Kaltenbrunner to Berlin to succeed the notorious Reinhard Heydrich as chief of the RSHA in Berlin. In this position, he directed the operations of the Nazi Secret State Police (*Geheime Staatspolizei* — Gestapo) and the Security Service (*Sicherheitsdienst* — SD). These operations involved the murder and mistreatment of prisoners of war and the civilian populations of occupied Europe; they also included the implementation of the so–called Final Solution, a program that called for the

183

physical extermination of the European Jews. In view of Heydrich's assassination in 1942 and Himmler's suicide in 1945, the victorious Allies chose Kaltenbrunner to represent the SS on the dock at Nuremberg.[1] Even when comparing him with his codefendants, observers found Kaltenbrunner particularly unappealing. Author Evelyn Waugh noted in his diary that "only Kaltenbrunner looked an obvious criminal."[2]

What makes a man like this tick? Kaltenbrunner came from the German–Austrian professional middle class of the Habsburg Monarchy. His father and his grandfather had been highly respected lawyers: the latter had been the mayor of the Upper Austrian town Eferding, while the former had been a partner in the most prestigious law firm in Linz, the Upper Austrian provincial capital. A Linz schoolteacher, whose part Jewish ancestry and affiliation with the Austrian Social Democratic Workers' Party rendered him unlikely to be sympathetic to Kaltenbrunner by nature, remembered the future RSHA chief as a pleasant and wellbred middle class youth. In fact, a quick glance at Kaltenbrunner's social and intellectual background reveals no propensity towards socially aberrant or criminal behavior, no hint at all at the future development of his career.

Yet perhaps we should take a closer look. The German–Austrian middle class of the Habsburg Monarchy formed part of a German ethnic group that was accustomed to enjoy political and cultural dominance in a multinational state. During the last decades of the nineteenth century, as the other Habsburg nationalities (Italians, Hungarians, Croats, Czechs, Slovaks, Serbs, Romanians and Jews) pressed (and as the state yielded to) claims for equal civic status, linguistic parity, equal economic opportunity and political patronage, many members of the German ethnic group, particularly from the middle classes, sought refuge in a sullen and later militant obsession with their national identity. Seizing upon an old German Romantic nationalist theme, they found compensation for their eroding political and social status in a yearning for German national unity. Incorporating the then popular Social Darwinist theory of the inequality of the races and their absolute struggle for survival into the vision of a united German nation, German nationalists in Austria called for a national union of the German speaking provinces of Austria with the German Reich on the principle of racial purity. Discarding the other Habsburg ethnic minorities as culturally and biologically inferior, these obsessed souls denounced as mortal enemies those who opposed their utopian ideal. These "enemies" — Catholics and Marxists, Slavs and Italians, and, above all, Jews — all had international affiliations that they allegedly used to undermine German national aspirations.

The Jew represented a unique threat to German–Austrians insecure

about their national identity. Lingering German Romantic nationalist pre-
conceptions of what characterized the genuine member of the German
nation, or *Volk* — the noble peasant and the honest village artisan —
combined with the survival of medieval restrictions on the Jewish population of Central Europe to render it unlikely that the Jew could ever fit into
the Romantic nationalist ideal of German life. Moreover, Jews were
linked in the public mind to two nineteenth century bugaboos of the
German–Austrian middle classes (as well as middle and lower middle
classes throughout Central and Eastern Europe): large scale financial capitalism (by virtue of the stereotyped image of Jews as particularly adept in
money matters) and Marxian Socialism (by virtue of the fact that many
individual Jews sympathized with, supported or held leadership positions
in the European labor movement). Austrian Jews were identified
specifically with the Habsburg status quo under which German nationalists were beginning to feel so insecure; for the constitution of 1867 had
granted Austrian Jews complete civic equality. Finally, the concepts of
racial inequality and Aryan superiority, developed by the French diplo-
mat Joseph Arthur de Gobineau, lent a pseudoscientific legitimacy by
their application to an intellectually perverted version of Darwin's theory
of evolution and gave rise in Central Europe not only to a positive doc-
trine of racial inequality, but also to a Messianic nationalist obsession
with absolute victory over enemies that could be achieved only through
biological struggle with the aim of maintaining racial purity.

   Those who subscribed to the ideal of a united, racially pure German state
perceived in the Jew a triple threat. From the East the Jew encouraged
Slavic pressure on German political supremacy, economic status and cultural dominance in the Habsburg state. From the Western plutocracies he
imported Liberalism, democracy and financial capitalism which undermined the supposedly healthy economic, social and political mores of
German life. From within he exploited the civil rights and economic opportunities granted to him by the system of 1867 to achieve dominance in
domestic economic and cultural life, thus insidiously extinguishing the
national identity of the Germans. With this paranoid world view in mind,
German nationalists of Habsburg Austria came to believe that their
ethnic–racial identity could be preserved only within a unified, racially
pure German national state.

   The most ardent advocates of this *Weltanschauung* were the German
nationalist students at the Austrian universities. Many of the students
were organized in dueling fraternities, or *Burschenschaften*. Three traits
of *Burschenschaft* life reinforced the violent nature and inflexibility of the
concept of German national–racial union. First, *Burschenschaft* politics

lent to that concept the ardor of youthful idealism embodied in the student movement, thus molding an ideology whose adherents found difficult to compromise. Second, the dueling ritual[3] imbued the fraternity student with a standard of harshness towards himself and towards others. Finally, questions of who was worthy of offering or accepting a challenge, known as *Commentfragen*, bred an elitist contempt for "unworthy" types, who came to be totally excluded from fraternity society. Among those deemed "incapable of giving satisfaction" were opponents of the *deutschnational* (German nationalist) ideal and members of races considered to be inferior. Though Jews had joined the Austrian fraternities during the 1860s and early 1870s, they were gradually denied membership in the 1880s, and finally refused the right to give satisfaction by means of the duel in the 1890s — on the grounds that, as Jews, they had no honor worthy of defending.

The *deutschnational* ideal took root in the German–Austrian professional middle class because many of the younger doctors, lawyers, teachers and engineers had been members of nationalist student fraternities before they graduated and entered their chosen professions. Between 1893 and 1898 — five years which saw the final expulsion of Jewish students from *Burschenschaft* life, fierce German nationalist agitation against Habsburg governments that sought to integrate Czechs, Slovenes and Poles into the ruling structure of the Monarchy, and the beginning of the high tide of success for the violent, confrontational politics of the nationalist, anti–Semitic Pan–German Party of Georg Ritter von Schönerer — Hugo Kaltenbrunner, the father of Ernst Kaltenbrunner, attended the law school at the university in Graz and served as a fraternity officer in the German nationalist *Burschenschaft* "Arminia." And while his responsible integration into a still stable and confident middle class society blunted his youthful radicalism, he carried his *Burschenschaft* ideal of a unified Germany and some of his *Burschenschaft* practices — contemptuous rejection of the Catholic hierarchy and Catholic teaching and refusal to associate socially with Jews — into his family life in provincial Upper Austria.

The ideology of the *Burschenschaft* did not fail to influence Hugo Kaltenbrunner; it was adopted as a political–cultural faith by his son Ernst, who under drastically changed circumstances joined the *Burschenschaft* Arminia as a first semester chemistry student in the autumn of 1921. Under the strain of defeat in World War I the Austro-Hungarian state had disintegrated, leaving behind a rump German–Austria, whose capacity for economic survival in the postwar world was viewed with skepticism by most of its citizens. Aggravating this crisis of confidence were a rampant inflation that undermined the economic base and the peace of mind of the urban middle class, severe unemployment due to drastic cutbacks in the civil service and the loss of economic markets in the Habsburg successor states, food shortages in the cities, and the specter of Bolshevik upheaval spreading from neighboring Hungary and Bavaria. Postwar German *Burschenschaft* students perceived these chaotic conditions as demonstrable proof of the point made by their predecessors a generation earlier: that the survival of German culture, and the German race in Austria depended upon a racial-political union with a Germany purged of alien races and influence. The *Burschenschaft* nationalists raised the banner of hysteria and hatred not only against the Austrian Jews but also against World Jewry. They proclaimed that the postwar world was the successful result of an insidiously clever Jewish conspiracy. Jewish capitalists, they maintained, had manipulated the Anglo–American and French leaders into adopting the Versailles Treaty system, whose sole purpose was to keep Germans divided and weak. Having prevented Austrian economic recovery by forbidding the yearned for union with Germany, the Jewish conspirators used the League of Nations to provide usurious loans that artificially maintained Austrian economic life at a substandard level. This nationally humiliating and economically unstable condition left Germans defenseless in the face of the alleged culture–annihilating trend surging westward from Soviet Russia and spearheaded by Jews who led Soviet revolutionary regimes in Hungary and Bavaria — and threatened the same in Austria. Such was the *Burschenschaft* myth that came to be accepted as gospel by many in the German-Austrian professional middle class.

The solution to tiny Austria's political, social, economic and cultural crisis was as simplistic as the myth-world upon which that solution was predicated: the creation of a unified, racially pure German Reich. The means by which this end should be achieved — struggle against the Jews as the biologically determined foe of the German race and against their Catholic, Socialist and Slavic agents — appealed to young men insecure about their social status and economic future and caught in a general identity crisis that did not leave their elders untouched.

As a fraternity member and officer in Arminia, Ernst Kaltenbrunner helped plan gratuitously vicious demonstrations against those perceived to be enemies of Germandom: Jews, Slavs, Italians, Marxists, Catholics and Habsburg legitimists. For example, after an anti–Semitic professor had fussed publicly over an alleged insult by Jewish students in the autumn of 1923, Kaltenbrunner and other fraternity officers directed gangs of student thugs to surround lecture halls and to physically prevent Jewish students from attending lectures until the identities of the culprits were made known. Though the latter were never discovered, the student leaders seized the opportunity to stage a demonstration protesting the very presence of Jews at the Graz university and to claim later that the incident had demonstrated how "professors and students stood united in the struggle against Jewry."[4]

Although Kaltenbrunner temporarily abandoned this political atmosphere when he took his law degree in 1926, he returned to it at another time of general economic, cultural and social crisis when he joined the Nazi Party in October 1930 and the elite SS in August 1931. He needed but little indoctrination in the Nazi ideology. As a fraternity student, he had already developed a conviction of German racial superiority, a belief that national survival depended on national unity and racial purity, a hatred of the perceived enemies of Germandom (Jews, Catholics, Slavs, and Marxists), a conviction that these enemies were absolute and could offer no compromise acceptable to the German nation, and, finally, the consciousness of belonging to the elite of the German race, worthy to serve in such a Praetorian guard as the SS.

After joining the Austrian Nazi Party and the Austrian SS in 1930–1931, Kaltenbrunner rose rapidly through the ranks. Active as a speaker in the Upper Austrian electoral campaign of March-April 1931, he was appointed commander of the Linz SS *Sturm* (Company) in the summer of 1932. After the abortive Nazi putsch against the Austrian government on July 25, 1934, he was able to exploit the temporary prominence of the Upper Austrian Nazi leadership, which had a degree of immunity from Austrian police persecution not enjoyed by other provincial leaders of the now banned and fragmented Austrian Nazi Party, to make a name for himself outside his native Upper Austria.

Operating behind the cover of respectable German nationalists on the Upper Austrian political scene, the Linz SS leader took over and reorganized the entire Upper Austrian SS. He also became a secret courier bearing intelligence on Austrian political matters and conditions to SD leaders in Berlin; in this capacity, he had the opportunity to cultivate contacts with *Reichsführer*–SS Heinrich Himmler and the chief of Security Police and SD, Reinhard Heydrich. In January 1937, Himmler appointed Kaltenbrunner chief of the entire Austrian SS; after the *Anschluss* of Austria in March 1938, Kaltenbrunner was rewarded for his service with the post of Higher SS and Police Leader for Vienna, Lower Austria, and Upper Austria.

In his new position, Kaltenbrunner supervised the activities of all SS and police forces based in his region and took direct command over them in the event of a national emergency. Though his rival, RSHA chief Reinhard Heydrich, effectively excluded him from executive control of Nazi Jewish policy in Austria, Kaltenbrunner nevertheless had in Vienna an inside view of and some opportunity to assist in the implementation of the early stages of the Nazi program to eliminate the Jews from German life: expropriation and concentration. He opposed the unauthorized personal plunder of Jewish property in which, under the cover of the aryanization program, some of his comrades in Vienna had indulged themselves. He preferred authorized theft by bureaucratic means.

In the summer of 1938, Kaltenbrunner used his authority to curb arbitrary acts of confiscation and outright robbery by individual party members, threatening future perpetrators of such unauthorized actions with police prosecution. Then he ordered the Nazi Party and all of its formations to have their members deposit in a bank for later redistribution bank books, currency, jewelry and securities confiscated from Austrian Jews by individual Party members in the first months after the *Anschluss*. The office of the Higher SS and Police Leader would be provided with an exact list of all items deposited. Finally, Kaltenbrunner legalized these thefts by decreeing the plundered valuables to be "confiscated property of enemies of the state . . . in view of the special circumstances of the times."[5] Likewise, he sought to put an end to the indiscriminate looting that followed in the wake of the *Kristallnacht* riots of November 1938 by ordering police patrols to guard Jewish-owned businesses in Vienna and Linz. He then legalized another round of theft, informing the police president of Vienna that the Jewish firms and shops that had been attacked had been taken over by the Reich and were to be regarded as state property.[6]

In early 1941, Kaltenbrunner was an inside witness to the first concrete steps towards achieving a goal that he had called for since his student years: the expulsion of Jewry from Austria. On March 20, he was informed by the Deputy *Gauleiter* of Vienna, Karl Scharizer, that according to a decision of Himmler himself, the Jews of Vienna would be deported to the *Generalgouvernement*, that part of Poland occupied by but not directly annexed to Nazi Germany. From then on, one freight car packed with Viennese Jews would be attached to each train leaving Vienna for Cracow.[7] By late 1942, 47,555 Austrian Jews had been deported to ghettos, labor camps and extermination centers in Poland, White Russia and Latvia.[8]

During his years in Vienna, Kaltenbrunner inspired the respect and earned the approval of *Reichsführer*–SS Heinrich Himmler. On January 30, 1943, seven months after the death of Reinhard Heydrich, Himmler summoned Kaltenbrunner to Berlin to take over the RSHA. In choosing

Kaltenbrunner to run this key agency, whose purpose was to define, expose, and eliminate enemies of the German race and the Nazi regime, Himmler knew that he had selected a loyal paladin skilled in political intrigue and an ideological soldier prepared to combat the perceived enemy on the home front with the most drastic means.

From the beginning of his tenure at the RSHA Kaltenbrunner was thoroughly acquainted with the extent and scope of the Final Solution of the Jewish Question — that is, the Nazi program to exterminate the European Jews. In the spring of 1943, his office provided statistical data on Jews who either had emigrated or had been exterminated to the Reich Inspector for Statistics for a status report on the progress of the Final Solution. As early as February 1943, the new RSHA chief demonstrated his own ideological zeal in this matter. He proposed to Himmler a loosening up of the group of Jews over sixty years of age living in the Theresienstadt Ghetto in Bohemia by shipping 5,000 of them to the Auschwitz–Birkenau extermination center. He reasoned that the deportation of elderly and ill Jews from Theresienstadt would free up for forced labor 4,800 able bodied Jews presently engaged in caring for them.

Despite such arguments, which were persuasive on ideological and practical grounds, Himmler rejected Kaltenbrunner's suggestion. He wished to maintain the Theresienstadt Ghetto as a convenient showcase of German civilization for the benefit of international relief organizations and curious Germans who might ask what kind of work an octagenarian or a disabled Jewish war veteran might be expected to do in the resettlement camps in the East.[9]

Kaltenbrunner assisted in the murder of the European Jews because he believed that as a race, Jews were committed to the destruction of the German race. He left hints of this conviction when questioned in his Nuremberg prison cell only a month before his death. Lecturing his interrogator that, in Eastern Europe and the USSR, the Jews alone possessed the intellectual capacity and managerial ability to provide the inferior Slavic nations with the potential to destroy Germany, he explained that in Slovakia there was "no cobbler, no tavern keeper, no tailor, no baker, no business at all that was not 100 percent Jewish. . . An American would not believe this, but it is so." In the Soviet Union, he maintained, the situation was worse yet: all sabotage, espionage and partisan activity was organized by the Jew, who was the "decisive element in every hostile action." If the reports of the mobile killing units of the Security Police and the SD, or *Einsatzgruppen*, indicated that several hundreds of Jews were killed in Russia after a given operation, this "was to be expected; it corresponded to local conditions and did not constitute a will to annihilate."[10] Kaltenbrunner the administrator, driven by an obsession that haunted Kaltenbrunner the student, became Kaltenbrunner the implementor of a program of mass murder.

The apparatus for the systematic annihilation of the European Jews had been operative for nearly eighteen months when Kaltenbrunner took over the RSHA on January 30, 1943. Three distinct yet interrelated programs made up the process of annihilation. The mobile killing units of the Security Police and the SD — the so-called *Einsatzgruppen* — were responsible for the murder by shooting or by gas wagon of approximately 1,400,000 Soviet and Central European Jews on Soviet soil between June 1941 and the late summer of 1943. Between December 1941 and the end of summer 1943, some 2,000,000 to 2,500,000 primarily Polish but also Dutch, Belgian and Greek Jews were exterminated in the course of Aktion Reinhard (Operation Reinhard), directed by Odilo Globocnik, the SS and Police Leader of the District Lublin in occupied Poland. Most of these Jews were gassed in the death camps at Treblinka, Belzec, Sobibor, and Chelmno. Finally, most of the Jews deported from France, Belgium, Holland, Norway, Italy, Greece, Croatia, Slovakia, Hungary and the Reich itself were rounded up and shipped to the gas chambers, primarily at Auschwitz–Birkenau, but also at Treblinka and Sobibor. This last segment of the operation was carried out by SS-*Obersturmbannführer* Adolf Eichmann's Jewish affairs department of the RSHA (RSHA IV B 4), which was subordinated to the chief of the Gestapo, Heinrich Müller, who in turn reported to Heydrich and, later, Kaltenbrunner. Approximately 2,000,000 Jews fell victim to the organizational talents of Eichmann and his colleagues. Since the annihilation process was in full swing by the time he came to Berlin, Kaltenbrunner was not required to make innovative changes, but merely to supervise the mechanics of the operation and to provide political clout wherever and whenever his subordinates ran into snags.

In Greece, the Eichmann team needed such support as early as February 1943. His subordinates' protest compelled Kaltenbrunner to pressure German Foreign Office officials to dissuade the Italians from offering Greek Jews fleeing the German zone of occupation asylum in the Italian zone. After the destruction of the Warsaw Ghetto in the spring of 1943, Kaltenbrunner gave direct orders to the commander of the security police in Warsaw to deport the survivors of the uprising to Treblinka. Four months later, he adopted a hard line on the deportation of the Danish Jews despite the protest of the German plenipotentiary in Copenhagen, Werner Best, that the action would compromise relations between the German occupation authorities and the Danish administration. The Danish authorities were able to spirit most of the Danish Jews off to Sweden before the Eichmann team struck; but Kaltenbrunner steadfastly refused to yield to requests that the 450 Jews and half–Jews rounded up by Eichmann's men on the night of October 1–2, 1943 be transferred to the care of the Danish Red Cross. Finally, spurred by the frustration of his subordinates at the refusal of the Bulgarian government to permit the deportation of the Bulgarian Jews, Kaltenbrunner demanded that the German Foreign Office "exert stronger pressure on the Bulgarian government with respect to the Jewish question in order to solve this problem as soon as possible through evacuation to the East." An official of the Foreign Office replied that to apply such pressure was "hopeless."[11] In fact, Himmler had grown so impatient with the intransigence of Hungary, Romania and Bulgaria on the deportation issue that he ordered Kaltenbrunner in May 1943 to "prepare the ground" by cranking up ritual murder propaganda in these countries.[12]

Kaltenbrunner's most spectacular and successful intervention in the process of the Final Solution occurred in Hungary. Until the German occupation of their country on March 19, 1944, the Hungarian authorities had refused to bend to German pressure for the deportation of the Hungarian Jews, whose numbers, swelled by Slovak, Polish, Romanian and Yugoslav refugees, approximated 900,000 in the spring of 1944. Three days after the occupation of Hungary, Kaltenbrunner arrived in Budapest. He induced the newly installed, pliant and pro–German prime minister, Döme Sztójay, to place two notorious anti-Semites, László Endre and László Baky, in charge of a new office of Jewish affairs in the Hungarian Ministry of the Interior. To Baky and Endre, Kaltenbrunner offered general guidelines for the roundup and deportation of the Hungarian Jews to the Auschwitz–Birkenau extermination center. Eichmann's experts took care of the details; and, between mid–May and June 30, 1944, 381,600 Jews were evacuated from Hungary. Over 200,000 of them were gassed at Auschwitz–Birkenau.

Even as the Third Reich began to collapse around him, Kaltenbrunner did not slacken his effort to annihilate the Hungarian Jews. Though the extermination apparatus in the death camps had staggered to a halt in the autumn of 1944 (lack of facilities has closed the operations in Belzec and Chelmno; prisoner uprisings stilled the death factories in Sobibor and Treblinka; and Soviet troops were fast approaching Auschwitz in the fall of 1944), Kaltenbrunner still sought to extract Jews from Hungary in order to exploit them for forced labor in defense of the threatened Reich.

On October 15, 1944, an SS inspired *coup d'etat* against the regime of Regent Miklós Horthy, who had sought to extricate Hungary from the

Axis alliance, brought to power a government controlled by the rabidly anti–Semitic Arrow Cross movement; its prime minister was Ferenc Szálasi. Horthy had halted the deportations in July under international pressure and Allied threats of reprisal; but Kaltenbrunner expected the Szálasi government to be more cooperative. On October 17, he sent Eichmann to Budapest with the suggestion that 50,000 Jews be deported immediately and that the remainder of the Budapest Jews be concentrated in designated places on the periphery of the city.

Since transit by train had become difficult due to Allied bombings and the advance of Soviet troops and since Auschwitz itself was threatened by the Soviet advance, Eichmann suggested that the Hungarian Jews be marched on foot to the Austrian border, where they would be put to work on fortifications construction. Kaltenbrunner gave the necessary orders; and, with the cooperation of the Arrow Cross Minister of the Interior, Gábor Vajna, the marches began on October 20, 1944. Lacking food, adequate clothing and adequate footwear, some 30,000 Jews, many of them women, were marched off from Budapest towards the Austrian border in rain and sleet. Approximately 5,000 collapsed or were shot on the way. Kaltenbrunner's personal responsibility for this cruel and brutal policy is revealed by his indignant note to Horst Wagner, the chief of department *Inland II* of the German Foreign Office, in which he complained that an emissary of the Swiss legation had distributed special passes among the members of a marching column, whom the Hungarian police had then permitted to vanish.[13] Protests from the Vatican and the Swedish legation finally induced Szálasi to halt the marches on November 21; but this shift in policy did little to deter bands of Arrow Cross hoodlums from slaughtering hundreds of Jews remaining in Budapest and dumping their bodies into the icy Danube. The fall of Budapest to Soviet troops on February 13, 1945 put an end to these massacres.

Though ideologically somewhat more rigid than others in Himmler's inner circle during the last months of the war, Kaltenbrunner too was susceptible to the idea of bartering the lives of the Jews still under German control initially for war materiel, later for a negotiated peace with the Western Allies, and finally for a personal alibi. In the late summer and autumn of 1944, he cooperated briefly with Himmler and *SS–Obersturmbannführer* Kurt Becher in the infamous Jews for trucks deal, whereby Hungarian Jews were to be offered transit to the West in return for Allied trucks and other war materiel. He denounced the plan to Hitler in October, however, when he realized that it would prove abortive.

Kaltenbrunner also negotiated with representatives of the International Red Cross in March 1945, offering the lives of the remaining Jews in the

concentration camps in exchange for political initiatives towards a negotiated peace with the Western Allies. On April 24, 1945, six days before
Hitler's suicide, he offered to permit, free of any obligation, Red Cross
aid to reach and insure the survival of 14,000 Jews imprisoned at Gunskir-
chen in Wels, Upper Austria. The late hour of this concession lent it the
aura of a clumsy effort to establish an alibi.

To the last day of the war and beyond, Kaltenbrunner naively hoped
that the Allies would recognize his value as an intelligence expert on
Eastern Europe and would recruit him for service in the conflict that he
expected to break out between the Anglo–Americans and the Soviet
Union. He was shocked when the Allies put him on trial as a major war
criminal. Himmler's ideological soldier broke down at Nuremberg, and
sobbed that no one would understand or defend him. During the course of
the trial, however, he recovered and put on a vigorous defense that surprised judges and prosecutors alike. Maintaining that he had been summoned to Berlin specifically to reorganize the intelligence service of the
Reich, Kaltenbrunner denied having exercised executive control over the
Gestapo or having participated in the Final Solution. He went so far as to
deny his personal signature on an incriminating document. The tribunal
judges were impressed but unconvinced by Kaltenbrunner's defense;
they convicted him on counts of war crimes and crimes against humanity
and sentenced him to death. On the night of October 15–16, 1946, he was
hanged at the Nuremberg prison.

One historian has described Kaltenbrunner as a "gangster filled with
hatred and resentment," a "cold and ruthless killer."[14] A psychotherapist
and a political scientist presented the opinion that Kaltenbrunner and his
co–defendants at Nuremberg "were not psychologically normal or
healthy individuals."[15] Another historian, referring to Hannah Arendt's
often misinterpreted phrase, "banality of evil," concluded in his dissertation that Kaltenbrunner was "a commonplace, run–of–the–mill chap"
who, drawn into mass murder by his position in the state and the SS
bureaucracy, "ended his life as a convicted war criminal."[16] Each of
these statements flatly contradicts the others, but each includes a part of
the truth.

Certainly Kaltenbrunner participated coldly and ruthlessly in the murder of thousands of human beings; he thus appears as a killer without a
conscience. And who can doubt that the crime of genocide presupposes a
degree of psychological abnormality on the part of the perpetrators? Yet
the meticulous attention paid by the latter to the technical detail of murder
and their gruesome ability to reduce the moral problems raised by such
murder to a question of bureaucratic management and execution obscure

the image of the heartless supercriminal or the insane killer on the rampage and can conjure up the picture of a faceless, commonplace bureaucrat who has few thoughts concerning his assigned tasks except that they must be carried out.

How can we reconcile the insanity of the crime and its ideological foundation, the methodical rationality of its means and the complex of undeniably human motives in its perpetrators? How could Kaltenbrunner and his colleagues — I am not speaking of the men who personally shot their victims or pushed them into the gas chamber, but rather of the managers of these operations, without whom the killing would hardly have been so systematic or successful in scope — behave like normal bureaucrats at their desks during the day and like normal fathers and husbands with their families at night and yet have committed such a shockingly abnormal crime beside which the acts of bona fide insane killers like Richard Speck or David Berkowitz pale into insignificance? This writer cannot claim to have satisfactory answers to these questions, but would like to offer some perspective on them by allowing the managers of the Final Solution to speak for themselves.

To maintain that these men were without conscience or even human feeling may be to jump too quickly to an easy conclusion. The killers may in fact have had qualms about the nature of their activities. In praising Hitler's chief of *Wehrmacht* operations and fellow co–defendant Alfred Jodl, Kaltenbrunner explained to an American interrogator at Nuremberg how a "political soldier" had to overcome personal doubts and qualms to carry out a policy which was consistent with his *Weltanschauung*. The political soldier[17] will, if he is of firm character, follow each order exactly

> but will experience [internal] resistance in doing so. He will make his decisions based on subjective, indeed political thought.

If such a general comment seems insufficient in dealing with this issue, let us go straight to the point. Odilo Globocnik, the SS and Police Leader in Lublin and the manager of *Aktion Reinhard* (which cost more than 2,000,000 Jews their lives), was reported to have confessed private misgivings to a friend in 1943:[18]

> My heart's no longer in it, but I am so deeply involved in such things that I have no alternative but to ride to victory with Hitler or go under.

When the infant twins of SS–*Hauptsturmführer* Hans Höfle, Globocnik's expert on the evacuation of the Polish Jews, died of diphtheria in the spring of 1943, the stricken father broke down in the cemetery after the funeral and cried: "That is the punishment for all my misdeeds."[19] Even

Rudolf Höss, the commandant of the Auschwitz–Birkenau extermination center, was "tormented by secret doubts."[20]

Heinrich Himmler was aware of such misgivings and even perceived them to be signs of decency in his subordinates. Hoping to preserve such decency in the face of the difficult tasks that his executioners had to carry out, he expressed to his commanders "a personal wish that after an execution the execution commando be provided with a diversion of spiritually valuable content."[21] The *Reichsführer* expressed both his understanding for occasional outbreaks of human sympathy among his subordinates and his pride at the ability of the latter to conquer such feelings for the good of the Greater German Reich. Speaking to his SS generals in 1943, he compared the resolve needed to exterminate the Jews with that required by the first act of mass murder committed by the SS, the Röhm purge.[22]

> In all frankness, I would also like to bring a very grave matter [i.e., the "evacuation" of the Jews] to your attention. Among ourselves, we can for once speak of it quite openly, yet we will never discuss this publicly. Just as we did not hesitate on June 30, 1934 to perform our duty as required and to stand our comrades who had gone astray up against the wall and to shoot them, so we have never spoken about it and we will never speak about it. . . . We were all horrified, but each one of us understood completely that he would do it the next time if such orders were issued and if it were necessary.

In the same speech, Himmler offered his subordinates the conscience saving formula for their actions: they had "the moral duty toward our race to kill this [Jewish] race that wanted to kill us."[23]

Perhaps most telling about the need of these managers of murder to justify their acts within an imaginatively created framework of moral decency was the indignant response of the Commander of the Security Police and SD in Minsk, *SS–Obersturmbannführer* Eduard Strauch, to those who would denounce the deeds of his executioners. As he told a conference of German civilian administrators in Minsk on April 10, 1943:[24]

> I can conclude with the assurance that we [i.e., the Security Police and the SD] are doing all we can here to assist the *Gauleiter* [sic] and [to do] our duty for our nation and [our] Führer. It is true that we must carry out harsh and unpleasant tasks sometimes; but it offends me when some people believe that they can look down their noses at us. We do not understand that, gentlemen. We can carry out this occupation [i.e., Security Police and SD service] only because we are convinced that someone must carry out these tasks. I can say with pride that my men, regardless of how evil these tasks are, behave in a correct and decent manner, and can look anyone in the eye and [return] home

to be fathers to their families. They are proud to have been active for their Führer out of conviction and loyalty.

One can draw from such statements the inference that, in addition to their need for moral justification, the managers of the extermination process were concerned that the basic tenets of civilized society that they had been taught in their middle–class youth by their middle–class parents might have a deleterious effect on their ability to implement the uncivilized act of genocide, which they perceived to be not only a necessary political–military operation, but also an inevitable development in the history of mankind. They could not have been concerned had they had no misgivings about that which they felt they had to do. They were, after all, killers with a conscience; and that conscience may have impelled them to the meticulous thoroughness with which they carried out their tasks. Consciously, however, they placed their sense of wrongdoing "in partial suspense,"[25] and through this deliberate act revealed themselves not as insane individuals, but sane murderers killing with a deliberate purpose. An insane person would not have required such elaborate rationalizations for his crimes.

If we must discard as inaccurate the simplistic explanation that the SS leaders were insane criminals, we must be equally wary of the thesis that they were banal evildoers who routinely managed an extermination operation as if they were issuing welfare checks or collecting taxes. The personal initiative and inventiveness that the SS leaders put into the implementation of the Final Solution scarcely fit the image of the dull, unimaginative bureaucrat implied by a banality thesis.

Kaltenbrunner and his colleagues participated in genocide with open eyes; the crime was a logical, if not exactly inevitable extension of the aim that German racial nationalists had proclaimed in the nineteenth century: the expulsion of the Jews from Europe. In response to the general social, economic, cultural and psychological crisis that had plagued German nationalists for nearly a century and that had been aggravated by defeat in World War I, and economic instability and cultural despair in the interwar years, the Nazis had created — or rather adopted — a mythical crisis, pitting German against Jew and defining the Jew as the source of all Germany's woes.

Maturing in the conditions of genuine crisis, Kaltenbrunner perceived in the simplistic solution to the mythical crisis the final solution to the genuine crisis: since the Jew was the mortal enemy of the German race and the historically determined source of its lethal cultural illness, the Jew had to be eliminated in order to insure the survival of the German people.

Kaltenbrunner became an accomplice to genocide because he consciously and actively embraced a political myth that postulated that Jews and other "inferior" races were by ancestry enemies of the German nation and that the destruction of these biological competitors would bring to a German dominated Europe a utopian era, forever free of crisis. He and his colleagues believed that the fulfillment of this inevitable historical destiny produced an exceptional state of emergency in which by calling for the suspension of all recognized and normally respected standards they could and did present the extermination of European Jewry not as a crime but as a moral imperative, as an action that stood in accordance with the biological law of nature. Only in such a light could we understand — should we ever wish to — the twisted, pathetic last statement of Rudolf Höss, who when he received the order to annihilate the Jews of Europe could only say *Jawohl*, and who wanted the world to know that the commandant of Auschwitz "had a heart and that he was not evil."[26]

Notes

1. For further biographical details see Peter R. Black, *Ernst Kaltenbrunner: An Ideological Soldier of the Third Reich* (Princeton: Princeton University Press; forthcoming).

2. *The Diaries of Evelyn Waugh*, Michael Davie, editor (Boston-Toronto: Little, Brown and Company, 1976), p. 646.

3. A challenge to a duel was usually a response to a real or imagined insult to one's personal honor or to the honor of a fraternity. The contest was normally fought with dull blades, though especially serious insults called for sharp sabers or even pistols. During the contest the body was held motionless; only the saber arm up to the shoulder could be moved. Victory was achieved by drawing blood. Collective or individual honor was restored regardless of defeat if the loser did not flinch or cry out as the blade parted his skin. Fraternity students wore their facial scars as symbols of their manhood and their character.

4. *Festschrift zum 60. jährigen Stiftungsfest der Grazer akademischen Burschenschaft "Arminia," 1868–1928* (Graz: Verlag der Grazer akademischen Burschenschaft "Arminia," n. d.), p. 116.

5. Order of Kaltenbrunner, August 6, 1938, Microfilm Group T–580, Roll 62, Ordner 304, National Archives, Washington, D.C.

6. Millesi [Police President in Vienna] to Barth [Staff of the Reich Commissar for the Reunification of Austria with the German Reich], November 21, 1938, Nuremberg Trial Document 2237–PS, National Archives, Washington, D.C.

7. Scharizer to Kaltenbrunner, March 20, 1941, File 1456, Dokumentationsarchiv des österreichischen Widerstandes, Vienna.

8. Radomír Luža, *Austro–German Relations in the Anschluss Era* (Princeton: Princeton University Press, 1975), p. 225.

9. Kaltenbrunner to Himmler, February 1943, Microfilm Group T–175, Roll 22, Frames 2527354–2527356, National Archives, Washington, D.C.; Brandt to Chief of Security Police

and SD, February 16, 1943, ibid., Frame 2527353; Raul Hilberg, *The Destruction of the European Jews* (Chicago: Quadrangle, 1961), pp. 283–284.

10. Interrogation of Kaltenbrunner, Nuremberg, September 19, 1946, pp. 16–17, ZS–673, Institut für Zeitgeschichte, Munich.

11. Wagner to Kaltenbrunner, August 31, 1943, Nuremberg Document NG–3302, National Archives, Washington, D.C.

12. Himmler to Kaltenbrunner, May 19, 1943, in *Reichsführer . . . Briefe an und von Himmler*, Helmut Heiber, editor (Munich: Deutscher Taschenbuch Verlag, 1970), pp. 266–268.

13. Kaltenbrunner to Wagner, November 11, 1944, No. 393, in Randolph L. Braham, *The Destruction of Hungarian Jewry: A Documentary Account* (New York: World Federation of Hungarian Jews, 1963), Vol. II, p. 810.

14. Eugene Davidson, *The Trial of the Germans* (New York: Collier, 1972), pp. 320–321, 327.

15. Florence L. Miale and Michael Selzer, *The Nuremberg Mind* (New York: Quadrangle, 1975), p. 287.

16. Wendell Robert Houston, *Ernst Kaltenbrunner: A Study of An Austrian SS and Police Leader* (Houston: Rice University, Ph.D. Dissertation, 1972), p. 190.

17. Interrogation of Kaltenbrunner, September 12, 1946, p. 8, File ZS–673, Institut für Zeitgeschichte, Munich.

18. Quoted in Heinz Höhne, *The Order of the Death's Head* (New York: Ballantine, 1971), p. 440.

19. Quoted in Hilberg, *Destruction of the European Jews*, p. 332.

20. Rudolf Hoess [Höss], *Commandant of Auschwitz* (London–Sydney: Pan Books, 1974), p. 172.

21. Circular of the Higher SS and Police Leader East [signed Krüger], "Anweisung für dies Durchführung von Exekutionen," August 14, 1940, R 70 Polen/180, p. 62, Bundesarchiv, Koblenz.

22. Speech of Himmler to SS-Gruppenführer at Posen, October 4, 1943, Nuremberg Document 1919-PS, National Archives, Washington, D.C.

23. *Ibid.*

24. Speech of Strauch, April 10, 1943, in "Protokoll über die Tagung der Gebietskommissare, Hauptabteilungsleiter und Abteilungsleiter des Generalkommissars in Minsk vom 8. April bis 10. April 1943," July 16, 1943, File R 93/20, pp. 137–146, Bundesarchiv, Koblenz.

25. Hans Buchheim, "Command and Compliance," in Helmut Krausnick et al., *Anatomy of the SS State* (New York: Walker and Company, 1968), p. 362.

26. See Hoess, *Commandant of Auschwitz*, p. 205; G.M. Gilbert, *Nuremberg Diary* (New York: Signet, 1961), p. 230.

9 ATTITUDES TOWARD THE PROSECUTION OF NAZI WAR CRIMINALS IN THE UNITED STATES

Allan A. Ryan, Jr.

This paper deals with the attitudes toward the prosecution of Nazi war criminals in the United States. To a large extent it is based on the author's experiences as Director of the Office of Special Investigations (OSI) in the U.S. Department of Justice. The paper focuses on the activities of the United States government, the Department of Justice and the OSI, relating to the investigation and after many years the prosecution of those who gave a new and terrifying meaning to anti–Semitism.

Under the cover of war, Germany and her collaborators conducted a social offensive whose goal was the death of an entire people and an entire faith. The eradication of a people is called genocide; there is no word in our dictionaries to describe the eradication of a religious belief and tradition, yet this is what was intended — not only the death of all Jews but the death of Judaism itself. It is also known that these attempts very nearly succeeded.

Following the defeat of the Nazis, the United States and other Allied nations, acting under the auspices of the United Nations Organization, then in its infancy, opened their doors to the refugees of that war, and of the Iron Curtain that descended across Europe in its aftermath. Over four hundred thousand Europeans came to the United States between 1948 and 1952 under the Displaced Persons Act to resume their lives. In that number, however, were many people — no one knows how many — who were not the victims of the Holocaust but the perpetrators of it. Although these people — concentration camp staff, auxiliary storm troopers, SS murderers, and government officials — were specifically ineligible to enter the United States under the law, they succeeded in misrepresenting their whereabouts and activities during the war years and in passing themselves off as former farmers, students, bookkeepers or prisoners of war. In the often chaotic DP camps of occupied Germany, thorough background checks were seldom possible and these people succeeded in sailing to the United States, with immigrant visas in hand, often in boats crowded from rail to rail with their once intended victims.

Once in this country, they slipped quickly into the relative anonymity of large cities and unobtrusive lives and were never heard from again. During the 1960s, secure in their new country, many of them became naturalized American citizens, careful not to reveal the dark story of their pasts to the authorities.

The government of the United States did nothing regarding this infiltration. Indeed, there was no general public awareness of the infiltration of former Nazis and persecutors into our country. In 1977 and 1978, Elizabeth Holtzman, an outspoken representative from Brooklyn, and Joshua Eilberg of Philadelphia led Congress in the first public hearings ever conducted on this record of inaction. From these hearings two provisions emerged — the first law in our history making participation in racial, religious or political persecution a ground for deportation, and an appropriation of $2.3 million to the Department of Justice to investigate and prosecute Nazi war criminals in this country.

In 1979, the Attorney General established the Office of Special Investigations and gave it the authority to take whatever legal action might be appropriate against those now in this country who had engaged in persecution in conjunction with the Nazi regimes of Europe during the years 1933 to 1945. In 1981, the Office of Special Investigations had a staff of 50 people, including 20 attorneys and a full complement of investigators, historians, researchers, translators and support staff, dedicated to this long-neglected task.

To call the perpetrators of the Holocaust war criminals is a sort of convenient shorthand, but of course it is a misnomer, because what they did had very little to do with the war. They were not carrying out a military policy but a grotesque social one. As Simon Wiesenthal has said, in a true war, soldiers take risks. They can kill, but they can also be killed. These people were not soldiers, and they took no risks; to call them war criminals is misleading, although it is often done.

What is the legal basis for the United States' action now? Because the United States has no jurisdiction to prosecute these persons for crimes that took place in Europe against European citizens, the emphasis of OSI's activity has been to bring cases to court, seeking to revoke citizenship on the grounds that it was obtained illegally or by fraud. By proving in court that a defendant was in fact engaged in persecution during World War II, we can establish that his entry into this country and his subsequent naturalization was illegal. If the OSI succeeds in this task, the second and final step is to seek their deportation.

The obstacles to success in any given case are great. Forty years ago the Supreme Court held that the precious right of American citizenship could be revoked only upon the clearest and most convincing proof that it was illegally obtained (US vs Schneiderman, 1943). The Court reiterated that principle in 1980 in revoking the citizenship of a former guard at the death camp at Treblinka — a man who came to this country by claiming he had spent the war years as a farmer (Fedorenko v. U. S., 1981). Added to this is the fact that it is a formidable task to prove in an American courtroom the commission of crimes that took place four decades ago and half a world away. Documents are held in foreign archives and the witnesses who survived are scattered from the United States to the Soviet Union to Israel. It can often be difficult to go into a courtroom in New York and obtain a conviction for a murder that took place on a public street a mile away six months earlier. Compare this to the task of going into the same courtroom and proving a murder that took place in a Nazi death camp five thousand miles away forty years ago. If witnesses can be found, they live in the Ukraine and Lithuania or Israel and often don't speak English. Now you can appreciate some of the obstacles the OSI faces.

Nonetheless in the first two years that the OSI was in operation, it achieved some success. In the United States Supreme Court, the OSI won the denaturalization of Feodor Fedorenko, a guard at Treblinka, and in so doing it established a crucial point — that any person who took part in Nazi persecution was ineligible by that reason alone to enter the United States and therefore was disqualified from obtaining American citizenship. The Supreme Court also ruled that there could be no defense on the grounds of ''I was forced to do it.'' It also ruled that it was irrelevant whether the defendant had spent 30 years as a law–abiding citizen in the United States (refer to Appendix II5).

In Philadelphia, the OSI won the denaturalization of a member of the Ukrainian auxiliary police (U. S. v. Osidach, 1980). In 1981, the OSI won a similar case in Brooklyn (U. S. v. Derkacz, 1981), and in March, a third case in Florida (U. S. v. Koziy, 1981).

On Long Island, the OSI won a judgment revoking the citizenship of the commandant of a concentration camp in Estonia (U. S. v. Linnas, 1981).

In Cleveland, a man who operated the first gas chamber at Treblinka was stripped of his citizenship by a federal court (U. S. v. Demjanjuk, 1981).

In Detroit, one of the leaders of the Iron Guard movement in Romania surrendered his citizenship rather than face trial (U. S. V. Trifa). In October 1982, he consented to an order of deportation.

In California, a German who as an SS officer wrote memos to Adolf Eichmann on how to solve the Jewish question surrendered his citizenship when the OSI confronted him with the results of its investigation (U. S. v. von Bolschwing, 1981). He died a few months later.

The OSI won a case ordering the deportation of the Minister of Justice and Interior in the Nazi puppet regime of Croatia — a man responsible for the deaths of hundreds of thousands of Jews, Gypsies and Serbs (U. S. v. Artukovic, 1981).

In 1981, the OSI completed trials and is waiting verdicts in two cases: to deport a member of the Latvian political police (U. S. v. Laipenieks), and to revoke the citizenship of a Ukrainian in Philadelphia who carried out anti–Jewish actions in his native country (U. S. v. Kowalchuk).

In short, the OSI won all nine of the cases that were tried before 1982 and has brought to court some 18 additional cases that are expected to be tried in the early 1980s. The OSI has investigated over 500 people in this country, and is continuing to open new investigations every month. The Reagan administration has given the OSI its full support, and the budget request for the OSI for fiscal 1983 is the largest one to date, some $2.75 million, or 20 percent more than the original budget for 1980.

In the course of this effort, the OSI has made some unusual breakthroughs. In Moscow in 1979 I negotiated the first agreement ever made allowing representatives of the American government to take testimony from Soviet citizens. Since then, the OSI representatives have taken the videotaped depositions of 75 Soviet witnesses, and the OSI has used them in court in several cases. The OSI has placed on the public record, for the first time in federal courts, the sordid record of Nazi persecution. The OSI obtained the full cooperation of the government of Poland — a cooperation that has continued in full force even since the imposition of martial law in December 1981. The recently documented anti-Semitic propaganda of the military regime there is not shared, so far as it can be ascertained, by those offices that have provided and hopefully will continue to provide assistance to the OSI.

The OSI has established a very close working relationship with Israel, and indeed a member of the OSI's staff is stationed full time in Jerusalem, at Yad Vashem. The OSI has worked closely with the government of West Germany, and I plan to meet, for the first time, with officials in East Germany and Czechoslovakia in an attempt to secure their assistance as well.

The OSI's greatest frustration so far has been that only one of the accused has been deported by early 1983. (Hans Lipschis, a guard at Auschwitz, was deported to the Federal Republic of Germany in April 1983.) The system of appeals and hearings that have grown up in this century with regard to denaturalization and deportation cases is complex and terribly time consuming. It encourages and rewards delay. One sometimes marvels that anyone can be deported from the United States for any reason. One hopes that the months ahead will bring the first deportations but that process, when it begins, will be a trickle, not a torrent.

Let us raise one final matter. Many people have asked, "Why now?" Why should the United States government, so many years after the end of World War II, be prosecuting Nazis? Isn't it a little late for that? What's the point in ruining the lives of a bunch of harmless old men who have lived decent lives here for thirty years, raising families, paying taxes, minding their own business? Aren't there more important things that the Department of Justice could be doing with its 2.75 million dollars a year?

Many of the people who raise these questions are not anti–Semitic in the conventional sense. They do not make light of the Holocaust and they do not harbor overt prejudices against Jews, at least as far as one can tell. But their questions require an answer that goes beyond the instinctive reaction.

The Holocaust was mass murder as political policy, and civilized people must reject it in every form, lest it appear as if we are forgetting it, or worse, legitimizing it. Of the hundreds of thousands who carried out this campaign in Germany and in Europe 40 years ago, those who remain in the United States today are only the aging remnants. Yet we know they are here and we know that they broke the law to come here and stay and live here in peace. To say that they pose no danger to anyone because they are old men misses the point entirely. We are proceeding against them under the law not because of what they might do in the future but because not to proceed against them would be to forgive what they did in the past. What we are doing today should have been done more than 30 years ago. To grant these people repose from the law in the 1980s would mean that their 30 years of silence and our 30 years of inaction somehow combine to legitimize their awful crimes, and that justice is the result. We should not accept that insidious logic, nor can we accept it merely because the criminals are fewer and older today.

What we are doing today is perhaps the last action that we as a people can take that is not only symbolic but it is an action that demonstrates our commitment that this shall not be allowed to happen again. What we are doing is enforcing the law against the very people who violated it, the very people who violated not only the United States' law of immigration and citizenship, but the law of humanity. We can charge in court only the former, but the latter can never be far from our minds.

And so to those who ask "Why now?" I say "If not now, when?" Shall we do nothing now and await instead, God forbid, some new Holocaust that will give us a new generation of Nazis, a younger, longer list of defendants? However late the date, it is still within the power of our nation, still within the reach of the law, to call into account those criminals who still live among us. It can yet be done. That is why it must be done.

Appendix

DIGEST OF CASES IN LITIGATION: US OFFICE
OF SPECIAL INVESTIGATIONS

December 1, 1982

I. Denaturalization Cases

1. JUODIS, JURGIS

Case Pending: U. S. District Court for the Middle District of Florida; Civil Action No. 81–1013–CIV–T–H.

Date Filed: October 26, 1981.

Date and Place of Birth: October 22, 1911, Kebliskiai, Kaunas District, Lithuania.

Entry Date: July 21, 1949, under the Displaced Persons Act of 1948.

Immigration Status: Naturalized February 8, 1955 by the U. S. District Court for the Eastern District of New York.

Summary of Allegation: During the Nazi occupation of Lithuania and Byelorussia, from 1941 until 1944, defendant served in the SS-controlled Lithuanian Auxiliary Police (*"Schutzmannschaft"*), in which he ultimately was commissioned as an *Oberleutnant*. While so serving, defendant personally commanded and participated in the assault, arrest, detention, and murder of unarmed Jews and other civilians. Defendant subsequently concealed and misrepresented his wartime activities when applying for entry to the United States and later when applying for naturalization as a United States citizen.

Progress to Date: On June 17, 1982 the court denied defendant's motion to dismiss the complaint. Depositions in Scotland and Lithuania were completed in August 1982. A status conference before the judge will be held December 29 to request a trial date and to decide various motions by both sides.

2. KAIRYS, LIUDAS

Case Pending: U. S. District Court, N. D. Ill.; Civil Action No. 80–C–4302.

Date Filed: August 13, 1980.

Date and Place of Birth: December 24, 1920, Svilionys, Lithuania.

Entry Date: May 28, 1949, under the Displaced Persons Act of 1948.

Immigration Status: Naturalized July 16, 1957 by the U. S. District Court, N. D. Ill.

Summary of Allegation: From 1942 to 1944, defendant served with the SS auxiliary guard units (SS *Wachmannschaft*) at Trawniki, Poland, the SS Comando Lublin, and the SS forced labor camp in Treblinka, Poland, where thousands of Jewish civilian prisoners were murdered by the SS *Wachmannschaft*. Defendant concealed these facts when applying for entry and for naturalization.

Progress to Date: Trial commenced on June 14, 1982, and concluded on July 7, 1982. A decision is pending.

3. KARKLINS, TALIVALDIS

Case Pending: U. S. District Court, C. D. California, Civil Action No. CV 81 0460 LTL.

Date Filed: January 29, 1981.

Date and Place of Birth: June 16, 1914, at Madona, Latvia.

Entry Date: July 23, 1956, under the Refugee Relief Act of 1953.

Immigration Status: Naturalized January 25, 1963 by the U. S. District Court for the Central District of California.

Summary of Allegation: While serving as a member of the Madona (Latvia) District Police, in July and August, 1941, defendant assisted in the persecution and murder of unarmed Jewish civilians and committed crimes including murder and assault. From September 1, 1941 until the fall of 1942, defendant was the Commandant of the Madona Concentration Camp, which was operated under the command of the chief SS officer in Latvia. During defendant's tenure as Commandant of this camp, unarmed inmates of the camp were starved, beaten, tortured, murdered and otherwise brutalized by defendant and/or by persons acting under his direction and control. Defendant subsequently misrepresented and concealed his activities during this period when applying for entry to the United States and later when applying for naturalization as a United States citizen.

Progress to Date: Defendant's answer to OSI's complaint was filed on March 30, 1981. Defendant's deposition was taken on April 9, 1981, at which time he refused to answer any questions relating to his wartime activities or to his entry or naturalization. On August 4, 1981, the judge ruled that defendant does not have to answer questions about his background or about his activities during World War II. Defendant was ordered, however, to answer questions relating to his immigration and naturalization. Depositions were taken in Latvia in November 1981. Trial has been set for March 15, 1983.

4. KOWALCHUK, SERGEI

Case Pending: U. S. District Court, E. D. Pa.; Civil Action No. 77–118.

Date Filed: January 13, 1977.

Date and Place of Birth: March 15, 1920, Kremianec, Poland.

Entry Date: February 2, 1950, under the Displaced Persons Act of 1948.

Immigration Status: Naturalized November 30, 1960 by the U. S. District Court, E. D. Pa.

Summary of Allegations: Defendant served as a member of the Nazi–controlled Ukrainian Police in Luboml, Poland during the years 1941 and 1942. While serving in this capacity, defendant participated in the persecution of, and the commission of crimes or atrocities against, civilians. Defendant concealed these facts when applying for entry and for naturalization.

Progress to Date: Depositions of six witnesses were taken in Lutsk, U. S. S. R. in January 1981. Trial was held, in Philadelphia, on October 19–28 and December 11, 1981. Post–trial arguments were heard on January 18, 1982. The decision in this case is now pending with the District Court.

5. KOZIY, BOHDAN

Case Pending: U. S. Court of Appeals, Eleventh Circuit; Civil Action No. 79–6640–CIV–JCP.

Date Filed: October 20, 1979.

Date and Place of Birth: February 23, 1923, Pukasiwci, Ukraine.

Entry Date: December 17, 1949, under the Displaced Persons Act of 1948.

Immigration Status: Naturalized February 9, 1956 by the Supreme Court, State of New York, at Utica. Denaturalized by United States District Judge James C. Payne in Southern District Florida on March 29, 1982.

Summary of Allegation: During the period 1942–1944, defendant served as a Ukrainian policeman stationed in Lysiec, Ukraine, and participated in the murders of unarmed civilians. He concealed these facts when applying for entry and naturalization.

Progress to Date: Depositions of witnesses in Poland were taken in January 1981, and additional depositions were taken in the Soviet Union in March. Trial in this case commenced on September 15, 1981 and ended October 2. A decision in favor of OSI was rendered on March 29, 1982 revoking defendant's citizenship.

Defendant filed post–trial motions for a new trial, to vacate the decision of the court, and to amend the decision of court. All were denied. On June 10, 1982, the defendant filed his notice of appeal. Because preparation of the transcript was delayed, Koziy's brief is due in early January.

6. KUNGYS, JUOZAS

Case Pending: U. S. District Court for the District of New Jersey; Civil Action No. 81–2305.

Date Filed: July 22, 1981.

Date and Place of Birth: September 21, 1915, Reistru, Silales, Lithuania.

Entry Date: April 29, 1948, under the Immigration Act of 1924, as amended.

Immigration Status: Naturalized February 3, 1954 by the U. S. District Court for the District of New Jersey.

Summary of Allegation: Defendant, in association with the armed forces of Nazi Germany, participated in the killing of approximately one hundred civilians in or near the village of Babences (Babenus), Lithuania in July 1941. In July or August 1941, defendant led an armed group of men which forced the approximately 3,000 Jewish civilian inhabitants of Kedainiai, Lithuania from their homes into a ghetto and then confiscated their property. Later that year, defendant organized, led, and participated in the killing of some 2,000 unarmed civilian Jewish men, women, and children at a mass grave site near Kedainiai. Defendant subsequently misrepresented and concealed his wartime activities and other material facts when applying for entry and for naturalization.

Progress to Date: Defendant's answer to OSI's complaint was filed on October 2, 1981. On October 14, 1981, the District Court denied defendant's motion for a protective order against the taking of depositions in Lithuania. Depositions taken in Lithuania were concluded in April 1982. The case has been set for trial in September, October and November, 1982, and each time has been delayed because of the press of criminal cases on the court's docket.

7. PALCIAUSKAS, KAZYS

Case Pending: U. S. District Court, Middle District of Florida; Civil Action No. 81–547 Civ. T–GC.

Date Filed: June 15, 1981.

Date and Place of Birth: September 11, 1907, Zagare, Siaulia, Lithuania.

Entry Date: April 19, 1949, under the Displaced Persons Act of 1948.

Immigration Status: Naturalized November 11, 1954 by the U. S. District Court for the Northern District of Illinois.

Summary of Allegation: On June 25, 1941, German armed forces occupied Kaunas (Kovno), the capital city of Lithuania. From approximately that date until May 1, 1942, defendant served the Nazis as mayor of Kaunas. While serving in that position, defendant assisted the Nazis in persecuting civilians by ordering the internment of the Jewish population of Kaunas (more than 20,000 persons) in a ghetto under inhumane conditions. In his capacity as mayor, defendant promulgated orders regulating the lives and activities of the Jewish population. One such order required all Jews to wear a conspicuous yellow Star of David symbol on their chests. Defendant also was responsible for the confiscation of Jewish–owned homes and the collection and counting of Jewish–owned valuables. These homes and possessions were then turned over to the German authorities and to others. Defendant concealed and misrepresented these facts when applying for entry and for naturalization.

Progress to Date: OSI filed its complaint on June 15, 1981. Defendant filed his answer on September 24, 1981. Defendant was deposed on September 21, 1981, at which time he refused to answer any questions, pursuant to a claimed privilege under the Fifth Amendment. OSI has filed a motion to compel defendant to answer its questions. A decision on this motion is now pending with the court.

Depositions were completed in Lithuania in April 1982. On July 12, 1982, the court set trial for December 1, 1982 in Fort Myer, Florida. That date was continued to December 7, 1982.

8. SCHELLONG, CONRAD

Case Pending: U. S. District Court, Northern District of Illinois; Civil Action No. 81 C 1478.

Date Filed: March 17, 1981.

Date and Place of Birth: February 7, 1910, Dresden, Germany.

Entry Date: February 23, 1957, under the Immigration and Nationality Act of 1952.

Immigration Status: Naturalized July 17, 1962 by U. S. District Court, N. D. Illinois. Denaturalized September 7, 1982 by the same court, following trial.

Summary of Allegation: During the years 1934–1940, defendant served in various *Schutzstaffel* ("SS") guard companies at the Sachsenburg and Dachau concentration camps in Germany. Defendant served first as a guard and later as company commander of several of these units. Defendant's duties at both camps included the guarding of thousands of civilians interned there by the Nazis because of their race, religion, or political beliefs. At Dachau, where defendant rose to the rank of SS–*Hauptsturmführer* (Captain), he was responsible for the training of new SS recruits for concentration camp guard duty. When applying for entry into the United States, defendant concealed his activities during that period at Sachsenburg and Dachau. When later applying for naturalization, defendant falsely swore that he had never served in a concentration camp. Defendant also concealed the fact that, from June through November, 1932, he had been a member of the *Sturmabteilung* ("SA"), a paramilitary unit of the German Nazi Party.

Progress to Date: Trial commenced on May 25, 1982 and concluded on June 4. On September 7, 1982, the court handed down its judgment in favor of OSI, ruling that Schellong had concealed his service at Dachau and Sachsenburg and revoking his citizenship. On October 6, the court denied the defendant's motion for reconsideration and new trial. Defendant's deadline to appeal the decision is December 6, 1982.

9. SOKOLOV, VLADIMIR

(a/k/a Vladimir Samarin)

Case Pending: U. S. District Court for the District of Connecticut; Civil Action No. 82–56.

Date Filed: January 27, 1982.

Date and Place of Birth: March 2, 1913, Orel, Russia.

Entry Date: June 27, 1951, under the Displaced Persons Act of 1948, as amended.

Immigration Status: Naturalized May 21, 1957 by the United States District Court for the Eastern District of New York.

Summary of Allegation: From approximately December 1942 until August 1944, defendant was employed by propaganda units of the armed forces of Nazi Germany in Nazi–occupied areas of the Soviet Union as a writer, literary editor, and deputy editor of the Russian–language newspaper, *Rech*. In writings authored by defendant and published in *Rech*, he urged that all Jews be physically persecuted and completely annihilated and that Nazi rule be extended to the United States and throughout the world. From approximately August 1944 until April 1945, defendant was employed in Berlin, Germany as a writer for the Nazi government–sponsored Russian–language newspaper, *Vola Naroda*. Defendant misrepresented and concealed all of the above facts when applying for entry and for naturalization.

Progress to Date: Defendant's answer to OSI's complaint was filed on March 29, 1982. OSI's motion to compel answers to interrogatories and to strike defendant's jury demand is before the court.

10. SPROGIS, ELMARS

Case Pending: U. S. District Court for the Eastern District of New York; Case Number 82 Civ. 1804.

Date Filed: June 23, 1982.

Date and Place of Birth: November 26, 1914 at Jaunjelgava, Latvia.

Entry Date: November 1950, under the Displaced Persons Act of 1948, as amended.

Immigration Status: Naturalized April 16, 1962 by the U. S. District Court for the Southern District of New York.

Summary of Allegation: Sprogis served as Assistant Chief of Police of the city of Gulbene, Latvia in 1941, during which time the Latvian Police assisted the Nazis in murdering Jews and confiscating their property. Sprogis personally ordered and assisted in the murder and arrest of Jews and the confiscation of their property. Sprogis was later the Police Chief of Madona, Latvia, where he supervised and took part in the killing of Soviet prisoners of war. He also participated in a punitive expedition in Byelorussia in which villages were burned and innocent villagers arrested or shot.

Progress to Date: The defendant's answer to OSI's complaint was received on August 23, 1982. Depositions were taken in Latvia from November 15–19. Discovery is proceeding.

II. Deportation Cases

1. ARTUKOVIC, ANDRIJA
Case Pending: U. S. Court of Appeals for the Ninth Circuit; Civil Action No. 81–7415.

Date Filed: May 9, 1951.

Date and Place of Birth: November 29, 1899, Klobuk, Herzegovina (now Yugoslavia).

Entry Date: July 16, 1948 as temporary visitor for pleasure, under the Immigration and Nationality Act of 1924, under the name Alois Anich.

Immigration Status: Overstayed visitor; File No. A7 095 961.

Summary of Allegation: Defendant was Minister of the Interior and Minister of Justice of the Nazi "Independent State of Croatia." In that capacity, he signed decrees authorizing executions and persecution and had direct complicity in massacres of hundreds of thousands of Serbs, Jews, Gypsies, and others.

Progress to Date: An order of deportation has been outstanding against defendant since 1952. In 1953, the Board of Immigration Appeals upheld the order and specifically found that Artukovic was responsible for the mass persecution of Serbs, Jews, and others. In 1959, however, defendant was granted withholding of deportation, pursuant to §243(h) of the Immigration and Nationality Act of 1952, 8 U. S. C. §1253(h), upon a determination by an INS Special Inquiry Officer that defendant's deportation to Yugoslavia would subject him to "physical persecution." Efforts made during the 1950's to secure Artukovic's extradition to Yugoslavia were similarly unsuccessful.

In 1978, Congress amended Section 243(h) to make it unavailable to those who had taken part in persecution under the Nazi regimes of Europe (P. L. 95–549, 92 Stat. 2065). In October 1979, OSI moved to revoke the §243(h) order withholding deportation.

On July 1, 1981, the BIA decided in OSI's favor, revoking defendant's stay of deportation and ordering that he be deported. The Board specifically ruled that defendant had offered no new evidence sufficient to call into question the soundness of the BIA's 1953 determination that Artukovic had been a leader in the Nazi puppet government in Croatia and that he had, in that capacity, participated in the persecution of Serbs, Jews, and others.

On July 1, 1981, defendant filed a petition with the U. S. Court of Appeals for the Ninth Circuit seeking a review of the decision of the Board of Immigration Appeals. Oral argument on the appeal was heard on January 4, 1982 in Los Angeles, California. The decision is pending. Defendant's deportation is now automatically stayed, pursuant to 8 U. S. C. §1105(a), pending disposition of his appeal.

2. DEMJANJUK, JOHN
Case Pending: Immigration Court, Cleveland, Ohio.
Date Filed: August 25, 1977 (denaturalization); July 2, 1982 (deportation).
Date and Place of Birth: April 3, 1920, Dub Macharenzi Ukraine.
Entry Date: February 9, 1952, under the Displaced Persons Act of 1948, as amended.
Immigration Status: Naturalized November 14, 1958 by the U. S. District Court, N. D. Ohio. Ordered denaturalized by U. S. District Court, N. D. Ohio, on June 23, 1981.
Summary of Allegation: Defendant, while employed as a uniformed guard with the German SS at the Nazi death camps at Sobvobor and Treblinka, Poland in 1942 and 1943, assisted in the extermination of thousands of Jewish civilians. Defendant operated the gas chambers at Treblinka and abused and persecuted Jewish prisoners and laborers. Defendant misrepresented his background in applying for entry and naturalization.
Progress to Date: Trial was held in February and March of 1981 before the U. S. District Court for the Northern District of Ohio, in Cleveland (Civil Action No. C77–923). On June 23, 1981 the Court entered judgment for OSI, revoking defendant's United States citizenship on the grounds that it had been procured both illegally and by willful misrepresentation of material facts. The Court found that defendant, when applying for entry and for naturalization, had failed to disclose his wartime service under the German SS at both the SS Training Camp at Trawniki, Poland and the Treblinka death camp. The Court specifically concluded that the six eyewitness identifications of defendant as a notorious guard who operated the gas chambers at Treblinka were reliable.

On June 8, 1982, the court of appeals for the Sixth Circuit affirmed the decision of the district court. Demjanjuk's petition for Supreme Court review was denied on November 29, 1982. Deportation proceedings will begin January 10, 1983.

3. DERCACZ, MICHAEL
Case Pending: U. S. Immigration Court, E. D. N. Y.; Case No. 80 Civ. 1854.
Date Filed: July 7, 1980, denaturalization; August 4, 1982, deportation.

Date and Place of Birth: February 22, 1909, Zheldec, Ukraine.

Entry Date: May 18, 1949, under the Displaced Persons Act of 1948.

Immigration Status: Naturalized November 11, 1954 by the U. S. District Court, E. D. N. Y. Ordered denaturalized by U. S. District Court, E. D. N. Y., on February 2, 1982.

Summary of Allegation: From September, 1941 through August 1943, defendant was a uniformed police officer in the Ukrainian Police Command in L'vov, Ukraine, and was stationed in Nazi–occupied Jaryzow–Nowy, Ukraine. Defendant actively participated in beatings and executions of unarmed Jewish civilians in Jaryzow–Nowy. He concealed and misrepresented these facts when applying for entry and for naturalization.

Progress to Date: Depositions were taken in the Soviet Union in March, 1981. OSI filed a motion for summary judgment on June 2, 1981. On February 2, 1982, the Court granted the summary judgment motion, and ordered that defendant's citizenship be revoked. The Court found that Dercacz had persecuted civilian Jews while serving as an armed member of the Ukrainian Police in Nowy Yarchev. The court had further found that defendant had procured his citizenship both illegally and by willful misrepresentation of material facts. Defendant's time for filing a notice of appeal has expired. Deportation proceedings against defendant were filed in New York on August 4, 1982.

At a hearing on 10/21/82, the Immigration Judge set December 7 for the deportation hearing.

4. DETLAVS, KARLIS

Case Pending: Board of Immigration Appeals; File No. A7 925 159.

Date Filed: Order to Show Cause filed with the Immigration Court, Baltimore on October 1, 1978.

Date and Place of Birth: June 27, 1911, Latvia.

Entry Date: December 20, 1950, under the Displaced Persons Act of 1948, as amended.

Immigration Status: Permanent resident.

Summary of Allegation: While serving, from 1941 to 1943, as a member of the Latvian Auxiliary Security Police, defendant participated in assaults upon and murders of unarmed civilians, primarily Jews, in Latvia. From 1943, defendant served in the Latvian Legion. In 1950, when applying for admission to the U. S., defendant falsely swore that he had not advocated or assisted in the persecution of any person because of race, religion, or national origin.

Progress to Date: Deportation hearings were held during January and

February, 1979, prior to the creation of OSI. In February 1980, the Immigration Judge ruled in favor of defendant, and refused to order his deportation. The court held that the government had failed to prove by clear, convincing, and unequivocal evidence that defendant had engaged in persecution. The court further found that defendant's admitted misrepresentations were not "material." OSI appealed this decision to the Board of Immigration Appeals, and the appeal was argued before the Board on August 4, 1980. On October 15, 1981, the BIA dismissed OSI's appeal, holding that government had not established the materiality of defendant's misrepresentations by clear, convincing, and unequivocal evidence. Various possible courses of action are now under consideration by OSI.

5. FEDORENKO, FEODOR

Case Pending: U. S. Immigration Court, Hartford, Connecticut, File No. A7 333 468.

Date Filed: March 5, 1981 (deportation); August 15, 1977 (denaturalization).

Date and Place of Birth: September 17, 1907, Sivasch, Ukraine.

Entry Date: November 5, 1949, under the Displaced Persons Act of 1948.

Immigration Status: Naturalized April 23, 1970 by the Superior Court of New Haven County, Connecticut. Citizenship ordered revoked by U. S. Supreme Court on January 21, 1981. Denaturalized by order of the U. S. District Court, S. D. Florida, Ft. Lauderdale Division, on March 11, 1981.

Summary of Allegation: Defendant misrepresented his wartime service as an armed guard at the Treblinka death camp in Poland during the years 1942–1943, and his commission there of atrocities against prisoners.

Progress to Date: On August 15, 1977, the government filed suit seeking defendant's denaturalization. On July 25, 1978, the U. S. District Court for the Southern District of Florida entered judgment in favor of defendant, despite defendant's admitted service at Treblinka and subsequent misrepresentation of his wartime activities.

On June 28, 1979, the U. S. Court of Appeals for the Fifth Circuit reversed the decision of the District Court. The Court of Appeals held that the District Court had applied an incorrect test of "materiality," and that applying the proper test to the evidence revealed that Fedorenko's misrepresentations had in fact been material. The Court of Appeals further ruled that the District Court erred as a matter of law in concluding that it had authority to enter a judgment for defendant based upon "equitable considerations." The Court of Appeals directed the District Court to cancel defendant's certificate of naturalization.

On February 19, 1980, the U. S. Supreme Court granted Fedorenko's petition for a writ of certiorari, and on October 15, 1980, the Attorney General argued the case for the United States. On January 21, 1981, the Supreme Court, in a 7-2 affirmance of the decision of the Court of Appeals, held that Fedorenko's citizenship had been illegally procured and therefore must now be revoked. The Court ruled that Fedorenko's misrepresentation's were clearly material. The Court also held that section 2(b) of the Displaced Persons Act of 1948 (which prohibited the granting of visas to persons who "assisted the enemy in persecuting civil[ians]") required that visas be denied even to individuals who might have "involuntarily" assisted the Nazis in persecuting civilians; hence, the District Court's finding that Fedorenko acted involuntarily was irrelevant. Additionally, the Court ruled that once it is determined that an individual's citizenship was procured illegally or through misrepresentation, courts have no discretion to excuse the conduct and allow the defendant to retain his citizenship hence, Fedorenko's good conduct subsequent to entering the United States was irrelevant.

Deportation hearings were held on May 4-5 and July 7, 1981. Both OSI and defense counsel have completed presenting their respective cases, including submission of materials pertaining to defendant's application for discretionary relief from deportation under §244 of the Immigration and Nationality Act, as amended (however, in December 1981, the Act was amended to provide that §244 relief is now unavailable to persons who persecuted civilians on behalf of the Nazis and their allies). The decision has now been pending over one full year with the Immigration Court at New Haven.

6. HAZNERS, VILIS

Case Pending: Board of Immigration Appeals, File No. A10 305 336.

Date Filed: Defendant was served with an Order to Show Cause on January 28, 1977.

Date and Place of Birth: July 23, 1905, Latvia.

Entry Date: August 23, 1956, under the Refugee Relief Act of 1953, as amended.

Immigration Status: Permanent resident.

Summary of Allegation: As an officer in the Latvian Self Defense Group and later the *Schutzmannschaft*, a police organization under German supervision and control, defendant directed and participated in the arrests and beatings of Jews, and in their internment in ghettos at Riga, Latvia.

Progress to Date: Deportation hearings commenced on October 25, 1977, and continued on various dates until their conclusion on May 18, 1979, prior to creation of OSI. On February 27, 1980, the Immigration Judge terminated the proceedings, concluding that the government's evidence was insufficient to prove defendant's deportability. OSI appealed this decision to the Board of Immigration Appeals on March 5, 1980, and oral argument before the Board was held on September 4, 1980. On July 15, 1981, the BIA dismissed OSI's appeal and motion to reopen, holding that the record did not contain clear, convincing, and unequivocal evidence of Hazners' deportability. Various possible courses of action are now under consideration by OSI.

7. KAMINSKAS, BRONIUS

Case Pending: Immigration Court, Hartford, Connecticut; File No. A6 659 477.

Date Filed: October 13, 1976.

Date and Place of Birth: October 15, 1903, Kraziai, Lithuania.

Entry Date: May 7, 1947, under the Act of May 22, 1918, as amended.

Immigration Status: Resident alien.

Summary of Allegation: Defendant participated in the shooting of approximately 200 Jews in Lithuania in August, 1941, and in the selection of approximately 400 Jews for execution at another location in July or August of 1941.

Progress to Date: Defendant was examined by a government-appointed doctor, who concluded that defendant's ill health precluded his participation in deportation proceedings. The defense moved to dismiss the case on the grounds of defendant's incompetency, and OSI moved to adjourn indefinitely with periodic monitoring of defendant's condition. On January 30, 1981, OSI and the defendant stipulated that the case be adjourned *sine die*, and that the defendant would submit to periodic mental and physical examinations to determine his fitness to stand trial. On November 25, 1981, a government–appointed doctor again found Kaminskas unable to stand trial.

8. LAIPENIEKS, EDGARS

Case Pending: U. S. Immigration Court, San Diego, California; File No. A11 937 435.

Date Filed: June 2, 1981.

Date and Place of Birth: June 25, 1913, Rucava, Latvia.

Entry Date: March 9, 1960, under the Immigration and Nationality Act of 1952, as amended.

Immigration Status: Permanent resident (citizen of Chile).

Summary of Allegation: Between July 1941 and August 1943, during which time Latvia was under the occupation and the control of Nazi Germany, defendant voluntarily served in the Nazi–affiliated Latvian security police. While assigned to duty at the Riga Prefecture and at the Riga Central Prison in Riga, Latvia, defendant participated in the persecution of civilians because of their race, religion, national origin, or political opinion; such conduct included participation in the beating and killing of unarmed inmates. Defendant was arrested in 1946 by French military authorities in Austria in connection with these activities. He concealed and misrepresented all of the above facts when applying for entry into the United States.

Progress to Date: On June 2, 1981, OSI commenced legal proceedings seeking Laipenieks' deportation from the United States. Depositions were taken in Latvia in November–December 1981. Deportation hearings were held in San Diego from January 26 to February 18, 1982. On June 9, 1982, Immigration Court in San Diego found in favor of the defendant and ruled him not to be deportable. On June 17, 1982, OSI appealed the court's decision to the Board of Immigration Appeals. OSI filed its brief on September 8; Laipenieks' brief is due January 3, 1983. Oral argument by both sides before the Board of Immigration Appeals will be heard on January 19, 1983.

9. LEHMANN, ALEXANDER

Case Pending: U. S. Immigration Court, Cleveland, Ohio; File No. A11 218 851.

Date Filed: November 23, 1981.

Date and Place of Birth: July 21, 1919, Zaporozhe, Ukraine.

Entry Date: February 15, 1957, under the Refugee Relief Act of 1953.

Immigration Status: Permanent resident (citizen of Germany).

Summary of Allegation: From the fall of 1941 until October 1943, defendant, while serving as Deputy Chief of the First Section of the Ukrainian Police at Zaporozhe, Ukraine, personally ordered and assisted in the persecution and killing of hundreds of unarmed Jewish civilians in and around Zaporozhe. Defendant's wartime activities included his ordering, directing, and participating in the mass execution by rifle fire of between 300 and 350 Jewish men, women, and children in the spring of 1942 at a trench near the Baranov Stadium in Zaporozhe. Defendant concealed and misrepresented all of these facts when applying for entry into the United States.

Progress to Date: On November 23, 1981, OSI commenced legal proceedings seeking Lehmann's deportation from the United States. On December 9, 1981, a preliminary hearing was held in Immigration Court in Cleveland on OSI's Order to Show Cause. The government's motion to permit the taking of depositions in the Ukraine was granted. These depositions took place in July and August 1982.

10. LINNAS, KARL

Case Pending: U. S. Immigration Court, New York City, File No. A8 085 621 (deportation).

Date Filed: June 25, 1982 (deportation) November 29, 1979 (denaturalized).

Date and Place of Birth: August 6, 1919, Tartu, Estonia.

Entry Date: August 17, 1951, under the Displaced Persons Act of 1948, as amended.

Immigration Status: Naturalized February 5, 1960 by the Supreme Court of New York at Suffolk County. Ordered denaturalized by U. S. District Court, E. D. N. Y., on July 30, 1981.

Summary of Allegation: Defendant commanded or was a member of the security forces of a concentration camp at Tartu, Estonia from 1941 to 1943, where he supervised and participated in the physical abuse and execution of civilian prisoners. He misrepresented his activities during this period when applying for entry to the United States and later when applying for naturalization as a United States citizen.

Progress to Date: Depositions were taken in Estonia in March–April 1981. Trial was held in Westbury, Long Island before the U. S. District Court for the Eastern District of New York, in June 1981 (Civil Action No. 79 C 2966). On July 30, 1981, the court entered judgment in favor of OSI, and ordered that defendant's citizenship be revoked. The court found that defendant had taken an active part in atrocities committed against men, women, and children at the concentration camp at Tartu, and had subsequently procured his citizenship both illegally and by willful misrepresentation of material facts.

Defendant appealed the decision to the U. S. Court of Appeals for the Second Circuit, and on January 25, 1982, the Court of Appeals unanimously affirmed the decision of the District Court stripping Karl Linnas of citizenship. The U. S. Supreme Court denied Linnas petition for writ of cetiorari on October 4, 1982.

On June 25, 1982, OSI filed deportation charges against Linnas. Linnas will commence on December 2, 1982.

11. LIPSCHIS, HANS J. (a/k/a Antanas Lipsys)
Case Pending: U. S. Immigration Court, Chicago, Illinois; File No. A10 682 861.
Date Filed: June 8, 1982.
Date and Place of Birth: November 7, 1919 at Kretinga, Lithuania.
Entry Date: October 29, 1956, under the Refugee Act of 1953, as amended.
Immigration Status: Permanent Resident (citizen of West Germany).
Summary of Allegation: As a member of the *SS–Totenkopf Sturmbann* (SS-Death's Head Battalion), Lipschis served at the Auschwitz and Birkenau death camps from approximately October 23, 1941 until January of 1945. These camps were operated by and on behalf of the Nazi Government of Germany for the purpose of systematically exploiting and murdering large numbers of people because of their race, religion, political beliefs, and other characteristics. Lipschis ordered, incited, assisted, or otherwise participated in the persecution of these persons. In the fall of 1946, U. S. military forces in Germany placed Lipschis on a "List of Perpetrators" of war crimes, but avoided arrest.
Progress to Date: Defendant appeared before an immigration judge on July 13, 1982. Trial is scheduled for January 3, 1983.

12. MAIKOVSKIS, BOLESLAVS
Case Pending: U. S. Immigration Court, New York City: File No. A8 194 566.
Date Filed: December 20, 1976.
Date and Place of Birth: January 21, 1904, Mesteri, Rezekne District, Latvia.
Entry Date: December 22, 1951, under the Displaced Persons Act of 1948, as amended.
Immigration Status: Permanent resident.
Summary of Allegation: During World War II, defendant was employed as chief of the Second Police Precinct in Rezekne, Latvia. As chief of police, defendant participated in assaults upon and murders of Jewish and other Latvian civilians, including arrests and execution of the inhabitants of Audrini, Latvia, and the burning of the village. Defendant also ordered the rounding-up of all Gypsies in his police precinct.
Progress to Date: Deportation hearings were held in October and December of 1977. In April, 1978, the government sought an order from the Immigration Court permitting the taking of depositions of witnesses in Latvia. The Immigration Judge denied the government's motion, holding that fair depositions could not be taken in the U. S. S. R. OSI appealed this ruling to the Board of Immigration Appeals. On January 9, 1981, the

BIA reversed the Immigration Judge's decision, holding that depositions may be taken in Soviet territories, and that their admissibility, and the evidentiary weight to be given them, are to be determined by the Immigration Judge after they are taken.

Depositions were taken in Latvia in May 1981. Hearings resumed at the Immigration Court in Manhattan on July 20, 1981. The government completed the presentation of its case during that week. The defendant completed the presentation of his case July 12, 1982. The decision in this case is now pending with the Immigration Court.

13. PASKEVICIUS, MECIS (a/k/a Mike Pasker)

Case Pending: U. S. Immigration Court, Miami, Florida; File No. A7 497 596.

Date Filed: June 24, 1980 (deportation); January 17, 1981 (denaturalization).

Date and Place of Birth: September 26, 1901, Ukmerge,

Entry Date: June 15, 1950, under the Displaced Persons Act of 1948.

Immigration Status: Naturalized September 4, 1962. Denaturalized, pursuant to a consent judgment, on August 23, 1979 by the United States District Court for the Central District of California.

Summary of Allegation: While serving in the Lithuanian Security Police from 1941 to 1944, defendant participated in the murder, beating and extermination of Jews and other Lithuanian and Russian civilians.

Progress to Date: A complaint seeking the revocation of defendant's citizenship was filed by the government on January 17, 1977. Defendant subsequently consented to a judgment revoking his citizenship, and on August 23, 1979, the U. S. District Court for the Central District of California (Los Angeles) revoked the defendant's citizenship. In consenting to this judgment, defendant stipulated that he willfully and intentionally misrepresented facts to U. S. officials concerning his service as a member of the Lithuanian Security Police from 1941 to 1944.

On June 24, 1980, OSI filed an Order to Show Cause seeking defendant's deportation. The Immigration Judge ordered that physical and mental examinations of the defendant be conducted by a court–appointed doctor to determine if defendant is competent to stand trial. On December 16, 1980, the Court found that the defendant is mentally incompetent to stand trial. The Court based this determination on the report of the court-appointed doctor, on other submitted medical reports, and on the Court's own observations of the defendant on two occasions in court. The matter was thereupon adjourned *sine die.* However, defendant must submit to periodic mental and physical examinations to monitor his fitness to stand trial.

14. TRIFA, VALERIAN

Case Pending: Immigration Court, Detroit, File No. A7 819 396 (deportation); U. S. Court of Appeals for the Sixth Circuit, Civil Action No. 80–1762 (denaturalization).

Date Filed: October 29, 1980 (deportation); May 16, 1975.

Date and Place of Birth: June 28, 1914, Transylvania, Romania.

Entry Date: July 17, 1950, under the Displaced Persons Act of 1948.

Immigration Status: Naturalized May 13, 1957 by the Circuit Court for Jackson County, Michigan, at Jackson. Denaturalized, pursuant to a consent judgment, on September 3, 1980 by the United States District Court for the Eastern District of Michigan.

Summary of Allegation: During World War II, Archbishop Trifa served in Romania as a member of the fascist "Iron Guard" and as president of the National Union of Romanian Christian Students. Defendant also served as editor of the Newspaper LIBERTATEA, which openly identified itself with the Iron Guard and which advocated its anti–Semitic policies. From 1936 to 1941, defendant advocated the persecution of the Jews of Romania, and aligned the National Union of Romanian Christian Students with the policies and politics of the Iron Guard. On January 20, 1941, he issued a manifesto which advocated the replacement of all "Judah–like Masons" in the government and the establishment of an "Iron Guard" government; and in consequence, a rebellion took place in which hundreds of innocent civilians were killed. As an Iron Guard member, defendant was given sanctuary, protection, and care by the German SS in Romania and in Germany from January 1941 until August 1944.

Progress to Date: Defendant consented to denaturalization on September 3, 1980, and his certificate of naturalization was thereupon cancelled by the U. S. District Court for the Eastern District of Michigan.

Defendant filed an appeal of the consent judgment revoking his citizenship on October 31, 1980. On November 3, 1981, the Sixth Circuit affirmed defendant's denaturalization, and on May 17, 1982 the Supreme Court denied his petition for certiorari.

On December 15, 1981, OSI requested that the Immigration Court remove the previously-imposed stay on the commencement of deportation proceedings, and schedule the deportation trial for March 1982.

Trial actually commenced October 4, 1982 and after the third day, Trifa conceded deportability under the laws of the United States. He admitted concealing his Iron Guard activities and was ordered deported. He waived all appeals, and efforts are now underway to locate a country that will receive him.

III. Cases No Longer Active

1. DEUTSCHER, ALBERT

Case Filed: U. S. District Court for the Northern District of Illinois; Civil Action No. 81C–7043.

Date Filed: December 17, 1981.

Date and Place of Birth: August 18, 1920, Worms, Odessa District, Ukraine.

Entry Date: March 29, 1952, under the Displaced Persons Act of 1948, as amended.

Immigration History: Naturalized September 10, 1957 by the United States District Court for the Southern District of Illinois.

Summary of Allegation: On several occasions during January and February of 1942, defendant, while serving in the *Selbstschutz*, a Nazi-sponsored paramilitary organization, participated in the mass execution by shooting hundreds of unarmed Jewish civilians, including women and children, near Worms, Odessa Region, Ukraine. Prior to execution, these civilians had been unloaded from the railroad freight cars within which they had been forcibly transported to the Worms area from Nazi-occupied territories in Eastern Europe and the Soviet Union. Defendant concealed and misrepresented all of these facts when applying for entry and for naturalization.

Litigation of History: On December 18, 1981, one day afer OSI filed suit seeking the revocation of his United States citizenship, defendant was struck and killed by a train in Chicago. The coroner has ruled the death a suicide. The case was formally dismissed by the District Court on January 5, 1982.

2. OSIDACH, WOLODYMIR

Case Tried Before: U. S. District Court, Eastern District of Pennsylvania; Civil Action No. 79–4212.

Date Filed: November 20, 1979.

Date and Place of Birth: July 12, 1904, Wetlina, Galicia, Poland.

Summary of Allegation: When applying for entry into the United States and for naturalization, defendant concealed his wartime service as Commandant in the Ukrainian Police in Rawa–Ruska, Ukraine, and his involvement in the persecution and murder of unarmed Jewish civilians (specifically, his participation, directly and through subordinates, in the roundup and transport to extermination sites of Jewish civilians residing in Rawa–Ruska).

Litigation History: Trial was held in Philadelphia before the U. S.

District Court for the Eastern District of Pennsylvania, in September and October of 1980. On March 17, 1981, the Court entered judgment for OSI and ordered that defendant's citizenship be revoked. The Court found that Osidach had taken an active part in persecution and thus had illegally procured his U. S. citizenship. On May 12, 1981, defendant filed a notice of appeal of the denaturalization order with the Third Circuit Court of Appeals (Docket No. 81–1956). However, defendant died on May 26, 1981, before that appeal could be heard. On July 6, 1981, OSI filed a motion requesting that defendant's appeal be dismissed on the grounds of mootness. On July 22, 1981, that motion was granted.

3. TRUCIS, ARNOLDS

Case Filed: U. S. District Court, E. D. Pa.; Civil Action No. 80-2321.

Date Filed: June 20, 1980.

Date and Place of Birth: September 20, 1909, Valka, Latvia.

Entry Date: April 27, 1951, under the Displaced Persons Act of 1948, as amended.

Immigration History: Naturalized December 18, 1956 by the U. S. District Court, E. D. Pa., at Philadelphia.

Summary of Allegation: Between July 1941 and November 1943, defendant was a member of the Latvian Auxiliary Security Police, an organization which participated in the persecution of Latvian Jews. Defendant personally assisted in such persecution by guarding and abusing civilians. Between approximately October 1943 and October 1944, defendant held the German *Schutzstaffel* (SS) rank of *Hauptscharführer* (Master Sergeant), and served with the *Sicherheitspolizei* (Security Police), and the *Sicherheitsdienst* (or SD [Security Service of the SS]), which organizations participated in the persecution of Latvian Jews.

Litigation History: Defendant's answer was filed on July 19, 1980. At his deposition on September 22, 1980, defendant refused to answer any questions, invoking a claimed privilege under the Fifth Amendment. On October 31, 1980, OSI filed a motion to compel defendant to answer questions, and oral argument on this motion was heard on February 5, 1981. On April 16, 1981, the Court ruled that defendant has a privilege under the Fifth Amendment to refuse to answer questions concerning his wartime activities. Defendant was ordered, however, to answer all questions concerning both his entry into the U. S. and his naturalization as an American citizen. Depositions of witnesses have been taken in the United States and, in May 1981, in Latvia. Defendant's deposition was taken in Philadelphia on July 1, 1981, at which time he answered questions regarding his immigration and naturalization but again refused to answer questions concerning his wartime activities. Depositions were taken in Latvia in November 1981. However, defendant died on December 6, 1981, before his case could be brought to trial. The Court formally dismissed the case on December 14, 1981.

2. VON BOLSCHWING, OTTO ALBRECHT ALFRED

Case Filed: U. S. District Court, Eastern District of California; Civil Action No. 81–308 MLS.

Date Filed: May 27, 1981.

Date and Place of Birth: October 15, 1909, Schoenbruck, Germany.

Entry Date: February 1954, under the Immigration and Nationality Act of 1952, as amended.

Immigration History: Naturalized April 6, 1959 by the U. S. District Court, Southern District of New York. Denaturalized, pursuant to a consent judgment, on December 22, 1981 by the U. S. District Court for the Eastern District of California.

Summary of Allegation: When applying for naturalization, defendant concealed and willfully misrepresented his membership in the German Nazi Party and his role as an officer in the *Allgemeine SS* (where he ultimately rose to the rank of *Hauptsturmführer*) and in the SD (the security service of the SS) from 1934 until at least 1941. While serving in the SS and SD, defendant devised and advocated specific proposals for executing the SD's program of persecution and forced emigration of Jews from areas under Nazi control. From at least 1937 until 1939, defendant served in the "Jewish Affairs" office of the SD (Office II 112), where he provided information and advice to officials of that office, including Adolf Eichmann, on Jewish organizations and on forced emigration of Jews. In 1940–41, defendant served as head of the SD in Romania, where he encouraged and aided the fascist "Iron Guard" movement in its anti–Semitic pogrom of January 1941 and in other acts of persecution.

Litigation History: On December 22, 1981, von Bolschwing voluntarily surrendered his United States citizenship, admitting that he had been a member of the Nazi Party, the SS, and the SD prior to and during World War II. Under the terms of a consent judgment entered on December 22 by the U. S. District Court for the Eastern District of California, von Bolschwing must submit to annual examinations by a court–appointed doctor. Pursuant to the consent judgment, the government has agreed to refrain from instituting deportation proceedings so long as, in the opinion of that doctor, the progressive neurological disease from which von Bolschwing now suffers persists. Von Bolschwing died in a hospital in Sacramento, California in early March 1982.

INDEX

Welhaven, Kristian, 121
Welles, Sumner, 58
Weltanschauung, 185
What I Have Heard about Adolf Hitler
   (Bossman), 157
White Paper, 48, 49, 50, 68
Wiesenthal, Simon, 202
Winant, John, 58
Wingate, Orde, 50, 51, 58, 67
Wise, Rabbi Steven S., 56, 82, 97, 98
Work permits, 10–11
World Zionist Organization (WZO), 47

Yasue, Colonel Norihiro, 81, 83, 87, 90, 94,
   95, 99, 102
Yevtushenko, Yevglny, 153, 154, 155
Yishuv, Palestinian, 48, 57, 59, 60, 61, 67,
   69, 70

Zemba, Rabbi Menahem Zemba, 16
Zikman, Lew, 97, 98
Zionist Organization of America (ZOA), 50
Zirulnikov, Shlomo, 151
Zollinger, Alfred, 40
Zygielbojm, Szmul, 9, 10

Contributing Authors

SAMUEL ABRAHAMSEN is Professor of Judaic Studies at Brooklyn College, The City University of New York. He is the author of several books and pamphlets, including *Sweden's Foreign Policy* (Public Affairs Press, 1957). He has also published a considerable number of articles in a variety of journals, including *Jewish Social Studies, The American–Scandinavian Review,* and *The New Republic.*

PETER R. BLACK is a historian associated with the Office of Special Investigations, Criminal Division, U.S. Department of Justice. For a short while he served as instructor of European history at Columbia University. He is the author of several studies and review essays which appeared in the *Working Paper Series* of Columbia University's Institute on East Central Europe, and in the *Slavic Review.*

RANDOLPH L. BRAHAM is Chairman of the M.A. Program in International Relations and Professor of Political Science at The City College of The City University of New York. He also serves as Director of the Jack P. Eisner Institute for Holocaust Studies at the Graduate School and University Center of The City University of New York. He is the author, co–author, or editor of 27 books and has contributed to others. He has also published about two hundred notes and articles in various encyclopedias and professional journals. His two–volume work, *The Politics of Genocide,* was published in 1981 by Columbia University Press.

FRANCINE KLAGSBRUN has written or edited eighteen books, including *Voices of Wisdom, Jewish Ideals and Ethics for Everyday Living* (1980), *Free to Be . . . . You and Me* (1974) and *Too Young to Die: Youth and Suicide* (1976). She has lectured widely on topics relating to Jewish

235

ethics. Ms. Klagsbrun serves in an advisory capacity with numerous organizations, including the Jewish Museum, the Jewish Publication Society, and the Fund for Jewish Education.

WILLIAM KOREY is Director of B'nai B'rith International Policy Research. He is the author of several works, including *The Soviet Cage: Anti–Semitism in Russia* (Viking Press, 1973). His articles have appeared in *Foreign Affairs, Foreign Policy, Problems of Communism, Slavic Review, Saturday Review, Commentary, Midstream* and other journals. In the spring of 1983, Dr. Korey served as a Guest Scholar at the Woodrow Wilson International Center for Scholars (Smithsonian Institution).

DAVID KRANZLER is a Professor at Queensborough Community College, The City University of New York, where he serves as chief of the library's Social Science Division. He is the author of *Japanese, Nazis and Jews: The Jewish Refugee Community of Shanghai 1939–1945* (Yeshiva University Press, 1976) and a number of related articles that appeared in such journals as *Jewish Social Studies, Journal of Asian Affairs,* and *Japan Interpreter.*

MONTY N. PENKOWER is Professor of History and Chairman of the History Department at Touro College, New York. He is the author of *The Federal Writers' Project: A Study in Government Patronage of the Arts* (University of Illinois Press, 1977). His writings on American history and contemporary Jewish history appeared in many journals, including *American Jewish History, Jewish Social Studies, Midstream,* and *Prologue.*

WALTER F. RENN is Professor of History at Wheeling College, Wheeling, West Virginia. A specialist in Twentieth Century Europe and National Socialist Germany, Professor Renn authored a number of studies which appeared in the *Upper Ohio Valley Historical Review* and *The Wheeling College Annual.*

ALLAN A. RYAN, Jr. is the Director of the Office of Special Investigations, Criminal Division, U.S. Department of Justice, the unit created in 1979 to track down Nazi war criminals in the United States and take legal action against them. A *magna cum laude* graduate of the University of Minnesota Law School, Mr. Ryan served as a law clerk to Mr. Justice Byron R. White of the Supreme Court of the United States (1970–71). In 1977 he was appointed Assistant to the Solicitor General of the United States.

BELA VAGO is the holder of the Strochlitz Chair in Holocaust Studies and head of the Historical Documentation Center on East–Central

Europe at the University of Haifa, and a recognized authority on both the Holocaust and East–Central European history. He is the author or editor of a number of books, including *The Shadow of the Swastika* and *Jews and Non–Jews in Eastern Europe*. His articles appeared in a variety of scholarly journals, including the *Journal of Contemporary History* and *East European Quarterly*. Professor Vago serves, among other things, as a member of the World Council of Yad Vashem and of the Executive Committee of the Historical Society of Israel.